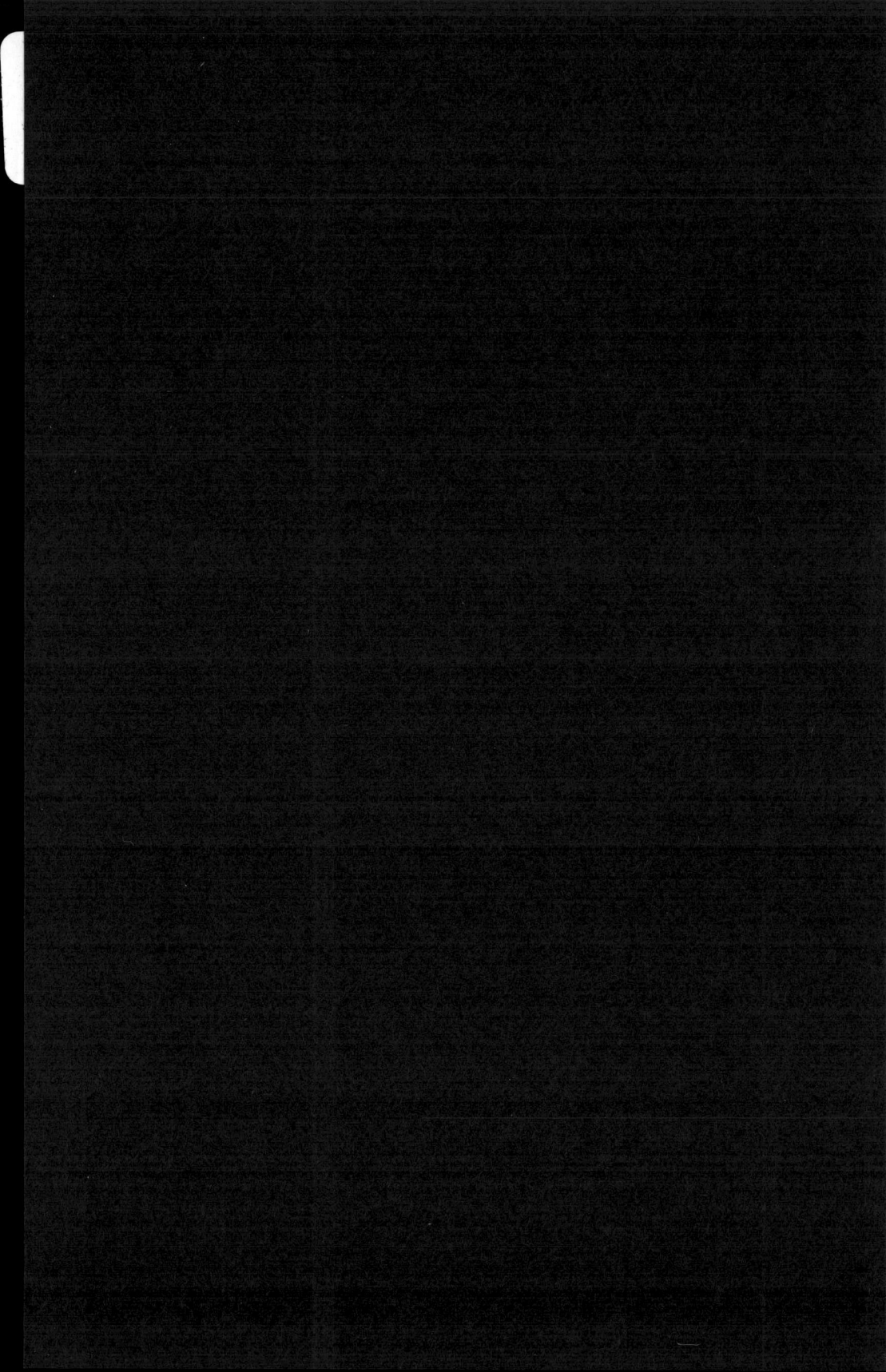

The Politics of Collegiality:
Retrenchment Strategies in
Canadian Universities

Declining enrolment, retrenchment (cutback) strategies, and demands from the public for increased accountability have forced university administrators to re-examine the efficiency of the university and adopt managerial techniques that advocate increased accountability, centralized authority, and objective resource allocation. Cynthia Hardy argues that this approach has failed to take into account the political realities of university life and the conflict that arises from competing demands for scarce resources.

In *The Politics of Collegiality* Hardy uses six case studies to explore how power and collegiality interact within institutional contexts during periods of fiscal restraint. Examining the funding cutbacks implemented by McGill University, Université de Montréal, University of British Columbia, Simon Fraser University, University of Toronto, and Carleton University, Hardy demonstrates that institutional context and retrenchment strategy are linked in such a way that what works in some institutions will not work in others.

By offering insight into how financial restrictions have been managed in particular universities, these individual case studies provide a conceptual framework for understanding institutional decision-making on a larger scale. She reveals that university administrators must recognize this broader context if conflict is to be avoided and the consensus needed to implement effective retrenchment plans created.

CYNTHIA HARDY is a professor in the Faculty of Management, McGill University.

The Politics of Collegiality

Retrenchment Strategies in Canadian Universities

CYNTHIA HARDY

McGill-Queen's University Press
Montreal & Kingston • London • Buffalo

© McGill-Queen's University Press 1996
ISBN 0-7735-1362-0

Legal deposit first quarter 1996
Bibliothèque nationale du Québec

Printed in Canada on acid-free paper

This book has been published with the help of a grant
from the Social Science Federation of Canada, using
funds provided by the Social Sciences and Humanities
Research Council of Canada.

McGill-Queen's University Press is grateful to the Canada
Council for support of its publishing program.

Canadian Cataloguing in Publication Data

Hardy, Cynthia, 1956–
  The politics of collegiality : retrenchment strategies in
  Canadian universities
  Includes bibliographical references and index.
  ISBN 0-7735-1362-0
  1. Universities and colleges – Canada – Finance – Case
  studies. I. Title.
  LA417.5.P64 1996   379.1'18'0971   C95-920993-X

Typeset in Sabon 10/12
by Caractéra inc., Quebec City

Contents

Tables and Figures

Preface

Strategic planning means reminding people in the midst of all the other things that are happening what we've got to do, and engaging in the political process of maintaining cohesiveness and cooperation. (University vice-president)

There's no need to do any planning unless you want to change something. So first find out what you want to change and then plan to obtain that change. Many people have the notion that planning is the production of a plan on paper and once you've done that you sit down and maybe take a few decisions to implement it, but it's then that things become political. (Dean)

This book has been a long time in the making. It began in 1983 with a grant from the Social Sciences and Humanities Research Council of Canada (SSHRC) to study retrenchment at McGill University and the University of Montreal. Additional grants from SSHRC and McGill University over the years enabled the inclusion of four additional universities. A series of articles followed, but a fuller treatment seemed to be the only way to do justice to the richness of the data. So, some ten years after the original research was begun, this book was written in an attempt to capture the complexity involved in the management of retrenchment. Ironically, perhaps, this study of Canadian universities during the 1980s is by no means out of date: not only do universities continue to face fiscal restraint, but there is still room to learn more about how power works within organizations; and there is always a need to nurture collegiality.

The author wishes to acknowledge the financial support of the Social Sciences and Humanities Research Council of Canada and McGill

University, and to thank all of the interviewees for their gracious participation in this study. The author would also like to acknowledge the comments of an anonymous reviewer, which were helpful in preparing the final version of the book. Michel Forand provided editorial suggestions.

CHAPTER ONE

Introduction

Changing enrolment patterns, funding restrictions, and demands for increased accountability from public paymasters have prompted a re-examination of the nature of university administration in recent years. Both administrators and government officials have expressed a growing interest in managerial techniques that introduce more of a business orientation into universities – techniques such as strategic planning, program evaluation, and performance indicators. One manifestation of these trends is the Jarratt Report (Committee of Vice-Chancellors and Principals 1985) in the United Kingdom. Similar patterns have been noted in other European countries and in Australia and New Zealand (Van Vught 1989; Watts 1992). While Canadian universities may have escaped the more extreme forms of government intervention and enrolment decline until now, they are nevertheless the object of similar concerns about their performance, particularly in the current context of scarce resources (Cutt and Dobell 1992).

These trends represent a move towards what is described here in general terms as "managerialism" – a concept that encompasses an increased emphasis on professional management, formal planning, systematic performance evaluation, centralized resource allocation, and directive leadership. Whether described as an industrial ethos (Jones 1986), executive management (Sizer 1987; Lee and Piper 1988), or managerialism, this concept advocates greater accountability, centralized authority, and objective resource allocation to improve performance.

Managerialism is predicated on a unitary perspective in which all interested parties are assumed to be bound together by a common goal. According to its proponents, rational analysis can, with the right kind of policies and procedures, be made to influence decisions and produce a corresponding improvement in performance. In this model, if opposition to rational decisions arises, it is usually attributed to inadequate communication or dismissed as some form of aberration instigated by troublemakers (Fox 1973; Burrell and Morgan 1979; Watson 1982). Indeed, critics have pointed out that the managerialist paradigm eschews the role that power, competing interests, and conflict play in real organizational settings. Since the unitary perspective pays little attention to the likelihood of conflict, it fails to suggest ways in which conflict might be avoided or overcome other than by enhancing communication or punishing troublemakers.

Challenges to the unitary model are not new. Writers have been criticizing its underlying assumptions since the 1950s (e.g., Lindblom 1959). One might ask, then, Why bring it up here? The reason for revisiting the unitary model is that, despite the criticisms and despite the wealth of empirical data showing that universities are subject to influences other than rational-analytic decision-making, the unitary model enjoys periodic resurrection. The managerialist philosophy that has been underpinning many of the recent changes in university circles is an example of this.

University circles are not unique in their fascination with the idea of a unitary model. A similar trend can be noted in the business world, where proponents of the "new management" (Lawler and Mohrman 1987; Hass and Philbrick 1988) have called on unions to abandon their traditional mandate to protect employee interests in order to support those of employers. In many respects, the desire for a world that conforms to the unitary model is understandable, since that model eradicates notions of conflict and simplifies the task of management. It promotes the idea (if not the reality) of objectivity and unity. The symbolism of common goals, a united team, and a happy family is seductive. Similarly, the emphasis on economic efficiency and rational analysis is reinforced by the dominant ideology in organization studies (Bryman 1984; Alvesson 1984).

Unfortunately, the unitary model also serves to obscure the political realities of our world, depriving administrators of the mechanisms needed to bring about change and making it difficult for employees to understand how power shapes their working environment. Thus there are both prescriptive and descriptive problems in ignoring the role that power plays in universities and other organizations (Hardy 1986, 1994).

MANAGERIALISM AND THE UNITARY MODEL

In what way are the underlying assumptions of the unitary model and its latter-day incarnation – managerialism – inadequate to address the challenge of managing universities under conditions of financial restraint? These assumptions are subjected to some scrutiny in the pages that follow. We discuss a number of areas where the unitary approach is seen to be deficient, and we demonstrate how it robs university actors of effective mechanisms for bringing about change. We also argue that the inaccurate depoliticization of university life embodied in this model will lead to recommendations that are unlikely to improve performance and may even jeopardize it (Hardy 1991a).

The first point to note about managerialism is that it emphasizes strategic planning – that is, a series of analytic techniques to assess organizational strengths and weaknesses, as well as environmental opportunities and threats, with plans then being formulated to address those factors. The emphasis is on formulation rather than implementation: the implicit assumption is that once the most rational plan has been identified, it will be implemented. Resistance to change is not taken into account, and even if it were, it would be consigned to obscurity – as irrational resistance to a rational plan by irrational people.

The emphasis on the value of strategic planning may be misplaced, however, since research on the link between formal strategic planning and financial performance in businesses indicates that it is, at best, tenuous (see Pearce et al. 1987). Even more damaging may be the lack of attention to the process whereby plans are translated into action, since implementation problems are common. After reviewing 33 strategic plans, *Business Week* (1984) found that 19 had been unsuccessful, mainly as a result of implementation difficulties. Over 30 different, highly sophisticated planning tools exist – with such exotic names as "nominal group technique," "dialectic inquiry," and "metagame analysis" – but fewer than a third give any consideration to how the plans can be put into practice (Webster et al. 1989). Indeed, estimates suggest that only a small proportion of strategic plans are ever implemented (Kiechel 1982; also see Skousen 1991).

As a result of these problems, business leaders have become aware of the need for "soft" or "people" skills to enable managers to translate plans into actions (e.g., Bruzzese 1991; Linder and Smith 1992; Foggin 1992). These skills include the ability to manage people and understand organizational politics, to promote team-building, and to span organizational and departmental boundaries. In addition to these analytic skills, managers also need interpersonal and political skills, which hinge on an understanding of "how things get accomplished within an organization and how to influence the changes" (Foggin 1992:8). If business needs such skills, so too does the university sector, where goals are more ambiguous, authority is less hierarchical, and power is more decentralized (Hardy et al. 1983), especially in the context of the likely continuation of financial restrictions. Given these requirements, the unitary model is unlikely to provide adequate answers.

A second thrust of managerialism is the need to take "decisive" action in the context of funding cuts. An analysis of weak and strong areas should be undertaken with a view to phasing out the former and redirecting resources towards the latter. The problem with this approach (e.g., Shirley and Volkwein 1978; Mayhew 1979; Dube and Brown, 1983; Mingle 1981; Heydinger 1982) is that it offers little advice on how to implement these actions in decentralized university settings. Nor does it take into account the damage that can be done to commitment and morale – and, in turn, to productivity and excellence (Hardy 1987a, 1990a). Whether in universities or in business (Hardy 1990b), managing cutbacks requires a delicate balancing of the need to maintain the morale of continuing employees and the implementation of difficult decisions. The rush to engage in radical resource reallocation and save money as quickly as possible overlooks the longer-term issues of commitment and morale, which are equally crucial in achieving satisfactory performance.

Third, managerialism tends to advocate a more central role for the president. Studies indicate, however, that strategies in universities are often based on bottom-up rather than top-down approaches (Hardy *et al* 1983). The diversified nature of large research institutions and the highly specialized nature of expertise require the involvement of the relevant professionals in generating strategic direction as much as, if not more than, the analytic techniques of central administrators. Thus centralizing power and increasing controls may serve only to hamper strategic developments. In a study of Brazilian universities, for example, rectors were found to have adopted a number of different leadership styles – from centralized to decentralized. The more effective research institutions were associated with a relatively decentralized form of leadership, while the rector with the most power was located in the university that was least productive in terms of research (Hardy 1990c, 1990d, 1991b).

The importance attributed to leadership is often overstated in the western literature on organizations. Much of this work represents the "great man" (and they usually *are* men) theory of management. In many respects, this approach is the artist's counterpoint to the science of strategic planning, and it makes many of the same mistakes by ignoring the myriad of actions that leaders and other members of the organization take in the context of its decision-making. While leaders clearly do influence decisions, the use of charisma and vision is only one way of doing so. First, leaders need to delegate work to other members of the organization, who may or may not carry out these orders. Second, even if these individuals do their duty, other employees must also subscribe to the changes. Finally, a ripple effect causes micro-level adjustments that are crucial to change but of which the leader may never be aware, particularly in the decentralized context of most universities.

Fourth, managerialism and the unitary model rest on an implicit assumption that more rational analysis somehow means less politics – that there is a right answer out there, if only we knew where to find it. As many writers have pointed out, however, what is considered to be "right," "rational," or "true" is socially constructed (e.g., Astley 1985). Knowledge is formulated on the basis of highly selective observations of the world. Sometimes, our idea of truth is unconsciously biased, simply by virtue of particular experiences that lead us to include certain observations and facts and to exclude others. At other times, seemingly "objective" criteria are consciously used to build credibility for certain actions at the expense of others (Sabatier 1978). Performance evaluation, for example, is not a neutral process, and very different pictures can be projected depending on the criteria that are employed (Cameron 1986). In fact, the very use of "objective" measurement focuses attention on factors that are easily measurable and quantifiable, while casting doubt on less tangible issues (Bowen 1977).

These criticisms suggest that universities (and other organizations) do not operate as rationally as some government officials and administrators might wish. "Biased" and "irrational" reactions are even more likely when resources are declining and the organization's members feel threatened. Given that possibility, university administrators might be well advised to temper proposals for action that view conflict only as a rare and temporary phenomenon and that ignore the diversity of those interest groups which influence university decisions. In addition, they need to consider the role that power plays in the successful implementation of cutbacks. Unfortunately, managerialism offers little help in understanding the politics of the cutback process, since it emphasizes analytic skills to the exclusion of political considerations. The present study represents an attempt to address this imbalance by applying a political perspective to retrenchment – that is, to a set of policies aimed at reducing costs within the context of government funding cutbacks.

UNDERSTANDING POWER AND POLITICS

Universities would seem ideal places in which to study the ebb and flow of organizational politics. There are many different groups, both inside and outside the institution, that influence university decisions – each with different world views, objectives, and interests. Decisions made by professors regarding research and teaching are influenced by professional affiliations and, increasingly, by research agencies and other external bodies. As governments become more preoccupied about funding and businesses become more involved in providing financial support, their influence on university decision-making increases. Internally, most major decisions (and, sometimes, some not so major ones) usually involve a collection of different professorial, administrative, staff, and student groups.

These groups are not necessarily bound by common goals and interests (Southern 1987): professors in different faculties may have different agendas, particularly when resources are scarce; professors and administrators often have conflicting goals; and external stakeholders, such as government and business, respond to pressures that are quite different from those to which universities are subjected. Accordingly, these groups are, potentially at least, in conflict with each other since they often perceive problems, solutions, and goals differently. They are not necessarily bound by a conception of the common interest; in certain circumstances, they may even pursue mutually exclusive goals.

More effective communication between these groups – one of the basic tenets of the unitary model – is unlikely to remove the potential for conflict. Even if the various groups understand each other perfectly, they will continue to view the world differently, to define problems and solutions differently, to protect different interests, and, at times, to pursue different objectives. Acting "rationally" does not help because rationality exists only in the eye of the beholder. As a result, organizational actors need to adopt political skills to bring about change. They must be able to recognize the relevant interest groups; analyse the relationships and distribution of power between them; and take actions that either create a common vision or enable them to prevail in spite of conflicting interests. In other words, organizational members must develop skills that either help them to avoid conflict by replacing vested interests with a common interest or enable them to prevail over opposition if conflict does arise.

While the concept of power is usually associated with the pursuit of vested interests and with overt conflict, it is important to note that power is also essential to collaboration and consensus (Burns 1961). Conflicting goals are not necessarily the result of greed and self-interest. Opinions may also diverge because individuals have different perceptions of the problems that exist and of the means to resolve them (Chaffee 1983a).

> Without perfect, unbounded, rationality it is quite feasible that individuals and groups may agree on ends without agreeing on how they are to be pursued (Walsh et al. 1981: 141).

This quotation describes conflict in a collegial setting: working for the good of the institution does not necessarily preclude differences of opinion, and thus power is needed to secure change in the face of these differences.

When considering the concept of power, managerialism tends to focus on instrumental power based on resource dependencies (Pfeffer 1981b) – that is, on formal controls such as line authority, the centralization of information and of resource allocation, hierarchy, budgetary controls, centralized reporting procedures, and so on. In most universities, however, central administrators are deprived of much of the formal, instrumental power often held by their business counterparts. The university setting turns formal controls into blunt instruments that may do as much to provoke conflict as to contain it.

At the same time, there are other sources of power that are far more conducive to collegiality. For example, if committees are used by administrators to consult with the professorial staff, power can be exercised in the way the members are selected, the terms of reference are established, the agendas are set, information is (or is not) provided, and deadlines are organized. The deans also represent a form of power. They are often opinion leaders in the university senate and in their faculties, linking central administrators to faculty members and helping to secure a wider, grass-roots commitment to the institution's goals (or alternatively to block initiatives undertaken by the central administration). Deans subjected to formal controls may become disenchanted with these strictures, but power can also be exercised through selection and socialization to produce deans that "fit in" and identify with the institution's perspective. In such cases, deans are more likely to abandon their parochial concerns and to support the administration's initiatives without the need for strict formal controls.

This form of power is unobtrusive and symbolic. It helps to avoid resistance by legitimating actions (see, for example, Hardy and Pettigrew 1985), and it creates collegiality by producing a commitment to the institution's goals. It differs from instrumental power in that it *evokes* cooperation by changing attitudes rather than by attempting to *enforce* cooperation by controlling behaviour directly. As a result, it is particularly appropriate to the university context, where the aim is to avoid conflict and secure collaboration (also see Chaffee 1985).

To understand universities – whether overtly political or apparently collegial – we need to adopt a concept of power that includes power to achieve common goals and not only power over others (e.g., Parsons 1967; Knights and Willmott 1985; Clegg 1989).

> In exploring the complexities of academic governance, we will not find any assistance in the type of political science of the last quarter century that reduced questions of power to the amount of influence that Person A has over B. Rather the conceptual sustenance is found in the growing amount of macro political analysis that seeks the specific structural location of legitimate influence, approaches that when combined point to three faces of power: the power of groups to prevail in overt conflict and explicit issues; the power of groups to keep issues off the agendas of action; and the power of groups to shape conceptions of what can and ought to be done (Clark 1983: 27).

A political perspective is needed, then, which recognizes that power can be mobilized to promote common goals as well as self-interest, and to prevent conflict as well as to prevail in the face of it. In other words, power should not be conceived as simply power over another individual or group: it also comprises a capacity to achieve collaborative outcomes. The political – or perhaps we should say politic – manager adopts a political perspective that gives credence to other actors within the organization and incorporates them into the management process, instead of merely ignoring them. In this way, an understanding of power and politics helps actors to realize their initiatives, while managerialism and the unitary model provide little help in managing the politics of either conflict or collegiality, or in realizing strategic change in higher-education circles.

CONCLUSIONS

In the face of funding restrictions and demands for accountability, many voices have advocated the adoption of managerial techniques in universities – that is, a business orientation in which centralized authority engages in such activities as strategic planning, performance evaluation, and objective resource allocation. This managerialist outlook rests on the unitary perspective, in which all interested parties are assumed to be bound together by common goals. It is argued here, however, that this model is an inadequate means of bringing about change because it fails to take account of the political realities of university life and ignores the role played by power.

The present study takes a different approach. It examines the retrenchment strategies adopted by six Canadian universities as a conduit to an exploration of the links between power, institutional context, and collegiality. These case studies – focusing on McGill University, the University of Montreal, the University of British Columbia, Simon Fraser University, the University of Toronto, and Carleton University – provide an insight into how financial restrictions were managed in particular universities and into the roles played by different actors. They also make it possible to construct a picture of the individual institutional context of each university. Conceptually, these contexts are derived from, and at the same time extend, the existing literature on university decision-making.

The subsequent analysis indicates that the nature of the institutional context, which comprises the presence of various organizational actors and their access to and use of power, influences the selection and implementation of retrenchment strategies. Thus context and strategy are linked through the distribution and use of power in the institution: decisions and actions are influenced by a number of different parties, and administrators wishing to implement their retrenchment plans must deal with these groups. Accordingly, we learn that retrenchment, like many other decisions in universities, cannot simply be imposed by the central administration.

Finally, a closer examination of the actions taken in the six universities reveals that many were taken to avoid opposition and conflict. These actions thus constitute a symbolic, unobtrusive use of power, where meaning is managed to create legitimacy and support for decisions that, in turn, will help to create and sustain collegiality. It is argued that this form of power is particularly relevant for university actors, since the traditional, instrumental sources of power are often limited in the academic arena. For actors to use this power effectively, however, they must have a thorough understanding of their institutional context in order to predict the symbolic effects of their actions and to estimate accurately how they will affect perceptions and meanings. To put it simply, what works in some institutions will not work in others. So, by understanding their own context, university actors can locate and mobilize sources of power that will help them to avoid conflict and create the consensus necessary to implement their retrenchment plans.

Before entering the subject of this book, however, it is useful to make clear what it does *not* examine. First, while the study focuses on power, it does not provide a neat, precise theory of power; nor does it present administrators with a series of steps on how to manage retrenchment. The definition and use of power have always evoked a considerable amount of controversy (Lukes 1974). One reason for this is the failure to acknowledge the complexity of power and a common tendency to limit what is an inherently general concept (Allison 1974). Bachrach and Lawler (1980) suggest that, rather than attempt to achieve a precise definition of the concept of power, we should use the term to reveal the complexity and multi-dimensionality of the phenomenon (also see Hardy 1994).

> Extant work on power usually attempts to impose on the concept a level of precision beyond that appropriate for a primitive term. Thus, we must ask not what is power but to what does the notion of power sensitize us. (Bachrach and Lawler 1980: 14)

Accordingly, attention is directed here towards asking what power comprises and how it produces results, rather than seeking to provide a precise definition. For the purposes of this book, a broad definition has been used that equates power with a force that influences outcomes. Politics is then defined as the use of power (e.g., Hickson et al. 1986). In this way, both instrumental and symbolic uses of power can be examined.

Second, while the study shows how power can be used relatively unobtrusively, it does not directly address the ethical implications of power that works invisibly to influence attitudes and manage meanings. Nor does it address directly the limits to this power or establish at what point the organization's members see the symbols for what they really are and become aware that their perceptions are being manipulated. Studies like the present one can help to increase the understanding of, and sensitivity to, power, and they can reveal the different ways in which power works to expose its hidden side. Ultimately, however, the outcomes of power will depend on the judgment and ability of the particular individual to employ it wisely, effectively, and ethically. (See Hardy, forthcoming, for a more detailed discussion of the ethical issues associated with the study and use of power in organizations.)

Third, in theoretical terms, the study attempts to extend the practical implications of Lukes's (1974) third dimension of power, which shapes perceptions, cognitions, and preferences. It does not explore more recent debates concerning the conceptualization of power – debates that could undoubtedly be applied to universities. This literature (e.g., Clegg 1989; Knights and Morgan 1991; Deetz 1992), based on the work of Michel Foucault (1979, 1980, 1982, 1984), views power as a web or network of power relations that holds all actors in its grip. It is far less "manageable" than the sovereign views of power that dominate most of the literature. Accordingly, while some actors may benefit from it, they are not necessarily able to manipulate it.

Fourth, this study does not concern itself with the implementation of retrenchment strategies. While university presidents unquestionably have a major impact on strategic change at times, in most situations they are simply one among many different players who contribute to change in organizations that are, by and large, characterized by a relative lack of centralized power. The discussion here examines the actions of the presidents, but in the context of many other, equally important factors. As the study shows, wielding symbolic power concerns not so much what a particular president does but whether his or her actions *fit* the institutional setting. Moreover, the use of symbolic power is not confined solely to university presidents and may be exercised by many different members of the university community.

Fifth, a number of parameters delimit the present work. The study has adopted a relatively broad-brush approach by focusing on an institutional level of analysis. It does not examine specific subcultures that may exist in different departments or faculties. Because the study is not a longitudinal one, it is important to remember that the descriptions here concern the universities as they were in the mid-1980s, during a period of contraction, with particular key players who were active at that time. It was not possible to update those descriptions. Space and time constraints also necessitated a focus on the academic community and made it impossible to go into much detail concerning cutbacks levied on nonacademic employees. There are even limits on the extent to which some of the issues mentioned in the case studies were pursued. The richness of the cases raises a number of interesting issues that, unfortunately, it was not possible to explore further.

Finally, the book has little to say about effectiveness other than as it pertains to the use of power. "Success" lies in the realization of intentions and, in the case of symbolic power, in the ability to avoid conflict although, even here, the term is problematic. The study shows how power can be exercised in an unobtrusive manner to influence outcomes; using the word "successful" to describe the hidden exercise of power in an attempt to obscure political issues hardly does justice to the complex, ethical implications that are involved.

The study does not consider whether the strategies adopted in the six universities constituted an effective way of dealing with retrenchment, for the simple reason that there is no consensus on what effectiveness is in this context and on how it could be measured. As Cameron (1985, 1986) has pointed out, different measurements lead to different conclusions. Consider, for example, the objections raised against the statistical methods used by *Maclean's* magazine in ranking Canadian universities. Even where ministry officials have succeeded in producing comparative statistics, as in Quebec recently, they have cautioned against drawing too many inferences from data taken from diverse institutions (*McGill Reporter* 21 October 1993: 1).

Although it might seem legitimate to consider effectiveness in financial terms in the context of funding cuts, how does one deal with the fact that some provincial government policies prohibit deficits while others prevent fee increases? How does one measure the situation of an institution with large deficits that are attributed to government "underfunding"? How does one account for an institution that has a large surplus but a high turnover of faculty or low morale? How does one explain the disparity between institutions that are able to launch large capital campaigns and those which have a less extensive and less wealthy alumni association?

While an exclusively economic perspective is inappropriate in the case of universities, academic indicators also present problems. When we look at the number of research publications, even on a *per capita* basis, we are focusing on one small component of a university's mandate. This measure is biased against smaller institutions, which do not have the high publishing rates and large grants enjoyed by their larger counterparts in such areas as medicine. Moreover, some observers have argued that a preoccupation with research diverts attention from undergraduate education. But even if teacher/student ratios are used as an indicator, should a high ratio be interpreted as a measure of a quality education or of inefficiency? For example, *Maclean's* 1993 study saw small classes as a sign of quality, whereas the U.K. system has given much greater weight to cost per student, advocating larger class sizes as an indicator of quality (see ISGUG 1993: 76). It is also worth noting that McGill, the top-ranked university in *Maclean's* 1993 study, had a deficit of over $70 million. In the context of retrenchment, this raises some interesting questions about whether McGill has been successful or unsuccessful in responding to fiscal restraint.

Clearly, then, there are difficulties in judging performance, let alone in establishing a causal link to a particular retrenchment strategy or institutional context. As a result, it was decided to leave the complex issue of defining and measuring effectiveness out of this study, although readers are free to form their own opinions, based on the data provided.

The remainder of this book presents and analyses the experiences of the six universities surveyed in the study. First, a brief introduction to the Canadian university system is provided, and the individual institutions are then described in separate chapters. The latter are interspersed with comparative "mini-chapters" to draw attention to particular issues that are explored in greater depth during the subsequent analysis. In particular, they reveal variations in institutional context; link these variations to differences concerning the choice and implementation of retrenchment strategies; and show how different facets of the institutional context can be used. These comparisons are designed to alert the reader to some of the issues discussed in the more extensive comparative analysis that appears in chapters twelve and thirteen. These two chapters explore in greater detail the relationships between institutional context, power, and collegiality. The final chapter argues that collegiality is an important component in the successful management of change in universities. Information on the methodology used in the study is provided in the appendix.

CHAPTER TWO

The Canadian Context

This brief introduction to the Canadian university sector and to its development provides a context for the case studies found in the following chapters. (For a more detailed and more comprehensive discussion of higher education in Canada, see Cameron 1991, on which the discussion in the first two sections of this chapter is largely based.) Since the book focuses on retrenchment strategies adopted in response to financial restrictions implemented during the early and mid 1980s, the following discussion describes the situation at that time. National developments will be described first, followed by specific information on the provinces of Quebec, Ontario, and British Columbia.

UNIVERSITY EDUCATION
IN CANADA

Higher education in Canada was first organized under the auspices of religious groups in the seventeenth century, but it was the nineteenth century that saw the creation of a number of universities that still exist today, including McGill (1821), Queen's (1840), the University of Toronto (1849), Laval (1852), Bishop's (1853), Dalhousie (1862), and St Francis Xavier (1866), among others. (Dates of origin sometimes differ between sources, some using the date when the charter was granted and others, the date when the institution opened.) Many other institutions failed to survive this early period because of the tensions arising from inter-denominational competition and secular politics. These forces also circumscribed the growth of those institutions which did survive: by 1867, only five institutions had at least 100 students. The *British North America Act* responded to the various religious and linguistic sensitivities by confirming the provinces' exclusive legislative responsibilities for higher education.

More institutions were established following Confederation. While some failed, others were more successful. The University of Manitoba was created in 1877 by provincial legislation as an examining body only, but it was given a monopoly over degrees granted in Manitoba, effectively amalgamating the four denominational colleges operating in the province. This bid to end denominational conflict and establish one provincial university proved successful, and it was later copied by the University of Alberta (1906) and the University of Saskatchewan (1907). Other universities were created during the fifty years following Confederation, both as newly formed institutions and through the amalgamation of existing colleges.

The First World War postponed further development in higher education, although it did give rise to the National Research Council in 1916, which came to be one of the major federal granting agencies. The 1920s were a period of growth and prosperity. Total enrolment increased from 23,000 to 33,000 during this decade, while revenues rose from $9 million to $14.5 million, and graduate study and research started to become significant activities. This period was followed by the depression of the 1930s, which ended university expansion. The return of armed forces personnel after the Second World War signalled an upswing in enrolments. An enormous impetus for expansion was created with the passing of the *Veterans Rehabilitation Act*, in which the federal government agreed to pay the tuition fees of veterans and to give an additional $150 per veteran to the university of enrolment. Over 20,000 demobilized military personnel increased enrolment by 46 percent in 1945–46 alone. In all, 136,000 veterans attended university over an eleven-year period under this plan. Higher civilian enrolment contributed to an even greater increase in student numbers – by 70 percent between 1944 and 1954, and by another 50 percent during the second half of the 1950s.

This growing demand put pressure on the universities' need for funds, and the federal government responded with a proposal to pay grants directly to universities. This move was quickly opposed by the Quebec government, which withdrew from the program on the grounds that it violated constitutional principles. The remaining provinces acquiesced to the new funding arrangements, despite some concerns about federal interference. Attempts were made to solve the jurisdictional impasse with Quebec, but it was not until 1959 that an agreement was signed whereby Ottawa granted tax concessions to Quebec to help that province fund its growing universities.

THE BEGINNINGS OF
PROVINCIAL UNIVERSITY
SYSTEMS

The growth in enrolment during the postwar period forced the provinces to consider how they should shape their higher-education systems to adjust to the greater demand. Newfoundland and Saskatchewan increased the number of university places within the framework of a single institution. In Alberta, the Calgary campus of the University of Alberta became an independent institution in 1966, and Lethbridge College gained full university status the following year. Two colleges affiliated to the University of Manitoba became Brandon University and the University of Winnipeg, also in 1967. New institutions were created in Ontario – Trent University in 1964 and Brock University in 1965. Colleges such as Carleton, York, and Guelph were given full university status as the Ontario system expanded to fourteen institutions. In British Columbia, the 1963 *University Act* – the first of its kind in Canada – set out in a single statute the powers, responsibilities, and internal structures of the province's four universities – Notre Dame University and the University of Victoria, both of them existing colleges given university status; the University of British Columbia; and Simon Fraser University, a new institution built in only eighteen months. In Quebec, the Parent Commission report in 1963 proposed a reorganization of the entire education system on the basis of widespread access to education and strong state involvement. This led to legislation in 1968 to establish the University of Quebec – a provincial network of autonomous campuses – and to end denominational control of other institutions.

Thus the 1960s were a period during which the foundations of revitalized provincial systems of education were laid down (Sheffield 1978). These systems included universities, ministries, and buffer bodies; and while different provinces adopted different measures, they all sought to increase the availability of higher education. The federal government continued to fund the bulk of university research uncontested, but the provinces rankled at the fact that operating funds went directly to the universities. To overcome this problem, *The Fiscal Arrangements Act* was introduced in 1967. It removed direct payments to universities and substituted a tax transfer to the provinces to fund the costs of postsecondary education. For the provinces, the new legislation meant the return of control and the promise of more money, and it acted as a further impetus in the formation of provincial university systems.

FINE-TUNING THE PROVINCIAL SYSTEMS

The 1970s saw the consolidation of provincial infrastructures. Newfoundland and Manitoba maintained their systems – the former, with its single provincial institution; the latter, with three. In the West, the Regina campus of the University of Saskatchewan gained independence, while British Columbia closed Notre Dame University in 1977, which left a system comprised of three universities (Campbell 1978; Leslie 1980; Cameron 1991). Ontario's transformation of a denominational college into Wilfrid Laurier University completed the provincial network, which now consisted of fifteen public universities and three specialized institutions – the Ryerson Polytechnical Institute, the Ontario Institute for Studies in Education, and the Ontario College of Art (Kymlicka 1978). University of Quebec campuses were opened in Montreal, Rimouski, Trois-Rivières, and Chicoutimi. In 1974, Sir George Williams University and Loyola College in Montreal merged to form Concordia University, resulting in a system made up of six independent institutions plus the University of Quebec (Whitelaw 1978).

In New Brunswick, the University of Moncton, a Catholic institution, was transformed into a fully public institution responsible for all French-language education in the province; the University of New Brunswick was its English-language counterpart, while Mount Allison University retained its connections with the United Church (Holmes 1978). In Nova Scotia, the provincial government played a less direct role in organizing its university system, and change was more incremental (Cameron 1991). There were, at that time, eight universities in Halifax and three elsewhere (Holmes 1978). Prince Edward Island merged St Dunstans College and Prince of Wales College into the public University of Prince Edward Island in 1969 (Holmes 1978).

Different provincial ministries evolved: in some provinces, all educational matters were combined under one ministry; elsewhere, university affairs fell under the responsibility of a separate ministry. Some provinces experimented with both models. The ten provinces also adopted different approaches to intermediary bodies. By 1968, all but Newfoundland and Saskatchewan had established intermediary bodies with varying compositions and responsibilities. Saskatchewan subsequently set up a Universities Commission in 1974, but dissolved it in 1983. Alberta and British Columbia dissolved their coordinating bodies in 1973 and 1987, respectively (Sibley 1982; Southern and Dennison 1987; Cameron 1991). Voluntary cooperative arrangements between institutions were developed in some provinces to provide information and establish lobbying groups such as the Conference of Rectors and Principals of the Universities of Quebec (CREPUQ) and the Council of Ontario Universities (COU). At the national level, the Association of Universities and Colleges of Canada (AUCC) was formed to represent all Canadian universities; the Canadian Association of University Teachers (CAUT) represented faculty members.

Funding arrangements varied across the country and over time. Formula financing, which linked funding to enrolments, continued to operate in Ontario and Quebec (although the formulae were different) but it was discontinued elsewhere. Some provinces – such as Newfoundland, Saskatchewan, and British Columbia – did not experiment with formula financing and allocated grants on a discretionary basis (Leslie 1980). Throughout this period, an underlying theme of the various financing arrangements was that universities were to retain a degree of relative autonomy. Typically, university administrators were (and still are) given a global budget and were free to decide how it should be spent. Most provinces controlled tuition fees, however, and institutions were rarely able to increase them without government approval. In some provinces, there was legislation to prohibit deficits and/or limit the right of faculty members to unionize.

The 1970s also saw the advent of new fiscal arrangements between the federal government and the provinces, with the introduction of Established Program Financing (EPF) in 1977. Provincial entitlements to federal funds were worked out for medicare, hospital insurance, and education. The *per capita* amount was indexed annually, in line with increases in the gross national product (GNP), and was multiplied by the current population of each province to arrive at that province's entitlement for a given year. The total was then divided into cash disbursements and taxation arrangements. The federal government introduced a new granting body in 1976, when the Social Sciences and Humanities Research Council of Canada was added to the Natural Sciences and Engineering Research Council and the Medical Research Council to dispense federal research funds.

GOVERNANCE AND STRUCTURE IN CANADIAN UNIVERSITIES

In 1906, the Flavelle Royal Commission, formed to make recommendations about the University of Toronto, established a bicameral governance structure, which was subsequently adopted by nearly all higher-education institutions in Canada (Cameron 1991). This structure consisted of a Board of Governors representing government and other interests, which was effectively responsible for financial and administrative matters, and a senate (or general faculties council), which was responsible for academic matters. The president of the institution was the chief executive officer. Faculty appointments, promotions, and dismissals were made by the board, but only on the recommendation of the president.

The 1966 Duff-Berdahl report endorsed this bicameral model but criticized its operation in Canadian universities because of unwieldy, ineffectual senates. It made a number of recommendations about such topics as streamlining and empowering senates, increased democratization, decentralized decision-making, and protection of tenure (Cameron 1991). These principles were quickly adopted as many universities began to review and revamp their governance structures, introducing elected senators, student representation, and departmental decision-making structures. The bicameral system was the basis of governance at nearly all institutions except Laval University and the University of Toronto, both of which adopted unicameral systems that combined the responsibilities of board and senate under the auspices of a single central body.

Today, there are over fifty Canadian universities.[1] Legally, they are private corporations deriving their powers from provincial legislation. Each institution hires its own staff, sets terms and conditions of employment, decides on program offerings, and determines course content and admission policies. Provincial governments provide operating funds,[2] and programs must be approved at the government level for funding to be awarded. Provincial funds for capital and research are separate. The federal government supports operating expenses through its transfer payments, and the direct costs of research through its research councils. So, although Canada has never had a national higher-education system, by the end of the 1970s a publicly funded provincial system was firmly in place with the support of a federal infrastructure.

During the 1950s and 1960s, the university sector underwent spectacular growth in other ways. Undergraduate enrolment increased fivefold between 1955 and 1975, doubling between 1962–63 and 1969–70 alone. Operating expenditures and graduate enrolments grew by a factor of twelve during this period, while capital expenditure increased twenty-three times between 1955 and 1966 (Leslie 1980). Government spending rose in line with these trends. The share of education in total government expenditure grew from 17.5 percent in 1964 to 22.2 percent in 1970, and the university proportion of the education budget rose from 16 percent in 1960–61 to 24.7 percent in 1967–68. In 1973, Canada was spending 7.1 percent of its GNP on education; on a *per capita* basis, only Sweden and the United States were spending more (Statistics Canada 1978).

AN ERA OF DECLINE

The 1970s marked a change in these trends. The first decline in student enrolments in twenty years was recorded in 1971; and although enrolments recovered the following year, they began to level off again in 1975. Projections at that time estimated a long-term decline in student numbers of 20 percent. Coupled with this was a change in governments' attitudes towards education, as political and economic factors transformed a desire for growth into a preoccupation with economy and efficiency (Langlois 1980; Leslie 1980; Hardy 1984). The proportion of government expenditure going to education fell from 22.2 percent in 1970 to 16.7 percent in 1975, and the university share of the education budget declined from 24.7 percent in 1967–68 to 19.5 percent in 1977–78 (Hardy 1984). The outlook predicted at the end of the 1970s was one of "a contraction in enrolments, a long period of shrivelling financial resources and external pressures to eliminate ... 'the redundant, the obsolete and the unnecessary'" (Leslie 1980: 5).

As Canadian universities entered the 1980s, the prediction of financial restrictions proved correct. Enrolment forecasts turned out to be inaccurate, however, and most universities continued to face increasing student numbers.

FINANCIAL RESTRAINT IN THE 1980S

In the 1980s, the universities were forced to juggle increases in student enrolments with decreases in government support. The 1981 recession made things worse, with all levels of government finding themselves hard pressed for cash. Accordingly, the federal government began to implement restrictions in transfer payments; at the provincial level, even where grants were increased they kept pace with neither inflation nor enrolment increases. The proportion of gross national expenditure spent on universities slipped from 5 percent in 1976–77 to 3.7 percent in 1986–87 (Cameron 1991), while enrolments rose by 27 percent and government support for basic operations grew by only 2.5 percent in real terms (1987 *Commonwealth Universities Yearbook*). All provinces except Prince Edward Island saw a reduction in the grant per student between 1976–77 and 1986–87, ranging between 14 and 28 percent (Cameron 1991).

These national funding pressures represent the financial backdrop for this study. They translated into different problems in different provinces, as the following discussion shows for each of the three provinces represented here – namely, Quebec, Ontario, and British Columbia.

Quebec

The Quebec system has six universities, in addition to the four campuses of the University of Quebec and various affiliated institutions. The provincial government provides operating funds on the basis of an enrolment-driven formula, as well as capital and research funding. Tuition fees are controlled by the government and remained fixed at a little over $500 for domestic undergraduate students from 1968 to the early 1990s. The universities were the responsibility of the ministry of education until 1984, when the department responsible for higher education was separated and became a ministry of higher education and science.

The provincial intermediary body is the Universities' Council (Conseil des universités), created in 1960s and consisting of seventeen members appointed by government, nine of which are university representatives. The council is responsible for advising the government on the needs and objectives of higher education, program approval, system coordination, and research direction. Relations between the universities and the council appear to have been mainly pragmatic.

> The universities cooperate with us but they don't always like us. I think they cooperate with us because they cannot do otherwise. If they didn't cooperate with us they would have to cooperate with the government. (Universities' Council representative)

The universities voluntarily belong to the Conference of Rectors and Principals of the Universities of Quebec (CREPUQ). During the 1980s, cooperation between them extended to joint demands for additional funding but did not fully overcome differences in institutional interest.

> The only coalition is at the level of "put more in the pot." The politicians see this not as a coalition of planners but a coalition of vested interests. For eight years the common CREPUQ response has been "more," but the individual institutions have said "more for me for this reason or more for me for that reason." (Ministry official)

Quebec operating grants failed to keep up with the increase in enrolments during the late 1970s: of the ten provinces, Quebec had the largest increase in operating grants – nearly 50 percent between 1975–76 and 1982–83 – but it also had the largest increase in students – 40 percent. As fees did not change, they dropped to only 2.6 percent of revenues. The overall decline of total operating income per full-time-equivalent student placed Quebec fifth among the ten provinces during this period (Skolnik and Rowen 1984). In 1981, the government announced plans to reduce funding by $180 million (out of a budget of around $840 million) over the next three years; as a result of this, total university grants were reduced by 13 percent between 1979–80 and 1983–84. The government left it to the universities to decide where they should make cuts by requiring them to submit retrenchment plans detailing how they would make the necessary savings. Fees were to remain at the same level, however.

Quebec universities were allowed to run deficits, and many did so. Between 1980–81 and 1983–84, the University of Montreal spent its $6 million surplus and incurred a $7 million deficit; McGill University spent $7 million of its unrestricted endowment fund (Hardy 1987b); and Concordia had an $11 million deficit in 1984–85 – 12 percent of its operating budget. The accumulated deficits of the Quebec system added up to $60 million (McGill Association of University Teachers *Newsletter* 17 March 12(3) 1986). Three years later, that figure had more than doubled (Cameron 1991).

The universities justified these large deficits by arguing that the funding formula was biased and resulted in some institutions being "underfunded." Outsiders were more inclined to see the deficits as a form of political pressure aimed at gaining increased funding for higher education. In this, the universities may have been prompted by the experience of Quebec hospitals. In 1985, the government reviewed the budgets of those hospitals which ran deficits (120 of the 200 institutions in the province) and promised additional funding if it decided that individual deficits had been caused by underfunding rather than bad management. The following year, the government wiped out an accumulated deficit of $260 million and added $133 million to hospital budgets.

> When you see the hospitals running up a deficit and getting away with it, inaction on the part of the government sends a signal. A university doesn't develop a deficit by absent-mindedness. I think many of the deficits developed because the universities thought that this was a message they could give the government. (Universities' Council representative)

If deficits were a form of political pressure, they achieved a measure of success. In 1986, the minister conceded that the deficits were largely the result of underfunding. A 1987 study showed that the precarious financial position of four Quebec universities and two affiliated institutions was the result of biases inherent in the funding formula. McGill University represented over half of the $32 million by which the system was estimated to be underfunded. The government began to earmark special funds for debt reduction, coupled with an increase in student fees. A 1986 parliamentary commission had uncovered overwhelming support for fee increases. Even some student leaders called for tuition fees to be raised to $2,500 over a five-year period (*The Montreal Gazette* 15 October 1986: A4).

> Facts say that tuition fees must rise. Almost everybody agrees. Even the students agree. (Ministry official)

Even with this consensus, it was not until 1990–91 that tuition fees were finally raised.

Ontario

The Ontario higher-education system is the largest in Canada, comprising fifteen universities in addition to various affiliated and specialized institutions. In the mid-1980s, three quarters of their revenue came from provincial operating grants, with tuition fees, which were controlled by the provincial government, contributing about one fifth. The universities had a considerable degree of autonomy in allocating their operating grants. They were awarded funds in the form of a global envelope, calculated on the basis of an enrolment-based formula, and were responsible for making their own decisions about internal resource allocation.

> The formula was a means of keeping the state and the universities apart. Academic autonomy and the autonomy of administration was [sic] well protected by this sterile formula. (Ministry official)

Ontario universities could run deficits but, unlike their Quebec counterparts, they did not do so during the 1980s.

Among interviewees, opinions differed as to how long the Ontario system had been subjected to funding restrictions, but the general feeling indicated a long gradual process of compression that began during the 1970s. A freeze was imposed on capital funding for new construction in 1970–71, and the universities' share of the provincial budget began to decline – from 5.8 percent in 1973–74 to 5 percent in 1980–81 (Skolnik and Rowen 1984; Axelrod 1982; Cameron 1991).

In 1978–79 the intermediary body – the Ontario Council on University Affairs (OCUA) – recommended an increase of 9.7 percent in government operating funds, but the universities received only 4.9 percent. In 1979, OCUA released a document entitled *System on the Brink: A Financial Analysis of the Ontario University System* to draw attention to financial problems in higher education. The main cause of these funding problems was an increase in student numbers, coupled with a small decline in government funding. Skolnik and Rowen (1984) show that Ontario sustained a 2-percent decline in provincial operating grants between 1974–75 and 1981–82, while increases occurred in all of the other provinces. Ontario also sustained the largest decline in real operating income per student during this period as a result of enrolment increases.

This situation continued into the 1980s, although attention seemed to be more firmly focused on the structure of the provincial system, notably on the extent of differentiation between institutions and on whether some form of reorganization would achieve better results. OCUA was among the first to raise the issue of rationalization. In 1980 its Committee on the Future Role of Universities in Ontario recommended that the system be restructured and that an additional $25 million be provided to redress funding problems. The government did not respond, however; instead, it formed the Bovey Commission in 1983 to examine the system within current funding levels. The commission nevertheless recommended that an additional $90 million be pumped into the system and also proposed an increase in tuition fees, limitations on access, and limited restructuring. The government rejected most of the commission's findings, and little was done in the way of either rationalization or additional funding (Cameron 1991).

With the advent of a new government in 1985 came a new minister and a new ministry in which responsibility for universities and colleges was separated from that for elementary and secondary schools. While the new government did not increase operating grants, it did provide an additional $50 million for targeted areas, with $25 million being allocated for undergraduate teaching, $15 million for research centres, and $10 million for faculty renewal. These funds were not added to base budgets (which were increased by 4 percent) but were made available over the following three-year period (which was subsequently extended). Despite these initiatives, the universities perceived little difference in their position.

> The old government said, "We don't think there's a crisis, but we still think the universities are valuable and we intend to fund them to the best of our ability." The new government says, "We think there is a

crisis but we are limited in what we can provide." The net result is about the same in terms of funding. (University administrator)

The result of some fifteen years of gradual compression led to a situation in which the universities felt strapped for cash but were unable to demonstrate a pressing need for more money.

> The universities face a crisis but it's very difficult to demonstrate. The universities are also saying that they are better than they ever were. It's very difficult to see what they are doing to deal with this crisis. The fact that professors tell you they are working harder and not enjoying it as much doesn't help us make the case. We have tried to develop output measures but we haven't been able to demonstrate decline. (OCUA member)

As a result, the government was not inclined to make any significant funding increases. In fact, there was a general lack of sympathy for the universities' so-called "crisis" (Skolnik and Rowen 1984; Skolnik 1986).

> Some of the senior members of the inner cabinet felt that universities weren't underfunded but unproductive. As a system of universities they weren't sufficiently rationalized or specialized. There was a lack of hard-nosed management, faculty were overpaid and underemployed. Generally speaking, there wasn't the toughness of governance or administration, and leadership was necessary to make them productive, efficient organizations. The period of affluence had left an image of universities among government that has never been wholly dispelled. (Ministry official)

The Ontario Council on University Affairs was an advisory body (Sibley 1982). It existed not by statute, unlike many of its provincial counterparts, but by order-in-council. Its members were appointed by the government, which also limited its terms of reference. OCUA tendered advice to the minister on such matters as the budgetary needs of the universities, but in fact the government completely disregarded its recommendations from the late 1970s onward.

> Our credibility is compromised by the fact that the government doesn't accept our funding advice. That is the most important thing. The fact that they accept other things doesn't seem to count. (OCUA member)

Interviewees indicated that the council's lack of influence had caused a considerable amount of disaffection in the university community.

An IMB [intermediary body] is supposed to be strong, sensible and act as a system of checks and balances. This is not what we have in this jurisdiction at this present time. OCUA acts as a check to the universities rather than a balance between universities and government. In practice, it has chosen to give advice only on those issues on which it has been asked to by the government, with a couple of exceptions. There's also a question of staffing and membership of OCUA, the resources they have, and the quality of people they can attract to serve. (COU member)

The universities themselves operated an umbrella group known as the Council of Ontario Universities, which collected and analysed data, and conducted public relations and lobbying on behalf of the universities.

We've always felt that COU would be ill served if it was recognized by the public or by government as an interest group. It probably is, but we feel we're not an interest group in the same way as the faculty associations or the teachers' federations, so we never become very strident. While we've been in a confrontation mode with the government, we felt we were locked into that relationship because ministers weren't advocates of the university system in a way that we felt they should be as part of their portfolio. I think we've talked tough in public, but we've tried to give credit where it was due and we've never gone to the barricades and thrown the body of a dead president on the steps of Queen's Park [the Ontario provincial legislature]. (COU member)

Resources were distributed between the universities by the enrolment formula, which was administered by OCUA. The formula had been a matter of dispute between the institutions for a number of years, and had largely been decoupled from enrolment changes by the government in 1978–79. OCUA proposed a new formula in 1983 but was again ignored by the government (Cameron 1991). The Council of Ontario Universities had also tried to negotiate a new formula with its member institutions, but that had only served to exacerbate divisions between the universities.

We haven't been able to agree on a new formula so we quit trying. (COU member)

In general, university presidents appeared satisfied with the role and performance of the COU, apart from its attempts to change the funding formula.

COU makes a difference. We all contribute fairly sizeably to it. It's not a small operation. It can lobby well and is very good at collecting comparable data across the country and assessing graduate programs.

They fool around with some things they shouldn't – such as the resource allocation mechanism. There's no way I can go to those sessions and agree to something unless I come out better off. They persist in doing this every so often, and it causes acrimony from time to time among the institutions. My feeling is that it's better to choose an agenda where there's a reasonable likelihood that you can agree, and stick with that. (University president)

British Columbia

At the time this study was conducted, the three universities in Canada's westernmost province – the University of British Columbia, Simon Fraser University, and the University of Victoria – operated under the 1979 *University Act*, which specified the main responsibilities and structure of each, such as the composition of the board of governors and senate, their members' terms of office, and the rules for appointments and elections. More detailed rules and regulations were left to the relevant bodies to decide. The universities received around 85 percent of their funding from the government. They had some latitude in raising tuition fees but could not run a deficit. Legislation also prohibited faculty unions.

A buffer body – the Universities Council of British Columbia (UCBC) – was also specified in the legislation. It consisted of eleven members and an executive director appointed by the government. Its main functions were to coordinate the universities' budget requests, transmit budget recommendations to the minister,[3] and allocate and distribute operating grants. It also made recommendations on capital expenditures and other funds, and approved new faculties and programs. UCBC had encountered a number of credibility problems, however.

Politicians like buffer bodies if they can blame them for the things they don't like and ignore them for those things they want credit for. The minister was very good at that – if it was a lousy decision he made good and sure it came out of Council; a lot of other times he ignored council. (Ministry official)

In particular, the Council faced difficulties in securing consensus among the three institutions, particularly with respect to financial matters. While they were willing to work together at drafting a joint proposal for government funds, they were less cooperative when it came to dividing those funds among themselves.

The universities all worked together to help us ask for as big a piece of the pie as they could get, but their institutional interests started to come to the fore when they worked with the Council on its division. As long as there was enough money to go around, the division wasn't too critical because even if everyone didn't get everything they wanted, there was enough to placate internal constituencies. Once the money started to get squeezed, the consensus fell apart. (UCBC member)

The Council also faced difficulties in securing common databases to support its financial recommendations.

The Council couldn't arrive at a common data base: if you ask the three universities, you get three different answers. (University president)

There was limited confidence in the chairman who was a highly political animal. [The Council] tended not to have particularly good support staff and so did not have good data, and it never tried to understand what's going on in each of the three universities. (Ministry official)

Only administrators at Simon Fraser University strongly supported the idea of an intermediary body.

UBC has always taken the position that it was the oldest and the largest and didn't need to worry about the smaller institutions. Victoria's view was that it was better to go it alone. (Ministry official)

UCBC has virtually lost all credibility with the universities now and the ministry as well. The universities have been reluctant until recently to rec-ommend it be done away with because conceptually the notion of having a buffer body is attractive, but we've always had trouble convincing the Council that it is not only the voice of government but also an advocate of the universities. Only Simon Fraser has tended to be an ally; both UBC and Victoria have been suggesting it be discontinued. (UCBC member)

This lack of support eventually led to the Council's demise in 1987.
    As far as relations with the provincial government were concerned, the universities felt themselves to be in an adversarial position, forced to defend their existence.

In British Columbia you have a tough time selling higher education in general – it's the land of the entrepreneur. All the universities felt themselves in the position where they had to defend their territory. We ended up in almost immediate confrontation. (University president)

There was more of a personal link to the government than in Quebec or Ontario.

> Politics is very much part of the fabric of day-to-day life in British
> Columbia. It's quite remote in Ontario and it's quite real in British
> Columbia. Everyone knows a cabinet minister or a member of the
> legislature or whatever. There's a real linkage into the political process,
> which basically means that politicians take things a great deal more
> personally. (University president)

As will be discussed in greater detail in chapter seven, financial
restrictions in British Columbia's universities were part of a general
restraint program implemented by the provincial government that
affected all parts of the public sector. It resulted in a period of sudden
and, in the Canadian context, dramatic contraction. During the 1970s,
British Columbian universities had received the second largest increase
in government operating grants (and total operating income) per full-
time-equivalent student between 1974–75 and 1980–81 (Skolnik and
Rowen 1984; Skolnik 1986). The situation changed radically in the
early 1980s as budgets were frozen in 1983–84, reduced by 5 percent
in 1984–85, and cut by another 5 percent in 1985–86 (Dennison 1987;
Cameron 1991). The drama was heightened by a threat to university
tenure as part of the government's efforts to reduce public expenditure
(Dennison 1987; Pedersen and Fleming 1984). This situation strongly
contrasted with the gradual compression experienced in Ontario.

> The essential difference has to do with the length of time during which
> the cutback has been felt and the means by which one goes about that.
> The manner in which it has been done in Ontario is much more humane.
> The whole climate in Ontario is one of more civility. British Columbia
> tends to be a province where polarization and confrontation are the
> order of the day. (University president)

Developments in British Columbia created the most dramatic situation
of the three provinces. Tuition fee increases of 22 to 31 percent and
the imposition of premiums for foreign students only brought fees in
the province up to the national average, and they failed to compensate
for the a real decrease in operating grant per full-time-equivalent
student of 18 percent between 1976–77 and 1986–87 – the largest
such decline in the country (Cameron 1991).

While fiscal restraint was a factor in all three provinces, it took on
different forms. In some cases, it was manifested in an actual cut in
funding; in others, budgets rose but student enrolments grew even
more. According to figures from the *Interprovincial Comparison of
University Financing: Tenth Report of the Tripartite Committee*

(published by the Ontario Ministry of Colleges and Universities, the Council of Ontario Universities, and the Ontario Council on University Affairs) between 1981–82 and 1985–86 – the period examined in this study – the provincial operating grant per student decreased by 7 percent in British Columbia and by 4 percent in Quebec, and rose by 20 percent in Ontario.

In reality, objective comparisons between the three provinces concerning the extent of fiscal restraint are difficult because of differences in the ability to raise student fees, in the "right" to run deficits, in access to private donations, and in the extent of research funding (which is estimated to increase overhead costs). Suffice it to simplify matters here and say that, in the perceptions of interviewees – which are supported by comparative data – fiscal restraint in British Columbia was rapid and gave rise to perceptions of crisis; restraint was gradual in Ontario, where it was traced back to the 1970s (between 1974–75 and 1981–82, the provincial operating grant per student more than doubled in British Columbia and Quebec, but only increased by 60 percent in Ontario); and it was moderate in Quebec.

CONCLUSIONS

While the federal government provides funding for operating and research costs, higher education is a provincial matter: provincial governments determine the number of institutions, provide most of their operating funds, establish or dissolve intermediary bodies, and have final approval over new programs. In the 1980s, recessionary pressures were forcing provincial governments to curtail university spending even though enrolments were increasing; and governments were becoming unsympathetic to the demands of the universities.

> Universities, while not overfunded, have given no proof that they have been significantly damaged by recent stringency in funding; [they seem] to acknowledge the stringent funding but decline to admit there has been any impact as the result of underfunding. (E. Neilsen, chairman of a task force on federal government spending, quoted in CAUT *Bulletin* April 1986: 1)

This was the environment facing the six universities examined here in the mid-1980s. The six case studies comprise both larger, traditional research institutions and smaller, newer universities. Tables 2.1 and 2.2 provide summary statistics concerning their situation in 1984–86. Each of the universities was facing, to a greater or lesser extent, financial restrictions and the prospect of cutbacks. Table 2.3 provides an overview of the main differences in environment, institutional context, and

Table 2.1
Comparative Statistics (General) on Six Canadian Universities, 1985–86

	McGill University	University of Montreal	University of British Columbia	Simon Fraser University	University of Toronto	Carleton University
Vice-presidents (number)	5	5	3	4	4	3
Faculties (number)	12	13	12	7	15	5
Board members (number)	44	24	15	15	50*	30
Political appointments to the board						
Number	0	8	8	8	16	0
Percentage	0	33	53	53	32	0
Senators (number)	80+	90+	80+	56	50*	60+
Deans on the Senate						
Number	12	13	12	7	0*	5
Percentage	15	14	15	13	0*	8
Faculty on the Senate						
Number	42	45	34	24	12*	36
Percentage	53	50	43	43	24*	53
Students on the Senate						
Number	18	6	17	12	8*	10
Percentage	23	6	21	21	16*	15
Professors (number)	1,500	1,500	1,900	450	2,000	640
Full-time students (in thousands)	17	26**	21	7	34	11
Total number of students (in thousands)	21	47**	27***	15	51	17
Part-time students (percentage)	18	45**	23	52	33	34
Graduate students (percentage)	27	20**	14	9	18	4
Foreign students (percentage)	9	2**	4	8	5	4

Source: *Commonwealth Universities Yearbook*, 1987.

*   Figures refer to the Governing Council.

**   Includes the École des Hautes Études Commerciales and the École Polytechnique. The total number of students at the University of Montreal was 35,000.

*** Excludes Continuing Education students.

retrenchment strategy. The next several chapters describe these institutions and the events that took place in more detail. Quotations taken from the interviews that were carried out (see appendix) are used to convey a picture of these institutions in the words of some of the people who worked in them at that time.

Table 2.2
Comparative Statistics (Financial) on Six Canadian Universities, 1984[1]

	McGill University	University of Montreal	University of British Columbia	Simon Fraser University	University of Toronto	Carleton University
Total income (millions of $)	241	236	269	87	517	106
Operating revenue (total income less research, millions of $)	183	199	214	79	341	95
Total research funds (millions of $)	58	37	55	8	111	11
Operating grant Millions of $	114	175	181	67	260	54
As a percentage of operating revenue	62	88	84	85	76	57
Total research as a percentage of operating revenue	32	19	26	10	33	12
Deficit (cumulative from 1980–81 to 1985–86, millions of $)	18	27	*	*	3.3	**
Deficit (as a percentage of operating revenue)	9	13	–	–	1	–

1   Figures compiled from university data. The six universities use different methods in compiling their data.
*   Deficits prohibited by provincial legislation.
** Surplus of $500,000.
–   Not applicable.

Table 2.3
Characteristics of the Six Universities

	Type	Fiscal restraint	Time period	Context	Strategy
McGill University	large, old	medium	1981–84	collegial	across-the-board formula
University of Montreal	large, old	medium	1981–84	technocratic	differential productivity formula
University of British Columbia	large, old	severe	1983–86	political	program terminations, dismissals of tenured faculty
Simon Fraser University	small, new	severe	1983–86	collegial, bureaucratic	reorganization of faculties
University of Toronto	large, old	gradual	from 1970s	federal bureaucracy	attempt to close a faculty
Carleton University	small, new	gradual	from 1970s	collegial, centralized	differential cutbacks

CHAPTER THREE

McGill University

What was McGill University's financial situation during the early 1980s? How did it respond? What were the reasons behind its choice of retrenchment strategy and what were the implications of that choice for the university? Before attempting to answer these questions, it will be helpful to provide some details about McGill's governance structure.

McGill University, established in 1821 with a bequest from James McGill, is one of Canada's oldest higher-learning institutions. In 1984 (the year when this study was conducted), it was a large research institution catering for around 30,000 students, 5,000 of whom were in graduate programs. About 1,500 full-time professors taught in twelve faculties. Its budget was over $240 million, of which 23 percent consisted of research grants.

A simplified version of McGill's organizational structure in 1984 is shown in Figure 3.1. The Board of Governors consisted of up to forty-four members, including the chancellor, the principal, and the president of the students' society as *ex officio* members. Twenty-five members were elected by the Board, five by the alumni, five by the university's Senate, three by full-time nonacademic staff, and three by students. The Board had "general jurisdiction and final authority over the conduct of the affairs of the University" and made all contracts and appointments (McGill Statutes 1987: 7).

The Board appointed the principal after consulting with a committee composed of Board, faculty, nonacademic, and student representatives. The principal was the chief executive officer of the university and was responsible for recommending appointments for vice-principals, deans, and professors to the Board. In the case of deans, the principal consulted an advisory committee that represented the various constituencies. In the case of professors and department heads, the principal consulted with the dean of the faculty concerned.

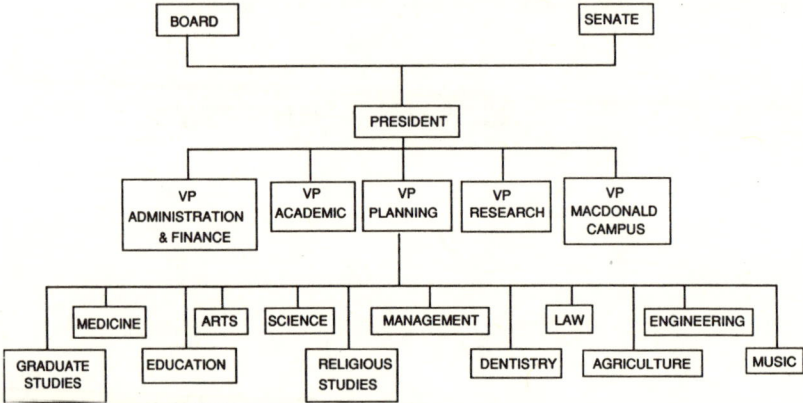

Figure 3.1
McGill University: Simplified Organization Chart (ca 1986)

Academic decisions were the responsibility of the Senate, which comprised over eighty members, including the chancellor, the chairperson of the Board, the principal (who was the Senate chairperson), the vice-principals, the deans (thirteen, including the director of Continuing Education), librarians (four), students (approximately eighteen), Board members (four), and some forty faculty representatives. The Senate was responsible for granting degrees, developing curricula, and approving courses. It made recommendations on academic policy and had the authority to create and terminate faculties and departments. In the event that the Senate and the Board disagreed, the matter under dispute was to be submitted to the Conference Committee, which consisted of the principal and five members each from the Board and the Senate.

FINANCIAL PROBLEMS
AT McGILL

In some respects, McGill University's current financial problems can be traced back to the 1970s:

> In the 12 years since 1970, costs which grew faster than government grants, coupled with a government imposed freeze on tuition fees, had placed the university in a seriously underfunded position ... [This] required budget cuts in real dollar terms for most of those years. (*Annual Report* 1981–82: 5)

Increases in government operating grants in 1977–78 and 1980–81 proved to be insufficient to meet salary increases.

The situation took on a new dimension in 1981 when the Quebec government announced that funding to universities would be reduced over the next three years and demanded from each institution a plan for balancing its budget. As a result of the cuts, total university grants in Quebec were reduced by 13 percent in constant dollars. McGill predicted that in order to break even in each of the following three years, annual budget cuts of 11.3, 5.9, and 5.9 percent would be necessary. At the same time as these financial restrictions were imposed, student enrolment increased – by 20 percent between 1978–77 and 1983–84.

MCGILL'S RESPONSE

Deficit Financing

McGill's central administration, supported by the Board, decided that the cuts necessary to balance the budget each year were unacceptable. It decided to embark on deficit financing in order to smooth out fluctuations in spending. This approach was articulated by a Budget Task Force established in 1981 to

> conduct an overview of the budget presented to the Board for 1981–2, an overview of the methods and steps already taken to achieve budget cuts for 1981–2, a consideration of whether further steps of a budget cutting nature are possible for 1981–2 and a consideration of preliminary proposals for budget measures for 1982–3. (Budget Task Force Report)

The task force consisted of one representative from each of the Board, the Senate, the central administration, and the academic and nonacademic staff. It presented its report to the Board in late 1981, advocating deficit financing to spread the impact of the cuts.

> The initial budget cuts indicated above, totalling 23.1 percent, are staggering and will not be achieved without considerable damage to the university … it is recommended that the cuts be more evenly spread over the 3 years, even though this will result in a deficit. (Budget Task Force Report)

By using deficit financing, the university could make more or less equal cuts of 7.3, 7.9, and 7.9 percent over a three-year period. The next question to address was, How were the cutbacks to be distributed?

Formula Funding

Administrators did not change the method for allocating resources to the different faculties and departments, and they continued to rely on a mechanism that had been used since the beginning of the 1970s – the funding formula. Simply put, that mechanism worked by applying to the previous year's budget a standardized formula that provided higher allocations for those departments or faculties with an increased student intake, and lower allocations for those with declining student enrolments. The budget determined by the formula was then "normalized" to equal an amount that was slightly lower than that of the projected budget for the university as a whole.

The difference went into a small discretionary fund that the university could use to make differential allocations between units. Deans could apply for a slice of this discretionary allocation when additional base funding was needed to support new developments, for example. These applications were evaluated by the Budget Planning Group, which consisted of the principal, the vice-principals, and one dean.

The discretionary allocations were intended to offset the negative effects of formula funding, which allocated resources solely on the basis of student demand. The combination of the two methods was an attempt to provide both the benefits of a standardized procedure and the opportunity to fund new initiatives.

> The budget walks a tight rope on this question [of discretionary funds], without the aid of a safety net. On one side is rigidity from overemphasis on a formula; on the other is the risk of accusations of preferential treatment, arising from discretionary allocation ... At McGill we have walked this tight rope with some success. Even in the years of our greatest austerity, even although to do so increased the austerity felt by all, we have each year reserved some discretionary funds for developmental purposes. (Armour and Desrosiers 1974: 24)

Between 1979–80 and 1983–84, the net budget cut required to meet government allocations totalled $13.8 million, but the actual budget cut to faculties and departments was $27.4 million. The difference was

> allocated to high priority areas to relieve the formula budget cuts and to provide development funds ... on a (non formula) basis which gave weight to the reports of the cyclical reviews and other expressions of

priority from the academic area. (Central administrator, in a written memorandum)

The discretionary budget was not used to reallocate resources on any grand scale, however, since only a small proportion of the budget went into this fund; in 1984–85, for example, it represented less than 4 percent of the budget.

The formula funding and the discretionary fund distributed resources – and resource cutbacks – on a university-wide basis. Overall, the university still had to slash its expenditures in line with its reduced funding, despite its use of deficit financing.

Expenditure Reduction

Hiring freeze. A hiring freeze was imposed in March 1981 but this lasted only briefly. It quickly became apparent that a freeze was not a desirable form of cutback.

> If staff who resign from areas that are already hard pressed are not replaced, the increased pressure on the remaining staff accelerates the rate of resignations. This self reinforcing negative trend could have disastrous effects on key areas. (Budget Task Force Report)

Tenured staff. Administrators at McGill explicitly stated their desire to avoid the termination of tenured faculty.

> We have tried and will continue to try to avoid solutions that will require methods of that kind. (Central administrator)

Terminating tenured staff at McGill required a resolution from the Board of Governors, but it could theoretically be done if a program was discontinued. It was felt, however, that

> tenure has such an aura around it that its cessation signals such a change in the university's circumstances that I think that we would continue to avoid making that kind of decision. (Central administrator)

A tripartite committee composed of Board members, executive members of the McGill Association of University Teachers (MAUT), and senior administrators deliberated the matter for about two years, but failed to arrive at any recommendations. Acknowledging that fact, the Budget Task Force explicitly ruled out any further efforts in that direction. Senior administrators felt that such actions would be highly damaging.

> I think that the consequences to the university in terms of resentment and morale from very valuable people who would be made insecure would be more trouble than it would be worth. (Dean)

Tenure quotas were an equally contentious issue. The Budget Task Force recommended a long-range policy to establish tenure ratios for departments, but the response of the university community was less than enthusiastic. An *ad hoc* Senate committee established to review staff policies recommended that the Senate debate the issue of tenure quotas, but the latter decided against initiating such a debate. Furthermore, although some central administrators were in favour of tenure quotas, others were completely opposed to them. The resulting university-wide stalemate removed the issue of tenure controls from the agenda.

Attrition. Between 1978–79 and 1982–83, 502 academic staff left McGill University. Of these, 308 were replaced; in addition, 54 new positions were created. As a result, the number of full-time academic staff decreased by 12 percent – a total of 140 positions, worth $5.2 million. The reduction of part-time jobs saved another $2 million, and the removal of 300 nonacademic jobs resulted in a further economy of $5 million. The total saving, including benefits, was $13.9 million. There were also some early retirements and a few special severance arrangements, although these did not play a significant role in reducing personnel numbers. In some cases, it was younger faculty members who bore the brunt of staff reductions when their contracts were not renewed.

> It has been our practice, in departments where budget pressures are unusually severe not to renew in these circumstances. This is a disquieting practice ... [but] we conclude regretfully that there is no way that this practice can be avoided or altered in our current financial circumstances. (Budget Task Force Report)

Salary policy. A major component of expenditure cuts was McGill's salary policy. Both staff and faculty associations agreed to forgo salary increases. Between 1977–78 and 1984–85, of the $44 million reduction in base budgets $7 million came from not paying salary increases (*McGill Reporter* 20 June 1984).

In summary, McGill University's response to financial constraints could be described as being more akin to an across-the-board approach than to highly differential or targeted cutbacks. The use of the funding formula, even when combined with the discretionary fund, resulted in cost trimming rather than radical surgery. The primary mechanisms for reducing expenditures were attrition and salary freezes. There were no closures of departments or programs for financial reasons, nor was there any formal statement of high- or low-priority areas.

THE REASONS

Why did McGill University adopt this particular strategy? The answer can be summed up as a desire by central administrators to avoid provoking conflict within the university.

> Our strategy all along has been to try to manage with diminishing resources in a way that reinforces some parts of the university but not others, [and] at the same time not dramatically disturb morale ... You constantly ask yourself whether you can accomplish the goal of trimming without throwing the campus into a state of turmoil. (Central administrator)

This conflict-avoidance objective had a number of components: maintaining a cohesive relationship between the deans; maintaining morale in the university community; reducing the likelihood of unionization; and retaining the decentralized nature of governance.

The Deans

The deans at McGill University were a highly cohesive group, even though one might have expected financial restrictions to increase conflict over scarce resources.

> Sure if I need money and another dean needs money I'm going to do my level best to get it, but not at his expense ... As things get tight it's necessary to develop a "me first" attitude but it's controlled by the people involved ... We understand one another, we tend to support one another as far as we possibly can. (Dean)

> I don't think there's a sense of guarding territory much there – there's a lot of collegiality, a lot of the sense that we're all in this predicament together and that we can help each other. (Dean)

The presence of the funding formula helped to protect this relationship by avoiding situations where the deans might have been in competition with one another.

> The way things operate, we don't compete in front of each other and so it's kept civil. (Dean)

The formula represented an "objective" approach to resource allocation, whereby the central administration could avoid accusations of preferential treatment.

> The formula is hoped to satisfy everyone, which means it satisfies no one, but you hope it satisfies no one about equally. (Board member)

In reality, however, such perceptions of objectivity were illusory.

> There is a fallacy in the formula. It's argued that the formula is objective but that's nonsense. The formula contains an element that says a graduate student counts twice as much as an undergraduate. Who made that decision? That's not objective; that's a decision to emphasize the graduate program. (Dean)

Nevertheless, formula funding was perceived by the deans to be a far more equitable – and acceptable – basis on which to make cuts than selecting units for closure or formally establishing priority areas. Even the discretionary budget did not provoke competition since the deans applied privately for funds.

> We never get into an open forum where we have to compete. We deal privately with the Budget Planning Group. I think the decisions are taken in a discrete and fair way. (Dean)

Thus cohesion within the group of deans was maintained in a way that might not have been possible with targeted funding and more selective cutbacks.

> Now if you go to differential funding that's something different. There will be much more competition and ... it would change the relationship. (Dean)

The Employees

Apart from a few small groups, neither faculty nor staff at McGill University were unionized. The McGill Faculty Union had a limited membership of about 100 and had failed to win collective-bargaining rights. The academic staff were represented by the McGill Association of University Teachers and nonacademic staff by the McGill University Non-Academic Staff Association (MUNASA). Relations between each of these groups and the central administration were relatively cordial, as evidenced by the willingness on the part of both associations to give up wage increases in order to help the university reduce expenditures.

> I think MUNASA is much more considerate than other unions are. I don't think you'd find any other union in Quebec willing to forgo 5 percent [in wage increases]. But I think that is a reflection of the staff at McGill and their attitudes and loyalty to the institution. (MUNASA official)

> There's not much antagonism between MAUT and administration. We believe decisions made by the Board are fair. (MAUT official)

This relationship with the associations resulted in more flexibility for McGill, making it easier to reduce expenditure through such methods as the salary policy.

> I think one of the major ways in which McGill has coped with the cutbacks has been [the result of] a very good relationship between administration and the staff associations. Because we're in a nonunionized situation we have a great deal of flexibility which wouldn't exist with a standard labour contract and ... despite all the planning exercises the most significant instrument for dealing with cutbacks is salary policy – reaching a tacit understanding. (Central administrator)

McGill's administration was, as a result, reluctant to jeopardize its relationship with its employees in general, and with the two associations in particular. Selective cuts would have run the risk of threatening collegiality and loyalty, particularly if they had involved the dismissal of employees. Such an approach would have, according to one central administrator, been "writing a ticket for unionization."

> I think [breaking tenure] would be disastrous because the relations that we have with the staff associations are superb. They have been an enormous help to me – they've given me advice on what is the fair thing to do. Once we attack tenure we would lose that. (Dean)

Continued salary compression did, however, strain relations.

> The good faith that had been established between McGill University Non-Academic Staff Association and the Administration over our 10 year history has been severely strained by the events of the last year. The failure of the Administration to live up to its parity commitment, when all other Quebec universities have done so, has driven a wedge between [us]. (McGill University Non-Academic Staff Association Newsletter 1982)

These pressures were such that cost-of-living increases and merit raises were reintroduced in 1985.

Decentralization

Another reason for not making more selective cutbacks lay in the decentralized nature of McGill's governance and organizational structure. This decentralization can be seen at the levels of both the central administration and the faculties.

Within the central administration, the principal was not an authoritarian figure; instead, he saw himself as part of the group of vice-principals, which worked by consensus.

> This university is, for all the knocking of the collegial style of government, a decentralized place with a significant degree of participation by colleagues in decision making. There have been many questions when my views have not prevailed and I don't have difficulty with that at all. I don't see myself as the person with all the right answers for McGill ... [If] it's apparent to me that I'm not going to be able to persuade enough senior colleagues, that's right, and I accept that situation happily. (Principal)

McGill had changed in the 1960s from a "one-man benevolent autocracy" into a democratically governed institution (Frost 1983).

> The principal remains the chief executive but has much less power than his predecessors and often finds himself with little choice but to endorse the advice he receives from consultative bodies. (Thompson 1977: 43)

As a result, the principal lacked the necessary power to impose unilateral cutbacks and, instead, was more likely to engage in discussion and negotiate solutions with the vice-principals. It was suggested that the primary role of the principal was an external one – maintaining liaison with McGill's external constituencies and fund-raising. Internally, the university was run by the Principal's Advisory Group, which consisted of the vice-principals, with the vice-principals for academic affairs and for finance and administration playing key roles.

> He's not the kind of principal like Cyril James who did everything himself. In other words, he has delegated the day-to-day running to, depending on the field, either the vice-principal (academic) or the vice-principal (finance). They are usually pretty much on the same wavelength … Between the two of them the place either functions or it doesn't. The principal is fairly dependent on them because he's away a lot of the time. (Central administrator)

At the central level, therefore, power was shared and the principal did not assume an authoritarian position in running the university. These administrators saw McGill as a decentralized university with an active Senate and powerful deans and department chairmen. This perception was echoed throughout the university, and it was enhanced by the practice of giving faculties a one-line budget.

> Maximum autonomy is given to each budget administrator. A global budget allocation is made available to each Dean … The Dean is responsible for the distribution of funds to his individual academic departments where they exist as discrete budgetary units. Department chairmen are then responsible for the distribution of funds within their departments. (Armour and Desrosiers 1974: 7)

The deans felt they had as much (or more) autonomy from the central administration as their counterparts in other Canadian universities.

> Most of the time my fellow deans in Canada have much less latitude to act independently and creatively than I do: I would not [want to] be a dean at most other Canadian schools. (Dean)

Although the deans may have had considerable autonomy from the levels of authority above them (i.e., the central administration), their power was circumscribed by the hierarchy below them – by the department heads, who were particularly powerful individuals in the larger faculties at McGill University.

> It would be an intrepid dean who would go against a strong-minded department head … The real power in this university is, I think, the chairmen, and they are deferred to by everyone – deans and vice-principals – in their own area. (Dean)

Department heads had their own global budgets and were responsible for allocating resources within their departments. Thus McGill was

> extremely decentralized and traditionally so, where deans have a fair amount of autonomy and, in some faculties, it's the departmental chairmen who have the autonomy. (Central administrator)

Running the university – and managing cutbacks – had to conform to these decentralized processes.

> Unless you have the cooperation of the deans and the chairmen, you're not going to get very far: the place is just too big and we're not that arrogant to make all the decisions. It just wouldn't work. (Central administrator)

> [Decentralization is desirable] *especially* in years of financial constraint because I really do believe that people in the departments are the people who know best how to spend the money that's been made available to them to get the job done. I don't think that we in this [administration] building know whether [for example,] Chemistry really is better off to have a visiting lecturer as opposed to a computer terminal or a new secretary. (Central administrator)

This decentralized decision-making process was far more amenable to formula funding than to selective cuts. Decentralization does not tend to produce the hard decisions that are required for the latter. As one dean put it: "You can't ask people to commit suicide." So, central administrators chose to avoid selective cutbacks.

> Obviously the decision [to make selective cuts] is not going to come from within the faculty because they'll scream. So it's going to have to come from a central planning crowd and that's one reason why it will never happen at McGill. It's so decentralized that they've got no balls at the top. (Professor)

Access to Funds

McGill University's access to private funding provided a degree of flexibility that other Canadian universities did not possess. McGill had the largest endowment of any Canadian university – $163 million in 1983–84. The unrestricted part was used to fund the initial deficits.

The unrestricted endowment is intended to take us through rainy days or rainy years, and we have still managed to preserve a degree of flexibility in the university and we have not been forced to take that dramatic action which would cause us to close down schools and cause a great deal of demoralization. They have served the University well through many years in producing valuable operating income and in providing a buffer which made it possible to plan ahead with a measure of consistency, thus avoiding some of the worse effects of the volatility and uncertainties in government funding. (Vice-principal [finance], quoted in *McGill Reporter* June 20 1984).

The university also held a highly successful capital campaign in the early 1980s, which raised more than $61 million. This money was, however, explicitly used to fund new initiatives and was not absorbed into the operating budget.

The first principle was [that] any private monies had to be carefully related to priorities emerging from the regular operating budget. We wanted to treat private money as supplemental to, and enriching, the [operating] monies that are already part of the planning process. The second principle was [that] we wanted as much as possible to target the private monies to areas of excellence. (Central administrator)

In summary, McGill's choice of a response to the financial restrictions was shaped by the university's context and, in particular, by the high degree of collegiality that prevailed.

It is important to respect and even nurture this asset of loyalty and sense of the community ... McGill University enjoys at present a collegial model, or probably about as close as it is possible to come. (Thompson 1977: 44)

This collegiality manifested itself in the cohesiveness of the deans, an absence of unionization, agreement to salary freezes, and support for the central administration.

They've reorganized up there so that the financial guy is doing the financial side of it. You don't have some kind of czar there who's an ex-professor and who's running the place by whim and by tradition. You actually have a person – the head financial person in the university, who's a guy who could be a bank vice-president – in a good bank! (Professor)

[The vice-principal (academic)] is a star: he's a tough cookie and he's got his head screwed on right. (Professor)

I don't think you can have the financial problems of the university in better hands than they are in now. (Dean)

This context shaped McGill's retrenchment strategy in three ways. First, it provided options, such as salary freezes, that were not always available to other universities. Second, the administration's decision to protect and nurture the collegial environment emphasized fairness and ruled out more selective cutbacks.

I think the university has recognized its obligation: it has developed a formula that tries not to make cuts harshly ... It's a very humane way of dealing with it. It tries to let things settle into place over a longer period of time rather than making very rapid surgical cuts that can be very harmful to the institution. (Dean)

Third, the collegial model and the decentralization of power to the Senate, faculties, and departments made it difficult for central administrators to take the type of unilateral action normally associated with more selective, targeted budget reductions. We can see, then, that the collegiality that existed at McGill University acted both as a source of flexibility *and* as a constraint on the choice of retrenchment strategy: it gave administrators some options that were not always available elsewhere, but it also placed restrictions on them if they wished to preserve that collegiality.

It might be argued that McGill's response to cutbacks was solely the result of the flexibility enjoyed by the university thanks to its access to private funds. In other words, McGill could afford, in a strict economic sense, to engage in deficit financing and avoid selective cuts because of the existence of unrestricted endowment funds. This view is not entirely accurate, however. First, the lack of an endowment had not prevented other Quebec universities from engaging in deficit financing, although it may have made it more costlier for them to do so because of the resulting interest payments. Second, other universities had employed deficit financing but used a far more selective approach to resource allocation. Third, access to private funding may have helped McGill to develop new projects, but it did not reduce operating expenses. So, while economic factors may have increased McGill University's flexibility in choosing how to respond to cutbacks, they were not the only reason behind the choice of retrenchment strategy.

THE CONTEXT AT McGILL:
A CLOSER LOOK

The influence of contextual factors (collegiality and decentralization) on McGill's choice of retrenchment strategy can also been seen when examining two particular processes – formal planning and cyclical review. How did these processes further reinforce the support for across-the-board cutbacks?

Planning

McGill University has officially acknowledged the importance of planning to its resource allocation process.

> The unrelenting challenge ... was the question of how to do better with less ... obviously, planning is the answer: planning the most efficient use of resources for maximum benefit. (*Annual Report* 1981–82: 2)

By the mid-1980s, McGill had had a financial planning system for some time, following previous encounters with deficits. The university had run up deficits of $2 million in 1968–69 and 1969–70, reducing the unrestricted endowment fund from $22 million in 1959–60 to $13.6 million in 1969–70. As a result, "at the university-wide level, planning was imposed within McGill in the late 1960s by the pressures of outside events which led to a financial crisis and student unrest" (Thompson 1977: 49).

A budget task force established in the early 1970s had undertaken a line-by-line examination of all academic budgets and taken steps to slow down the expansion of the university.

> The process was not a popular one but, in retrospect, many would regard it as a necessary first step, (a) as an educative process for a budget committee in its first year, and (b) as a way of sensitizing the university community to the process of budgetary stringency that was to become a rather regular part of McGill life during subsequent years. (Armour and Desrosiers 1974: 3)

Later on, a Budget Planning Group was established, with responsibility for budget planning, policy, and implementation. The time was "opportune for McGill to undertake the planning and implementation of a long term programme of financial control" (Armour and Desrosiers 1974: 4). A four-year rolling budget was instituted, later converted into a five-year financial plan. This system of financial planning was extended with the creation of an operational research office – which later became the Office of Research for Planning and Development – and with the appointment of the first vice-principal responsible for planning. In 1970, a planning commission was created to explore alternative models for the operation of the university within these financial constraints. The commission later became the Academic Planning and Priorities Committee (a subcommittee of the Senate), which reported on goals, plans, and priorities.

Despite the earlier experience with financial planning, academic planning met with more limited success.

> The planning experience at McGill has not been a failure but it has fallen far short of its potential. For the most part, the structures and personnel exist; they need to be made more effective. (Thompson 1977: 55–6)

One reason for this was that academic planning in an institution such as McGill had to be decentralized.

> Planning is an activity in which every unit and each staff member must become involved. Plans imposed from above would not be decisions based on the informed opinion of those closest to teaching and research activities. (Planning Report)

> Effective planning requires *participation* at every level. Planning *for* people works badly in a university environment; what is required is planning *by* people. (*Annual Report* 1981–82: 3; emphasis in the original)

The problem was that the "people" were not always enthusiastic about planning.

> I see planning as an expanding bureaucracy, of very little assistance to me but capable of creating several structures of bullshit that I have to cope with. (Dean)

> Planning is a very political game: every vested interest in the university is trying to promote its own interests. (Professor)

Formal planning mechanisms were associated with bureaucracy and centralization.

> [The planning document] had a rough time in Senate because it was viewed as a mechanism for centralizing decision-making. It was also viewed as introducing another layer of bureaucratic red tape and paper

work to the workings of the university. I understand it was perceived as kind of putting all the deans in a row and making all of them into lieutenants, marching to the orders of the [central administration]. (Board member)

As a result, planning had limited credibility in the eyes of the academic community.

Planning has to be done in a very subjective and *ad hoc* way. The numbers are nice if you want to justify something after the fact. The real academic planning has somehow to be based on a lot of subjective factors ... that kind of planning does not make much use of statistical data. (Dean)

Cyclical Review

A mechanism known as "cyclical review" was instituted by the vice-principal (academic) in 1981 to evaluate and review the quality of all programs and units in the university. For a number of reasons, this process had considerably more credibility than the planning process.

First, the cyclical-review process was perceived as a decentralized one. The unit under review was required to produce a self-study document that was subsequently examined by the review committee, which also carried out interviews within the unit. Central administrators were not members of the review committees, which consisted mainly of professors from other units and of the dean of the faculty to which the unit belonged. The review committee was charged with drafting a report that was, in turn, reviewed by the Academic Planning and Priorities Committee, which also consisted primarily of professors, although it was chaired by the vice-principal (academic). The emphasis was on consultation. Deans received a copy of the report and were urged to discuss it with faculty members.

At a minimum, the recommendations of cyclical review reports should be made available to Faculty's planning committees in order to be discussed within the faculty. (Minutes of Academic Policy and Priorities Committee, 21 March 1984)

Second, the cyclical-review approach had an air of objectivity because it relied on external evaluators who came to McGill University to assess the unit under review and submit a report to the review committee, and on the presence of members of faculties other than that of the unit.

A third factor of credibility stemmed from the fact that the cyclical-review process was not publicly linked to the issue of cutbacks. It was emphasized as a form of quality control and a means of improving academic programs, even though it was informally recognized that poor quality could result in the phasing-out of programs while good reviews would help to protect units.

> We are likely to try and protect, as much as we can, an area that is doing extremely well in the estimation of peer reviews. (Central administrator)

> I think we have to assume that cyclical review is really a method by which you find out which are the excellent academic units in the university and which are poor; and if you find poor ones, well then I presume that you allow them to wither and die. (Dean)

> I think it's naive to suppose [the cyclical review and cutbacks] are not connected. Of course they are connected, because the people who make the financial decisions can't do it in the abstract. They need a vehicle of some kind of outside assessment or evidence or judgment and they can either accept it or not accept it. It's a mechanism for shifting resources. (Dean)

Central administrators were anxious to distance the cyclical-review process from the cutbacks for a variety of reasons. First, the process was designed to be continuous, to assess quality, and to help identify priorities in the years to come. This meant that a review would be conducted every five to seven years. In order to stimulate commitment to the cyclical-review approach, the central administration was reluctant, during this first cycle, to focus on the areas that might constitute candidates for cuts.

> You can't do all the weak areas the first time around, because if they all come out negative then nobody wants to participate [the next time]. (Central administrator)

In fact, if the cyclical-review process were to maintain its credibility, some units would have to be given additional resources.

> One of the dangers in cyclical review is that they may make some recommendation but if the university has neither the will or the resources to implement them, this will be seen as a futile exercise ... That will affect morale because the administration will be seen to be impotent in

its ability to strengthen areas where review committees with external referees are pleading for growth. (Dean)

Second, administrators did not want to use cyclical reviews to impose change from above but, rather, to promote change in the units under review by providing information and pointing out weaknesses. Their function was to be a catalyst, thus avoiding the necessity of intervention by the central administration.

> It isn't so much what you do with the review but what you hope is going to be the response of the unit. (Central administrator)

> The benefits are benefits that accrue to the departments and faculties simply by taking the time to look at themselves and what they are doing. (Dean)

Third, the review process did not, in itself, force comparisons between units. Each unit was evaluated separately, on its own merits. Thus the dilemma typically attached to the existence of scarce resources – that choices must be made *between* units – was not incorporated into the review process. As a consequence, during this period of financial restrictions no program or unit closures resulted from the cyclical review. Even units where such action was recommended were given one – and, in one case, two – last "chance" to redeem themselves.

Thus it can be seen that the attitudes towards formal academic planning rendered it an ineffective mechanism for establishing priority areas and implementing selective cutbacks at McGill University. While the cyclical review had more credibility, the central administration deliberately distanced it from the budget reductions. Where did this leave the question of selective cutbacks at McGill in the mid-1980s?

SELECTIVE CUTBACKS AT McGILL?

The university had often articulated an official commitment to selective cuts based on priorities.

> Early in the year, the vice-principal (academic) cautioned that budgetary problems will inevitably force McGill, as well as most other North American universities, to reduce some of its older, smaller or more costly programs, both to make room for needed new programs and technology and to cut costs. (*Annual Report* 1981–82: 3)

It is clear, however, that in the current financial situations, there are not enough resources to meet all of these needs. It is necessary to make choices, however, difficult these may be. (Report on the 1983 Planning Exercise)

We are certainly evolving as quickly as we can a strategy that will protect the areas that we consider top priority and, if we have to make cuts, make them more severely in areas that are not [priorities]. (Central administrator)

Moreover, central administrators maintained that the discretionary fund had enabled the university to make some selective decisions.

I think we *have* [stated priorities] because our financing arrangements are not simply student-driven ... We have certainly made discriminating judgments. (Central administrator)

Many interviewees disagreed, however.

I think they have not [made selective cuts], although I would say the same thing with respect to the faculty – we have not picked out certain areas and funded them comfortably and let other areas go. The deans haven't done it, the administration hasn't done it, and the chairmen haven't done it. We are all reluctant to make these major shifts in resources. (Dean)

I don't think we have reached the decision yet that we should cut back massively on a program ... It's difficult to determine what a university does well, what it does less well, and thereby make it concentrate on the better things. There are no really useful criteria available ... McGill doesn't know what its strengths and weaknesses are or, if they do, they are not telling. (Board member)

The university community was not convinced of the need to reduce the scope of its operations. For example, the following statement made by a subcommittee of the Academic Planning and Priorities Committee introduced the idea that the university should establish whether programs could be phased out:

Every program at every breadth of organization from specialized groups within departments to faculties should see to what extent its base can be narrowed for the purpose of maintaining quality by concentration of resources.

That statement was later amended by the Senate as follows: "should see to what extent, *if any*, its base can be narrowed without reduction of quality" (emphasis added).

Nor was it clear whether the university community would tolerate the degree of central intervention that would accompany make radical resource reallocation.

> Any real tough decisions have to be made top-down; they have to be. People are not going to say we need to be dissolved, or cut by 50 percent ... If budget cuts continue, then, sooner or later, someone up on top is going to have to [do something] ... but we're going to run into pockets of resistance. (Central administrator)

Few interviewees were receptive to the idea of central intervention.

> I wouldn't want to see [the allocation of posts] being done by central administration who almost by definition must have a different value system. (Professor)

> Any change that is imposed top-down will work but it will be so traumatic. (Central administrator)

> I used to think we should [make selective cuts]. I now think the cost of doing that would be so great, politically, that it would be damaging. (Professor)

So, while there was some grumbling in the university community about the reluctance to make "hard" decisions, the egalitarian, decentralized approach was generally accepted. As a result, McGill administrators would have been faced with considerable difficulty had they wished to institute a more selective approach to cutbacks. Indeed, they would have threatened the decentralized, collegial nature of the institution.

CONCLUSIONS

McGill University's strategy for retrenchment was chosen to protect morale and commitment within the institution. As a result, cuts were administered primarily in an across-the-board manner by means of a formula based on student enrolments. A discretionary fund enabled some resources to be diverted towards new developments, but the university did not formally establish high- and low-priority areas, nor did it make any radical reallocation of resources.

Administrators at McGill selected a retrenchment strategy in the early 1980s that, they believed, would help them to maintain a relatively loyal, nonunionized staff. They were able to capitalize on the existing loyalty and so, for example, were able to negotiate salary freezes to help reduce expenditures. McGill also had a degree of economic flexibility in its access to private funds. While this source of funding may have facilitated the choice of deficit financing, it was not the only factor behind the choice of strategy. As we shall see, other universities engaged in deficit financing and employed very different strategies, while others made similar general compressions without incurring deficits.

CHAPTER FOUR

The University
of Montreal

The University of Montreal was originally established in 1876 as part of Laval University but became independent in 1919. It was a Roman Catholic institution until 1967, when it received a new charter that converted it into a private institution although it continued to depend on government funding. In 1984, the university had thirteen faculties: Arts and Science (comprising nearly thirty departments and around 600 professors), Theology, Law, Medicine, Education, Music, Continuing Education, Pharmacy, Veterinary Science, Dentistry, Graduate Studies, Nursing, and Environment Design. Students numbered around 30,000, including some 6,000 graduates, and there were nearly 1,500 professors.

The annual operating budget exceeded $200 million, with over 90 percent coming from the provincial government. The university received $33 million in research grants, equivalent to 16 percent of its operating budget. The university awarded degrees on behalf of two affiliated schools – l'École des Hautes Études Commerciales (HÉC) and l'École Polytechnique. With 5,000 students, the latter is the largest engineering school in Quebec, while HÉC had more than 8,000 business management students. Both schools fall outside the scope of this study.

Budgetary cutbacks began to affect the University of Montreal in 1981. Although government funding had not kept up with inflation during the 1970s, the university nonetheless had a surplus at the end of 1980–81. That year, however, the government increased the university's operating grant by only 4 percent, even though salary increases (comprising more than 80 percent of the budget) of about 17 percent had been negotiated with the staff. The shortfall represented a budget cut of about 10 percent, according to university officials. The government also announced plans to decrease total funding to Quebec universities by 30 percent over the next three years.

The reductions in operating grants amounted to $30 million between 1981–82 and 1983–84. Government funding rose by only 6 percent during this period, against an inflation rate of 22 percent and a 9 percent increase in student enrolments. The university made its cutbacks on the basis of its "ability to cut expenses and not balance the budget" (in the words of a central administrator) and, not unlike McGill, engaged in a strategy of deficit financing. By the end of 1983–84, the University of Montreal had accumulated a deficit of $6.2 million, having spent the surplus of $7.2 million that had existed in 1981.

RESOURCE ALLOCATION

In the first year, 1981–82, there was a 3.5 percent reduction in faculty budgets and a 5.5 percent cut in services; during the same year, there was an additional 2.5 percent reduction in administrative units. These cost reductions were distributed across the board because, according to central administrators, the late announcement of the cuts – half way during the academic year – left no time to plan any other course of action.

> As it usually is [with the government], there is no way to plan in advance. (Central administrator)

Administrators estimated that these cuts saved about $12 million without causing too many problems.

> We knew we had extras that other people [in hospitals and secondary schools, also experiencing cutbacks] didn't have any more. (Dean)

There was dissatisfaction with the uniform nature of the cuts, however. Deans complained that across-the-board reductions encouraged mediocrity and penalized good departments. These criticisms became more vocal when it became clear that the cuts would continue, and there were demands for greater selectivity.

> Once the buffers have gone you have to "make choices," which is a very erotic term for a university. (Central administrator)

The central administration developed a formula to allocate differential reductions of up to 11 percent in 1982–83 and up to 7 percent in 1983–84. The magnitude of the reduction faced by any given faculty was determined by a "productivity" formula, where the criteria were research and teaching. The formula allocated larger cuts for such faculties as Education and Nursing, while others, such as Science, Economics, and Computer Science, were not affected by reductions (Bélanger and Tremblay 1982).

The 1982–83 formula was developed from a study conducted in 1981 by a committee on teaching and research priorities (Comité des priorités sur l'enseignement et la recherche, or COPER). The committee recommended that teaching resources be reduced in less productive units. The criteria developed to measure productivity formed the basis of the 1982–83 formula. They consisted of a number of indicators intended to help in assessing performance in research and teaching, and also included a qualitative component, whereby specified cuts were adjusted according to the constraints faced by individual faculties (such as the number of tenured staff) and in response to appeals from deans.

> The cut was on paper. Eventually, they would worry about your needs. It's one thing to have something for the university as a whole but when you sit down with a vice-rector and say, "We have to keep that person," it's a different ball game. They made various adjustments. (Dean)

> I remember having a battle and saying it was unjust; and I must have convinced somebody because I remember our allocation went up. (Dean)

The formula was refined the following year to reduce the number of criteria to three basic areas – teaching, graduate teaching, and research – in order to produce a more exact weighting.

> It was much more quantitative and mechanical. It did not take into account disciplinary traditions, disciplinary constraints, faculty constraints like tenure. Unlike the other [formula], where we looked [at these things and made] qualitative judgments. (Central administrator)

In summary, the strategy adopted by the University of Montreal in response to funding constraints placed a far more overt emphasis on differential funding than that followed by McGill University. A productivity formula was used to rank units according to whether they were high or low performers, and funds were distributed accordingly.

THE IMPLEMENTATION
OF THE CUTS

While the overall pattern of resource allocation was determined centrally through the formulae, the implementation of the cutbacks was largely left to the deans after the first year. The formulae allocated resources on the basis of figures calculated at the departmental level, but the deans received a global budget for all departments under their responsibility. It was left to them to decide whether to conform to the guidelines concerning individual units: they did not have to allocate resources between departments on the basis of the formulae.

Global budgets represented a change in the resource allocation process. Previously, deans had been more constrained by the central administration. For example, they had had to obtain central approval to hire. Under the new system, as long as they had money in their budgets, deans were free to recruit.

> We no longer had to argue with a vice-rector every time we wanted to hire a professor of something like that [as long as] we satisfied academic standards. (Dean)

Should a professor leave, the deans could also decide whether to replace him or her with an equivalent person or with a junior (and cheaper) individual, or to use part-time lecturers instead; they were also able to carry deficits and surpluses over to the following year. While the change represented some freedom from previous restrictions, in reality the deans had little room for manœuvre since most of their budgets were tied up in commitments to existing staff and salaries were negotiated centrally.

THE REDUCTION OF EXPENDITURES

The only way to save significant amounts of money was to reduce salaries, which represented 85 percent of the budget. Central administrators maintained that they had been unable to negotiate salary concessions with the faculty union. Union representatives argued that the administration had not made its requests "in such a way that the unions felt solidarity." Moreover, at the time of the request, newspaper articles appeared criticizing the high administrative costs of the university, including the rector's high salary and his chauffeur-driven car.

> The image of the administration of the university was [that it was] passing the buck. "Why should we pay when his chauffeur is still there." (Dean)

Thus the main form of expenditure reduction was a decrease in the number of employees. Between 1980–81 and 1984–85, the number of full-time-equivalent teaching posts fell by over 10 percent, and 425 nonacademic and 120 academic posts were removed from the payroll. This was done without breaking tenure or introducing tenure quotas: the Assembly (senate) debated the issue for a year and then rejected the idea. Consequently, attrition became the main mechanism for reducing personnel.

The administration did initiate steps to prevent the renewal of contracts of untenured staff. In 1982, more than 100 letters were sent to such employees, informing them that, unless otherwise notified, their contracts would not be renewed at the end of the academic year because of budgetary constraints. The administration maintained that the letter had to be sent in December 1982 because, according to the statutes, the university would otherwise have been unable to terminate legally the staff in question at the end of the following academic year. The letter made the headlines in the Montreal newspapers, and the university was forced to re-evaluate its position. The deans were given the possibility of finding other ways to reduce costs and, with the union agreeing to a 1 percent shortfall in the negotiated salary increase, the remaining positions were saved.

No major attempts were made to reorganize or merge units, and the administration was reluctant to initiate the closure of any units or programs. A study was undertaken by the central administration to examine each unit and to estimate how long it would take for its closure to produce savings for the university. The study concluded that the loss of income associated with the loss of students and the inability to fire staff would preclude any cost savings for a significant period of time.

> It would be difficult to cut a complete unit. I don't know how we could do it, how we could cut an academic unit because then we would lose students and lose more money. It would have to be a service ... We've done some analysis and in all cases we cannot cut expenditures enough to compensate for the loss of the grant ... because the staff has job security. (Central administrator)

Early retirement was not promoted to any great extent, and only a handful of people took advantage of this possibility. Individuals were not attracted by the monetary incentive, and since payments were made from faculty budgets, deans had little motivation to encourage individuals to seek early retirement.

> I must say we haven't convinced many people to retire before sixty five. (Assistant dean)

The university tried to attract more private funding. A new director was appointed to the development office in an attempt to professionalize fund-raising. A capital campaign during the early 1980s raised $25 million.

> We didn't have the people to [raise money]. We didn't have the people to build a system. We are doing that now. (Dean)

While the University of Montreal adopted a more differential process of resource allocation than did McGill University, the methods of expenditure reduction and revenue raising were similar. Attrition was the main cost-reduction mechanism and, although the university differentiated between high- and low-performing units, it avoided radical surgery.

DECISION MAKING

The University of Montreal's internal structure differed somewhat from McGill University's (see Figure 4.1). The rector and vice-rectors were appointed for renewable four-year terms. The Council was the equivalent to a board of governors, while the Assembly resembled a senate. The former consisted of twenty-four members, of whom eight were appointed by the government, two by the Archbishop of Montreal, and five by the Assembly; the remainder were appointed by the Council itself. The Assembly consisted of over ninety members, including twenty-two *ex officio* members, forty-five professors, six students, three nonacademic staff, and three Council members. Some academic matters were the concern of the Commission des études (curriculum board), which was responsible for the approval and coordination of courses. It consisted of nearly forty members, including the rector, the deans, and representatives of students and professors.

This division of responsibilities between the two academic bodies appeared to make the Assembly weaker than the Senate at McGill University, while the Council seemed more influential than McGill's Board. For example, while both the Assembly and the Senate could be overruled by the Council or the Board, that occurrence was unheard of at McGill but not uncommon at the University of Montreal.

> Sometimes [the Assembly members] think they are a deciding body – but not according to our charter. They make suggestions and recommendations and they are a powerful pressure group, but not a deciding body. (Central administrator)

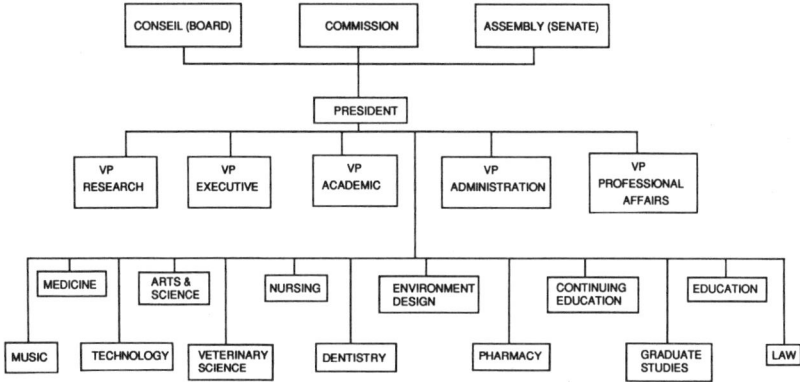

Figure 4.1
University of Montreal: Simplified Organization Chart (ca 1986)

It's the Council that takes the definitive decisions. (Dean)

The Council acted on the advice of the Executive Committee, which consisted of the rector, the vice-rectors, and the directors of the various administrative functions. Recommendations concerning financial matters came from the Budget Committee, a subcommittee of the executive committee. The key group, however, was the smaller "Régie," composed of the rector, five vice-rectors, and the university's secretary general, of which the Council was highly supportive.

The Régie knows the Council, it knows how to present things, it knows what to present, it knows not to present other things. The rector and vice-rectors are very powerful. (Dean)

I'm not suggesting the Council are rubber-stampers, but they act on information and that information reaches them from the Régie, which is a powerful group. (Dean)

As a result, power at the University of Montreal was centralized in the hands of central administrators.

The power play takes place at a level far beyond our influence. (Dean)

Even with the decentralization of resource allocations in the move towards global faculty budgets, the University of Montreal remained far more centralized than McGill. Deans were constrained by the unionization of academic and nonacademic staff. All salaries were negotiated centrally, and deans had to work within precise guidelines, procedures, and definitions. Department heads did not receive their own budgets, as they did at McGill, and were dependent on the dean for funding decisions.

> The department heads are not powerful enough – they don't have the support of central administration. The deans are not powerful enough. (Dean)

The process of determining the selective cutbacks was also relatively centralized. The committees established to develop the formulae and examine the closure of units were comprised, primarily or entirely, of central administrators, while committees at McGill University typically involved fairly equal representation from the Senate, the Board, faculty, nonacademic staff, and students.

Another difference concerned the deans, who were far less cohesive than those at McGill. While there was not much overt conflict between them, they did not perceive themselves as particularly united. Instead, they saw themselves as a fragmented group of separate units.

> It's an individual effort by each unit to try and do as well for itself as possible – sometimes, without doubt, to the detriment of the good of the overall university. (Dean)

> The deans have always been competitive in a gentlemanly way. No one bangs the table and says, "I want more money" ... [but] everyone has his own territory and doesn't enter into anyone else's. (Dean)

> There are lots of barriers surrounding each faculty. (Dean)

In addition, a number of specific actions taken by the central administration gave rise to particular concerns.

Termination Attempt

The attempt to terminate the contracts of untenured staff met with considerable criticism.

> It was a stupid way to solve a problem. It was mismanagement – they didn't think about it. You should see my junior staff. They are still afraid of what's going to happen. (Dean)

Decentralization

The move to decentralize the budget was also viewed with suspicion. Central administrators argued that it was part of an ongoing move towards decentralization initiated by the rector in 1975, and that the fact that it occurred at a time of fiscal constraint was a coincidence.

> Unfortunately, [decentralization] coincided with the period of cutbacks. (Central administrator)

Some deans agreed with this interpretation of events.

> [The rector], I think, secretly wanted to decentralize more. There was perhaps a battle between him and some of the vice rectors ... He jumped at the idea. (Dean)

Others, however, adopted a far more cynical view of decentralization, seeing it as a political move on the part of the central administration to diffuse the pressures created by the cutback allocations.

> It would relieve the pressure on the central administration because the tough decisions would be made by deans. If all the pressures had been put on central administration, then the deans, the faculty members, etc., would have been against a small group. Now with this decentralized system, the base is negotiating with the deans, the deans negotiate with the administration. (Central administrator)

> Some cynics said, Now they don't have any money left, they give the power to the deans; when they had money left, they kept the decisions to themselves ... I am one of those cynics. (Assistant dean)

Few interviewees thought that power had been decentralized in any meaningful way.

> Power is never given here, so if something was given, it wasn't power, it was administrative ... Decentralization [needs] a new style of decision-making which allows more knowledge and information to flow between faculties. (Dean)

> They started a style of management that was supposed to be decentralized. What they really decentralized were the problems, what they really centralized was the money. You can hire anyone you want as long as you have the money. Since you don't have the money, you can't hire ...

They keep an eye on you very closely ... We didn't increase our power very much. (Dean)

It was also pointed out that to decentralize during a period of cutbacks was counterproductive since central direction was required to allocate resources to priorities.

In my view the timing was bad: when a corporation is having problems, they don't decentralize, they centralize. (Dean)

Central administrators, on the other hand, argued that the granting of increased autonomy to the deans had helped them to implement the cutbacks more easily.

There are choices to be made when you have cutbacks. It is very difficult for the central administration to take them. Such decisions must be taken at the base. (Central administrator)

The decentralized approach has allowed us to do a lot more than us cutting directly in the budget ... we left that responsibility with the dean or the director to make his own cuts. (Central administrator)

A few deans agreed with this observation, although with some ambivalence.

It meant nothing because there was no more money left. Money was not decentralized – the problem was decentralized. But, after all, it was better; it was a way of permitting the faculty to keep on living. I prefer that, but I think the overall view was they were transferring the problem. (Assistant dean)

To some extent they were letting the basic units handle the problems. This is it: during prosperity *we*'ll handle it; during misery *you* handle [it]. But maybe it's better this way. If it was centralized it would have been worse. (Dean)

The move towards decentralization thus failed to secure strong decanal support.

Competition and Territoriality

Another complaint expressed by many deans was that the move to reduce costs resulted in an increase in amount of the competition between them.

The deans realize as the pie gets smaller, to get their share they have to fight with other deans. (Central administrator)

The overall amount of money was always the same, so each time we got one more dollar, someone else had to lose it ... We were always looking at each other: "Was he cut?" (Assistant dean)

This competition did not take the form of an all-out war so much as of barriers being erected to protect individual territories.

If I send a student to another faculty, I send money. So there is a tendency to build walls around each faculty. (Dean)

Many of the complaints were directed at an unfair formula rather than at other deans, between whom there was little overt conflict.

I don't think that we've ever been in the position where we're visibly competing with each other at the same time; we're always taken one by one. (Dean)

Thus while the financial restrictions increased the degree of fragmentation among the deans, they did not intensify the level of overt conflict between them.

Leadership

Many complaints were not directed at the cutbacks *per se* but stemmed from general dissatisfaction with the leadership of the university.

Leadership starts at the top. That has to be underlined. We haven't had that for a long time. My view is that if there is leadership there will be a restructuring of our faculties. (Central administrator)

With the management of this university, you have a hard time seeing where they are going. I'm not sure they know ... either. (Dean)

Crisis is a good opportunity to review what we're doing, where we are going and be a bit more creative. If we take it that way, I think we can get out of this mess. It's the leader's responsibility to develop that climate, and this is what we don't see in this university. The leadership is very weak. If we had better leaders who wanted to develop entrepreneurship, then I think things would go better. (Dean)

In summary, the University of Montreal was a more centralized institution than McGill. The Council had been known to overrule the

Assembly; the deans were fragmented and, despite some decentralization, lacked power; department heads did not have their own budgets; and much of the power within the university rested with the central administration and, in particular, the Régie. While centralization, coupled with specific issues in the handling of the cutbacks, had engendered some criticism, these actions had not intensified conflict between groups in the university, nor had they provoked widespread resistance against the central administration's handling of the budget cuts.

THE DIFFERENTIAL NATURE
OF THE CUTBACKS

While there were complaints about the way in which elements of the cutback process had been handled at the University of Montreal, there was no strong resistance to the *principle* of differential cutbacks. If anything, complaints revolved around a belief that the cutbacks did not go far enough to support priority areas and make meaningful choices between units.

The university had a tradition of setting up committees, consisting primarily of central administrators, that conducted quantitative studies into resource allocation that predated the formulae. In the 1970s, for example, an investigation into "orientation, direction et planification" had been conducted to plot a future course for the university. Since the study had been based on an assumption of future growth, it had little relevance to the reality of the 1980s. So, two new committees were established – COPER (Comité des priorités sur l'enseignement et la recherche), which investigated teaching and research; and COPAS (Comité des priorités dans les secteurs administratifs et les services), which examined nonacademic units.

Thus the idea of using quantitative studies was well established, but many people believed that these studies were a way of *avoiding* action rather than *taking* action. For example, COPAS recommended merging some services to save money, but these recommendations were not accepted, according to some, because of the threat to existing "territories." COPER's proposal to cut the number of elective courses was not adopted either. Nothing of substance came from either study.

> It was the first evaluation exercise in this university. People don't like to be evaluated, especially where there is a lot of money [at stake]. The attitudes are changing a bit. The report contained quantitative data and also qualitative value judgments. As a result, the rector received letters saying it doesn't make sense. There was some panic at the administration's level, especially at the rector's level. (Central administrator)

The study that considered the implications of closing individual units also came to the conclusion that no money could be saved this way because of the ensuing loss of students and of the inability to terminate tenured staff. Many individuals felt, however, that it was designed to "prove" a foregone conclusion.

> It was a theoretical exercise. No one tried to identify which are the fields offering good services, which are the fields we want to preserve, and which are the others and what we could do with the people. (Dean)

> It was designed to prove a point. Everybody was happy with it because it went through the Council and the rector could say, "Well, you've been asking me about this: here's the answer." (Central administrator)

Thus the quantitative studies conducted at the University of Montreal and the ostensibly differential approach were interpreted by the university community, not as an attempt to establish priorities but as a way of avoiding difficult decisions.

> Every time we set up an inquiry it is a way of taking no decision ... It prolongs the agony. (Dean)

> There is a big difference between making choices and just using the term. We did not make choices even with the criteria we had designed. It was not a formula conducive to choices. When you make choices there are value judgments ... there has to be a plan. Although the wording was used there was no plan ... It was just an image that some people wanted to project. (Central administrator)

Many interviewees thought that the formulae were used to legitimize decisions rather than to determine priority areas and establish where cuts should be made.

> They have used a formula to make the cuts look more logical ... [but] you had the impression that no one listened to what you were saying and that decisions were made ahead of time. (Dean)

> Now it is necessary for the university to find the courage to make selective cutbacks. The previous cutbacks were not selective but modulated cutbacks based on performance. They were horizontal cuts. (Dean)

A second complaint centred on the methodology for reducing costs, which some interviewees considered to be unfairly biased in favour of the scientific disciplines.

We thought that the criteria developed to grade the units did not apply very well to [professional schools]. (Assistant dean)

The formula was very unsatisfactory because the philosophy of the cuts was based upon performance in teaching, but there was a heavy weighting on [graduate] students and research. As a result of this, some departments were very highly penalized. (Dean)

There were serious methodological questions. The [formula] was prepared for the type of department in the arts and sciences ... It didn't give enough weight to practical work. (Dean)

Other interviewees, however, felt such criticism was inevitable from areas that had fared poorly.

They were criticized because they were making a judgment [on] the faculties ... They were ranking the faculties on research and many deans didn't like that. The ratios placed the faculties in a position where they had to be compared on the same basis. (Assistant dean)

There was lots of criticism of the productivity studies. Those who had [the] weakest productivity, they contested the numbers, they contested the data. (Central administrator)

Following two years of differential resource allocation, the university returned to across-the-board cost reductions in 1984–85, when a base cut of 2.6 percent was applied to all faculties. The central administration argued that it was impossible to continue with selective cuts.

We could not analyse and reanalyse the situation ... We felt we couldn't go through the process again, but we still had to cut. (Central administrator)

In general, the differential cutbacks were accepted by the university community despite some grumbling about the methodology and the weighting given to certain areas. What seemed to cause more concern was the belief that selective reductions were more window-dressing than a sincere attempt to establish and fund priority areas.

SELECTIVE CUTS AT THE UNIVERSITY OF MONTREAL?

When the retrenchment policies adopted by McGill University and the University of Montreal are compared, one can see that the latter adopted an ostensibly more differential approach to resource allocation during the period of cost reductions and used more technocratic analysis in the form of quantitative studies. These studies were carried out by committees dominated by central administrators. The principle of differential cutbacks and the use of quantitative studies to support them was, however, perceived to be legitimate; what was criticized was the unwillingness of the central administration to go far enough along this selective route. As a result, the idea of establishing formal priorities was far more acceptable at the University of Montreal than at McGill, and many people articulated a desire for the central administration to make more selective decisions concerning high and low priorities.

> The university directors will have to make some choices, some very difficult choices to be sure. It will be impossible for them to do otherwise. (Central administrator)

> If we are to continue, we must establish priorities. (Dean)

Most central administrators, however, showed a marked reluctance to adopt this strategy.

> If we wanted to go further, if we were put in the position where we had to cut more, then I think it would have to be done in a different way. We would have to cut in activities, cut a department, cut a program, cut a service. This [would have to be done] by the central administration. This would be difficult. It's much more difficult to cut a complete unit. (Central administrator)

> When you cut, those who are cut are never happy. They will always be very critical because all the statistical methods you know mean different outcomes. (Central administrator)

In 1985, a new rector was appointed, who represented a clean break with the previous administration. He was perceived by interviewees to be capable of providing the necessary impetus to force the university to focus on its priority areas.

> Everything is tied up with what the new rector has in mind. There is a feeling that he is someone who has a low profile but who is action-oriented. He doesn't like to talk about administration but he does administrate. (Central administrator)

The new rector was quoted as favouring evaluation by external experts and long-term planning, although he was cautious on the subject of eliminating departments.

> If we closed one department or another, it would not settle our deficit.
> (Rector, quoted in *The Montreal Gazette* 30 November 1985: B-4).

A new study on performance was conducted in 1985 to examine the research and teaching records of each unit and compare them with those of equivalent units in eleven other Canadian universities (Bélanger and Lacroix 1986). Quantitative data such as grants from the major research agencies, the number of courses taught, and the number of publications were used to evaluate performance. This study had more legitimacy than previous efforts because it compared "oranges with oranges" (as one dean put it) and used widely accepted indicators.

> If you don't get money [from the research councils], then you are no good – it's as brutal as that. (Central administrator)

It was also more acceptable because, unlike the other studies, this assessment was not commissioned by the central administration but by the Planning Committee, which reported to both the Council and the Assembly. It was believed that this study could be used to identify priorities within the university.

> The last phase is the comparison with other institutions and getting faculties to identify the areas they want to preserve. Maybe then we could make a few comparisons and a few choices. (Dean)

Thus the appointment of the new rector was welcomed with a considerable amount of optimism, stemming from the belief that the new administration would improve the management of the institution. His appointment signalled the possibility of change and the establishment of priorities. There was also a widespread feeling that the latest study was a legitimate mechanism for identifying priorities. It used a more sophisticated analysis than previous studies, by comparing the performance of the University of Montreal with that of other Canadian universities and using external indicators. Moreover, it was not commissioned by the central administration. It would appear, then, that in 1985 the University of Montreal had a "window of opportunity" to effect some significant changes in light of the credibility provided by new leadership and a "technology" in the form of the 1985 study on performance.

CONCLUSIONS

During the late 1970s and early 1980s, the University of Montreal relied extensively on the generation of quantitative data to justify resource allocation decisions. The various committees, studies, and reports, as well as the Office of Institutional Research, an office in the central administration that collected, generated, and analysed these data, can be considered as a centralized *technocracy* (Mintzberg 1979a) linking resource allocation to formal analysis on the basis of various forms of performance indicators. While this "rational" approach had considerable legitimacy among members of the university, central administrators did run into a number of problems concerning their implementation of the cutbacks. In particular, the overall high degree of centralization, the termination of untenured staff, and the symbolic gesture of decentralization to the deans at a time of budget cuts were criticized.

One of the reasons behind these criticisms lay in the lack of confidence in the leadership of the institution that existed during the time of the cutbacks. It would appear that, if the central administration management lacks credibility, quantitative criteria and rational analysis, no matter how legitimate, will not be enough to compensate. This view is supported by subsequent events. The technocratic approach, far from being abandoned, was strengthened in 1985 through a more sophisticated, national comparison of university performance in Canada. The legitimacy of this particular initiative appears to have been enhanced not only by the increased sophistication of the analysis, but also by the fact that it was sponsored by the Planning Committee. Moreover, the arrival of a new rector increased the belief that more would be done with the results of the study.

Chapters three and four show a marked difference in the institutional context at the two Quebec universities: at the University of Montreal, relatively centralized planning was accepted; at McGill University, planning at any level was frowned upon. Two very different formulae were used to respond to fiscal restraint: one was designed to accentuate differential cutbacks; the other was designed to minimize them. The following chapter examines explores some of the similarities and differences between the two universities in greater detail.

CHAPTER FIVE

Comparison: McGill University and the University of Montreal

McGill University and the University of Montreal are similar in terms of many of their structural characteristics and research mandates. In the face of budgetary restraints imposed by the provincial government, they adopted similar strategies to cope with these challenges but chose quite different processes of implementing those strategies (Hardy 1987b).

DEALING WITH THE CUTBACKS

The two universities chose similar mechanisms for reducing expenditures: since 80 percent of the budget was tied up in salaries and tenure, and since job security protected the majority of employees, reducing the number of posts through attrition was the main mechanism adopted by both institutions. McGill had some additional flexibility in freezing salaries since staff were nonunionized and agreed to give up wage increases, thus enabling the university to save $7 million. Both universities relied on hiring freezes as a temporary measure; and neither broke tenure, introduced tenure quotas, or changed sabbatical policy. Government policies prevented both universities from raising tuition fees, and both launched capital campaigns to increase their revenues. Research funding was also increased – by 60 percent at McGill University and by 52 percent at the University of Montreal – although this also raised overhead costs. So, in response to similar financial constraints, both universities chose similar strategies to save and raise money; in other words, the contents of their respective strategies were much the same. The processes employed to implement those cutbacks were quite different, however.

At the University of Montreal, across-the-board reductions were implemented in 1981–82 because, according to administrators, the late announcement of government funding cuts left little time to plan anything else. Faculty budgets were reduced by 3.5 percent; services, by 5.5 percent; and administrative units, by 2.5 percent. Over the next two years, differential cuts were made on the basis of "productivity" formulae developed by administrators to evaluate undergraduate teaching, graduate teaching, and research in each department. Differential reductions of up to 11 percent were made in 1982–83, and of up to 7 percent in 1983–84 (Bélanger and Tremblay 1982; Bélanger and Lacroix 1986).

McGill University did not use a special mechanism to implement cost reductions but relied on a formula that had been used to allocate resources for a number of years. This was based on student numbers: in general terms, faculties and departments with increased student enrolments received more money; those with fewer students received less. The previous year's base budget was multiplied by the formula to take enrolment changes into account, and this amount was then normalized to equal the amount available for expenditures. Budgets were reduced by slightly more than the amount necessary to meet funding cuts in order to provide a discretionary fund equivalent to about 3 percent of the budget.

DIFFERENCES IN CONTEXT

To understand why different implementation approaches were followed, one must examine the contexts in which they were applied. While the two universities were structurally similar, their institutional contexts were quite different. One area where this was particularly clear was in the use of formal planning and quantitative analysis.

At the University of Montreal, quantitative studies were common, and several committees were set up to report on budgetary constraints. In 1981, there were two committees on priorities in teaching and research, and in the administrative and service sectors. In 1982, one committee developed the productivity formula for 1982–83, while a second committee refined it for the following year. A committee in 1983 examined the cost and benefits of closing each department. And in 1985 a working group on priorities engaged in a major comparative analysis of research and teaching productivity in all disciplines against their counterparts in eleven major Canadian universities (Bélanger and Lacroix 1986). Each year, the Office of Institutional Research distributed a variety of publications devoted to these issues. All of these reports were lengthy, with considerable emphasis being placed on numbers and charts; for example, the 1985 report consisted of two volumes of text and tables, totalling 712 pages.

These committees were staffed primarily by administrators, and their reports contained a substantial amount of analysis that was used to justify resource allocation decisions. For example, the decision not to eliminate any units was explained with reference to the 1983 study. The 1985 study on priorities was a highly complex and quantitative exercise, which was viewed by deans as an essential step in planning priorities and resource allocations for the future. Thus formal planning and quantitative data were highly visible at the University of Montreal.

The situation was quite different at McGill University, where only two committees were created to examine the issue of cost reductions between 1981 and 1985. Both contained a representative of the Board of Governors, the Senate, the central administration, and the faculty and staff associations. Both produced reports that were brief (50 and 28 pages, respectively), contained few figures, and were characterized by general policy statements on how cutbacks should be handled (for example, the position on deficit financing and salary freezes) rather than by intensive quantitative analysis.

Formal planning and centralized direction did not play a prominent role at McGill (Thompson 1977). The deans were particularly suspicious of the technocratic approach, and administrators were reluctant to use overtly differential mechanisms that could lead to conflict between departments and faculties at a time of scarce resources. This approach was seen as a way to minimize conflict, since it had the appearance of objectivity and avoided any radical reallocation of resources. Even the discretionary fund promoted an image of fairness since the deans "never competed in an open forum" and the private negotiations were "kept civil."

THE OUTCOMES

What were the results of these different approaches to implementation? In terms of resource allocation between faculties, the two universities display similar results: there was no radical reallocation of resources in either institution (Table 5.1).

These similarities might seem surprising, given that the approach adopted by the University of Montreal emphasized differentiation while McGill's obscured it. There were three main reasons for these similarities. First, the University of Montreal's approach assessed differential cuts on a departmental basis but awarded global budgets to the deans; as a result, departmental differences tended to offset one another. Second, McGill's discretionary fund injected a differential element into the resource allocation process. Third, attrition was the main cutback mechanism. Since both universities were old, large, and had similar

Table 5.1
Changes in Budget, Student, and Staff Allocation, University of Montreal and McGill University, 1980–81 to 1983–84[1]

Faculty	Proportion of budget		Proportion of students[2]		Proportion of staff	
	1980–81	1983–84	1980–81	1983–84	1980–81	1983–84
University of Montreal[3]						
Art & Science	35	36	38	39	34	34
Dentistry	5	5	2	2	4	4
Education	7	6	2	1	10	7
Law	3	3	6	5	3	3
Medicine	25	25	15	15	20	22
Music	2	2	2	2	3	3
Nursing	1	1	1	1	2	2
Pharmacy	1	1	2	2	1	1
Planning	3	3	3	3	3	3
Theology	1	1	2	2	1	1
Veterinary Science	5	5	2	2	2	2
McGill University						
Agriculture	6	6	5	5	6	6
Arts	16	16	22	21	19	19
Dentistry	2	2	1	1	2	2
Education	9	9	9	8	12	10
Engineering	11	11	11	11	11	11
Law	2	3	3	3	2	3
Management	5	5	8	8	5	4
Medicine	21	21	14	14	16	18
Music	3	3	2	2	3	4
Religious Studies	1	1	1	1	1	1
Science	18	18	16	17	20	19

1 Figures from university budgets.
2 There are slight differences in the way the two universities calculate student credits.
3 Graduate Faculty and Continuing Education students have been excluded.

faculties, one would expect a similar demographic profile; indeed, most savings were achieved in areas populated with older professors.

As a result of their respective expenditure-reduction and revenue-raising strategies, both universities reduced their dependency on government funding and increased research revenue. McGill had slightly more success in diversifying its sources of income (Table 5.2) with the help of the interest from a large endowment ($163 million in 1983–84). Neither university balanced its books, however. The University of Montreal used up a $6 million surplus and accumulated a $7 million deficit between 1980–81 and 1983–84, while McGill used $7 million of the unrestricted portion of its endowment to fund operating deficits during the same period.

Table 5.2
Distribution of Sources of Revenues, McGill University and University of Montreal,
1980–81 and 1983–84[1]

	University of Montreal		McGill University	
	1980–81	1983–84	1980–81	1983–84
Fees	5	5	6	8
Quebec grant	77	74	57	49
Research	10	14	19	23
Private income	–	–	3	4
Other	8	7	15	16

1 Figures in percentages from university budgets.

CONCLUSIONS

The process used to implement retrenchment at McGill University – decentralized and ostensibly "fair" cutbacks – was designed to protect the collegial culture that administrators believed permeated the university. At the University of Montreal, the use of productivity formulae and selective reductions was an attempt to legitimize the cutback decisions. Administrators hoped that this "technocratic" approach would justify their decisions by linking differential cuts to performance and providing a rational basis for avoiding more drastic decisions, such as eliminating departments or faculties (Hardy 1988).

In effect, the different formulae used at the two universities were important more for their *symbolic* significance than for their substantive impact on resource allocation. They were different in form, rather than substance, because of differences in the context – the "technocratic" approach accorded legitimacy at the University of Montreal, while the "egalitarian" approach had more credibility at McGill University.

CHAPTER SIX

The University of British Columbia

The University of British Columbia (UBC) was initially established under the auspices of McGill University but gained full independent status in 1915. It is the largest university in British Columbia: in 1984, some 1,900 professors taught in twelve faculties; there were about 27,000 students, 4,000 of whom were graduates; and the university's operating budget was $215 million, augmented by research grants of over $50 million.

PROVINCIAL RESTRAINT MEASURES

The focus of the study here is on UBC's response to the provincial government's 1983 restraint legislation. The university had already had some experience with financial restrictions prior to 1983. Following an arbitration award, a 21 percent increase in salaries in 1981 had reduced the amount available for other operating expenses. The response was, according to one dean, to "freeze everything in sight." The following year, a presidential advisory committee was established to examine ways of reducing expenditures. Deans were asked to prepare a range of options with respect to budget reductions. The major donors of that exercise were the faculties of Education, Arts, and Medicine. In addition, tuition fees were increased.

In 1983, the newly re-elected government (Social Credit) introduced a provincial spending-restraint program that involved thirty-four legislative acts in all. Bill 3 – the *Public Sector Restraint Act* – specifically provided for tenure to be abandoned where it was deemed to be a source of financial problems. Following widespread protest, the government amended the legislation to exempt organizations where the intent to overcome such problems was retained through collective agreements. The UBC faculty association entered into negotiations with the administration to determine a procedure for the definition of financial exigency, but the initial attempt to establish criteria for this purpose failed. Negotiations then began to establish procedures for redundancy following a declaration of financial exigency. An agreement between the association and the administration was reached in 1984, but it failed to be ratified by the association's membership. Subsequent negotiations continued until an agreement was finally ratified in 1985 (see Dennison 1987 for more details).

The government's restraint legislation was accompanied by measures to reduce operating grants. Following a freeze in 1983, grants were subject to a 5 percent decrease in each of the next two years. By 1984, the president was predicting a deficit of at least $6 million. Since universities in British Columbia were not allowed to run deficits, it was clear that action to reduce expenditures further would have to be taken.

In 1984, the president established an advisory committee chaired by the vice-president for academic affairs, with four professors from Law, Science, Medicine, and Fine Arts as members. The committee examined the university's operations and assessed their strengths and weaknesses. The knowledge gained through the committee and from interviews with deans enabled the vice-president (academic) to send letters to the deans in November 1984, asking them to "show cause" why certain areas should not be discontinued. The deans were expected to respond early in the new year, but by this time the president had left and the vice-president (academic) had become president *pro-tem*.

At the same time, the Senate Budget Committee (SBC) was developing a procedure that was to be followed in the event of program discontinuance. The SBC's mandate was to advise the president on the budgetary process, but in 1982 it had been given a second term of reference – to assist the president and report to the university's Senate on academic priorities as they pertained to the preparation of the university's budget. The committee produced a comprehensive planning document that rated programs as core, core-related, and noncore on the basis of quality, cost, enrolment, uniqueness, and special value to the province and to the country as a whole.

In May 1985, a set of proposals for program elimination was presented to the Senate by the acting vice-president (academic) on behalf of the president's office, based partly on the recommendations made by the SBC. The Senate debated the proposals, and programs in Dental Hygiene, Industrial Education, Recreation Education, and Media Technology, as well as the Licentiate in Accounting and the Diploma in Agricultural Sciences, were discontinued. One proposal, regarding the

Landscape Architecture program – was not approved. In addition, a sum of $3.4 million was to be saved through unspecified cost reductions in Arts, Science, Medicine, Applied Science, and Education.

Some 100 faculty positions were eliminated, mostly by closing vacant posts. Twelve faculty members received termination notices, of whom nine were tenured. In the absence of an agreement on redundancy procedures, the administration acted on the assumption that it had the right to release faculty from programs that had been discontinued with the Senate's approval. The faculty association disputed this assumption but withdrew the arbitration demand when the university negotiated severance terms with the faculty members concerned. The decision to terminate tenured faculty did, however, cause wider protest, and a committee of enquiry was established by the Canadian Association of University Teachers. This led to new discussions between the faculty association and the administration and, eventually, to a set of redundancy procedures to be followed after a declaration of financial exigency that were finally agreed upon and ratified by the association's membership in 1985.

THE PROCESS OF PROGRAM ELIMINATION

The University of British Columbia is the only university in Canada to have laid off tenured faculty in recent times. In order to understand how and why UBC adopted this approach, it is important to clarify the roles of the various interest groups that were involved.

The university's governance structure (Figure 6.1) was laid down in the *University Act*. The president was appointed by the fifteen-member Board of Governors. Ten Board members were appointed by the government (two of whom were nominated by alumni); two were elected by faculty; one, by nonacademic employees; and two, by students. In addition to being responsible for financial decisions, the Board also considered recommendations from the Senate for the establishment and discontinuance of faculties, departments, and courses. The Senate, which was responsible for academic governance, had over eighty members, including the president, the academic vice-president, and the deans, as well as faculty and student representatives. The legislation also created the Universities Council – a buffer body between the three universities in British Columbia and the government, which was responsible for system-wide planning, coordination of budget requests, and approval of new programs.

Four groups were particularly visible as far as program closures were concerned – the Senate Budget Committee, the deans, the Senate, and

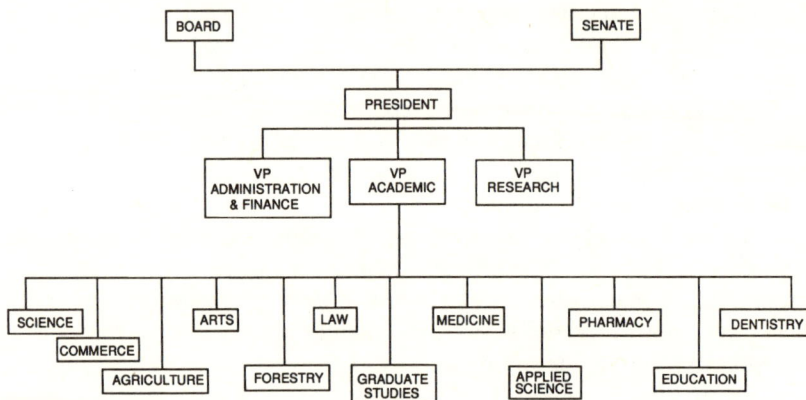

Figure 6.1
University of British Columbia: Simplified Organization Chart (ca 1986)

the Board of Governors. The actions of these groups and their influence on the cutback process throw light on the way in which UBC handled the decision to eliminate programs.

Senate Budget Committee

The members of the SBC were appointed following recommendations by a nominating committee whose members were elected by the Senate. The SBC developed a number of recommendations for program closure based on core/noncore criteria, which were submitted to the president. Not all of its proposals were then submitted to the Senate by the central administration, however. For example, the SBC had wanted more cost reductions than were actually proposed to the Senate; it had proposed specific cuts in Arts and Medicine, but dollar targets were instituted instead. So, while the recommendations for program elimination that were made to the Senate bore some relation to those proposed by the SBC, they were not exactly the same.

> I'm not sure about the SBC review and what subsequently happened. I think the current vice-president (academic) would like to argue that there is a relationship, but my own perception is that they are not connected. (Professor)

The SBC's influence over the president's decisions was circumscribed. It could not operate independently of him and was unable to initiate investigations at the Senate's request. Moreover, its advisory was to the president only.

> The SBC gives advice to the university president and advises Senate of its action. That's a sore point with some members of Senate – that it does not report to Senate. (SBC member)

As a result, it was up to the president to decide whether he wanted to use the SBC in planning financial cuts.

> The power of the SBC depends on how the president uses it. Here we ask the chairman of the SBC to come in, so that the SBC is taken into the confidence of the central administration on most elements. It comes awfully close to feeling, sometimes, that it's being asked to rubber-stamp. (Central administrator)

The committee also depended on the central administration for much of its information.

> The SBC cannot collect information independent of the president's office. (Faculty association representative)

The SBC would have found it difficult to initiate, let alone implement, change without central support.

> The SBC is not as influential as everyone thinks it is, in the sense that it is very difficult for us to generate anything. For example, there would be an absolute riot if we started to generate the data and impetus to try and get another retrenchment. We have to work with the administration and we have to serve as a check on them. (SBC member)

> The SBC isn't a group that decides things. So things are presented to Senate not as a *fait accompli*, but they comment on it. It would be without precedent [for the committee] to come up with its own view of what should be done independent of the administration. It's not an executive body, it's an advisory body. (Central administrator)

The committee also had difficulty in securing the support and cooperation of many of the deans, who held a great deal of influence in the university.

> The SBC is a committee of Senate, and I don't think many deans would be happy on being called by a committee of Senate. And we don't have

the power to summon the deans. We have to go through the president for everything. (SBC member)

Most of the deans expressed either indifference or antagonism towards the SBC, including one who referred to them as "a bunch of patsies."

The SBC did, however, help to shape program closures. Since the Senate had to approve program discontinuance and the SBC was made up of Senate members, it was an important opinion leader in the Senate.

The SBC is influential in so far as Senate is concerned and as far as the university is concerned. (Board member)

Thus the SBC was a mechanism whereby the administration could be seen to be consulting.

The SBC has been used to add a little legitimacy to the decisions of the president. The SBC has tended to be a cooperative body. (Central administrator)

The SBC advises the president on behalf of the academic sector of the institution. They are perceived to be people who can review the budget from the academic point of view. It lends propriety to the budget development process. Everything is run through them, probably more so than in the past. (Central administrator)

The SBC has never been particularly influential – it was just another committee. It was where the decision had to be seen to be coming from – not the deans, not the administrators but a group of senators representing the university. That was why it was so difficult to understand why there were accusations of a lack of consultation. The Senate really is the university. (Dean)

Without the SBC, the administration would have found it difficult to persuade the Senate to accept its proposals or to demonstrate that they were the result of consultation.

The SBC is moderately influential and valuable, of some importance but not central to budget activity. I don't think it's just window-dressing. They could make life very difficult for the administration if they felt it was wrong. (Dean)

In summary, the SBC appeared to be a driving force behind the retrenchment inasmuch as it prepared the criteria for discontinuance that served as a basis for proposals made to the Senate. In reality, however, not all of its recommendations were accepted, and its input into the retrenchment exercise was limited. It may have provided information to help the central administration to decide where effective cost reductions might be made, but it is worth pointing out that the vice-president (academic), later president *pro-tem*, had already chaired an earlier committee on cutbacks. It was suggested by some interviewees that the proposals for closure were based more on his knowledge of, and plans for, the university than on the work of the SBC.

> It was absurd to think that the committee was the engine that drove the retrenchment. It was a presidential retrenchment. (Dean)

If such was the case, the SBC's role was confined primarily to serving as a legitimizing mechanism used by the central administration to secure faculty and Senate support for its plans. Thus it is clear that the proposals submitted to the Senate were not influenced solely by the SBC: other players were involved.

The Deans

The deans were a particularly powerful group at the University of British Columbia.

> The deans at UBC have a reputation for being very powerful. The university was run more as fiefdoms. The deans had quite a bit of power … The university has always had a tradition of powerful deans right from the day it opened. (Senate member)

Their power stemmed not so much from a role in the governance of the university as a whole but from their position as powerful, independent faculty administrators, sovereign within their own area.

> At UBC the deans are not a senior policy team. On the other hand, individual deans could play a role. So, by dint of personality, influence, or interest a dean could be about as influential as he wanted to be, but the deans collectively are not built into the organization in the formal sense. The corollary is that the dean has a great deal more autonomy in his own faculty. (Central administrator)

The deans' role can be perhaps best described as that of chief executive officers (CEOs) of their respective faculties.

> I think they see themselves as CEOs of a subsidiary and they want to run their particular entity. (Dean)

The central administration had traditionally been relatively weak at UBC and, as a result, had left the management of the faculties in the hands of the deans. The latter had considerable latitude in allocating resources among the different departments in their faculties. The larger faculties – Arts, Science, and Medicine – were particularly renowned for their strong deans. Their autonomy had allowed the deans to develop their own methods of accounting, information collection, and purchasing, which had, in the view of the central administration, led to duplication and confusion.

> This university has prided itself on spending less on administration than any other university in the country. What they've really been doing is spending more on administration because a lot of jobs that should have been done in the president's office have been done in the deans' offices and department heads' offices. There was an extensive duplication of effort. If you could add up all the invisible costs, it added up to more than if it had been done centrally. (Central administrator)

The result of these factors was a high degree of fragmentation. Individual deans kept to their own territory – "one faculty did not know another's business," in the words of one dean – and they certainly did not form a united group.

> Deans didn't talk to each other very much. They tended to be very independent and somewhat isolated from each other. Information in the past has been very, very jealously guarded. (Dean)

This dynamic resulted in the relative politicization of the university as the deans fought with each other and with the central administration.

> UBC has a lot of antagonism in it. It is part of the confrontation politics. The departments shook a stick at the faculties who shook a stick at the president, and we are coming to answer for it. All the faculties fought and were vying with each other away from the centre. It was all shenanigans, old boys, slap-happy. (Dean)

The centre found itself relatively powerless vis-à-vis the deans. Obtaining detailed information from the faculties had been difficult either because it was not available – "when we wanted to get the overall financial picture we were using systems that were twenty years old and totally incompatible," according to one central administrator – or because deans were reluctant to provide it.

> In the past, information has not been widely shared; it's been kept in the dean's office. [There are] people who have never had to account for themselves. Some operate on the mushroom principle: you leave them in the dark and cover them with whatever it is you cover mushrooms with. (Central administrator)

The inability to compile detailed, global statistics also made it difficult to develop an institutional perspective. The deans viewed themselves as protectors of their own faculty and did not always identify with the larger organization and its needs.

> I think many of the deans feel that the faculties are the university and they are best run as faculties rather than integrated into the university framework. The more difficult the central administration makes running the faculties by imposing rules and bureaucracy that apply to everyone, the more deleterious that is to the faculties. (Dean)

The retrenchment exercise, however, demanded an institution-wide response. The extent of decentralization at UBC, the lack of an institutional perspective, and the weakness of the central administration hindered the development of such an institutional plan.

> UBC is too decentralized. Nobody sets priorities. The deans set priorities for their faculties, but no one sets priorities for the university or makes choices for the university. (Dean)

When it came to cutbacks, some deans were unwilling to provide central administrators with "information they didn't need" (as one dean put it). The deans of the larger faculties, in particular, had a monopoly on knowledge and information.

> Some deans were incredibly frosty and had obviously been dragged kicking and screaming to the SBC ... They saw it as a kangaroo court and felt the decisions should have been in their hands. (Dean)

> Some deans responded well, others not so well. Some did not want to say where they would cut. It's easy with the small faculties because you can see clearly where to cut – there's no room to play with. When you get to Arts and Medicine it's terribly difficult. (SBC member)

As a result, the central administration largely depended on the deans in formulating its closure proposals. It relied on them for information on where cuts should be carried out and on the implementation of these decisions. The deans had the opportunity to oppose these proposals in the Senate during the approval process; if they had mounted a concerted opposition, this would have led the Senate to vote against the proposals.

> If the deans had wanted to put up a fight on the floor of Senate, they could have got every one of those rescinded. (Senate member)

The recommendations that went to the Senate were not a simple application of the SBC's criteria: they were also a reflection of the power of the deans.

> In retrospect, the cuts were determined by how persuasive particular deans or department heads were. There were units to be terminated, but their dean made a fuss for whatever reason – and the unit was kept. No one really knows what the SBC recommended. There was significant overlap, but some units were taken off. Too much depends on the deans. A strong, persuasive dean who is likely to make trouble is likely to get off easier than he would if it were judged on need or quality. The process is not as objective as perhaps it should be. (Dean)

The central administration did not act on those SBC recommendations which were likely to incur outright opposition from a dean.

> The SBC wanted to discontinue more things that we were prepared to recommend to Senate. In some of those we didn't have the support of the dean. The last thing we wanted to do was get into Senate and end up arguing with the dean. (Central administrator)

For example, in a letter sent by the vice-president (academic), the Arts faculty was originally asked to justify the continuance of the Religious Studies program and to comment on a proposed major reduction in the Family and Nutritional Sciences program. Faced with the refusal of the dean to discuss those two issues, the administration withdrew these specific proposals and substituted a dollar target.

> Some of the deans were able to protect their faculties. They had intended to fire twelve people in the Religious Science department and half of Home Economics. The dean of Arts, to his credit, said, "Go to hell." (Professor)

> The dean ran Arts and no one else ran Arts, and there was no way he wanted the SBC getting in there and making a decision about his faculty. (SBC member)

Medicine, also renowned for a strong dean, similarly received a dollar target. The Education faculty, on the other hand, suffered specific cuts because, argued interviewees, the acting vice-president (academic) had previously been the dean and, therefore, had first-hand knowledge.

> I think the cuts were the result of what the former dean of Education perceived to be necessary in his own faculty. He was and remains interested in changing a [training-oriented] faculty into a research-oriented one. (Faculty association member)

The Senate's failure to approve the proposal to eliminate the Landscape Architecture program was further testimony to the strength of the deans. A number of arguments were voiced, including the fact that UBC's program was the only one of its kind in western Canada. A significant factor, however, was the opposition of the dean in the Senate.

> We got caught by the dean being less neutral that she'd led us to believe she would be. (Central administrator)

In summary, if central administrators were to secure Senate approval for the closures, they needed to have, at the very least, the tacit support of the deans in addition to that of the SBC. The recommendations that were made, with the exception of that concerning the Landscape Architecture program, largely accomplished that balance. The proposals that were put forward were those which had been suggested by the SBC *and*, at the same time, did not antagonize the deans.

> The president's office has to involve us, but they don't have to take our advice. Now they would have a tough time getting it through Senate. The only things they took to Senate were the things the SBC agreed to, except the Arts and Medical targets; otherwise their recommendations and ours were consistent, and ... where we differed they did not take [them] to Senate. It is true that the SBC wanted larger cuts than [did] the president's office. (SBC member)

The Role of the Senate

The UBC Senate had the formal power to approve or reject recommendations made by the central administration, but the support of the deans and the SBC reduced the chances of rejection. Nevertheless, the Senate could still refuse to discontinue programs. Its opposition to the elimination of the Landscape Architecture program was interpreted as a stand taken to assert its independence and make a symbolic gesture.

> In our opinion, Senate wanted to flex its muscles and show that it could delete a recommendation. (SBC member)

In other respects, however, the Senate was not perceived to be a particularly strong body.

> I was not surprised that the Senate accepted the recommendations; what surprised me was [that] they turned one down. As a general rule, when it is clear that the administration has seriously thought something through, that there is the involvement of academics – which was certainly the case here – and when an important committee of Senate itself has been involved, I'd expect Senate to accept it as a legitimate set of proposals. (Dean)

The Senate was given only a limited period of time to consider the proposals for program termination. A weekend meeting was arranged, and a decision had to be taken before the end of the meeting.

> Senate found itself in an awkward position: the background they had been given was scant, the time in which they had to take the decision was brief. Senate has difficulty in dealing with financial decisions when it doesn't have the financial background. Nevertheless, they realized the position the university was in, and the academic strength of some units was such that they could not continue. (Dean)

The Senate had to make this decision on the basis of complicated financial criteria and incomplete information.

> Senate didn't have all the information they conceivably might have had. The Senate also has a tradition of doing what the president tells it [to do]. (Professor)

The perceived crisis caused by the government's attack on tenure helped to legitimize the administration's action. Many people felt "something had to be done."

> Things were presented as a crisis, and they had to act now. They were deliberately given information at the last possible minute and although there was a free debate, they didn't know what they were debating. In particular, they didn't know that if they made certain decisions, the

university would go out and fire people. Senate was misled. (Faculty
association representative)

This crisis may also help to explain why the deans were agreeable to
at least some form of cutback: they too had become "aware of the
corporate problem" (in the words of one dean).

By avoiding opposition from the deans, securing the support of the
SBC, and responding to the need for rapid and complex decisions, the
central administration helped to increase the chances of successfully
closing some programs. This analysis does not, however, explain why
the administration chose this form of retrenchment in the first place.

THE REASONS BEHIND PROGRAM CLOSURE

The response of the University of British Columbia to the provincial
government's funding reductions – the elimination of selected programs
and the termination of tenured faculty members – looked like a major
and drastic act.

> Ideally, you'd like to do these things through attrition or any other way
> so as not to upset the apple cart but, in the case of twelve people, we
> upset the apple cart. (Board member)

At the same time, only twelve people lost their jobs, and the direct
saving achieved through program closures was minimal. The major
money-saving approach was attrition.

> The lucky departments are the ones that don't have anyone retiring or
> resigning around the time of budget cuts. It makes management look
> pretty weak – the line of least resistance. But when you have to cut at
> short notice, it is an expedient way of cutting. (Administrator)

Most interviewees indicated that they did not view the closures as a
real attempt to make differential cuts or establish priority areas.

> [The core/noncore investigation] was just an exercise that the adminis-
> tration was going through ... I think they were basically playing for
> time. The necessity of making difficult decisions had never been faced.
> (Faculty association representative)

> If you are going to bite the bullet and [take on] the ensuing problems,
> you might as well do it in areas where, if you are successful, you can

make major savings. There were lots of problems over minor savings. (Dean)

Administrators argued that while relatively few people were involved, the terminations signalled to the community that the administration was willing to make tough decisions.

> In the end, it was only nine [tenured] people who were terminated, so it did not solve the major budgetary issue. On the other hand, it was a sharp signal to the community that we were protecting our strengths. It was very important to say to the community, "Yes, we can take tough decisions." It may be that it hit the morale of individual faculty members, but it may have been a positive thing as far as administrators, department heads, and deans were concerned, because it showed that when times were tough the university could take tough decisions. It's an interesting question of deeply selective versus across-the-board cuts – you can argue that one both ways. Clearly, one has to be selective, but if you are too selective you will also destroy morale. (Central administrator)

More importantly, the administration's decisions were a signal to the external community that the university was responsive to the need for restraint. The provincial government was perceived to be highly suspicious of the way in which the universities were managed, believing them to be wasteful and inefficient.

> The impression was that not only was the government making deep cuts because of the fiscal problems, but that they were delighted to make the deep cuts because they did not value the universities. (Central administrator)

As a large, research-oriented institution, the university had already been criticized by the government for its apparently high staff/student ratios. Government officials also felt that the central administration was unable to run an efficient organization.

> UBC is like feudal England: robber barons ran the faculties; they gave token support but fought amongst themselves. They gave no control to the central office, so it couldn't do anything. (Provincial government official)

The decisive act of program closure was an opportunity to demonstrate that the administration was able to take action. It was "important to be seen to be cutting," as one dean put it.

> There was an element of "showing the government that we can take tough decisions." (Dean)

> [The closures] were good choices as an answer to government. If the government was going to play a game, we were going to play a game too. The twelve people were the sacrificial lambs too. They did a marvellous job of obfuscating – smoke and mirrors – in the sense that the cuts were so trivial while they looked much more dramatic from the outside. (Dean)

Government demands for action were keenly felt at UBC because most of the members of the Board of Governors were government appointees and strong supporters of government policy. The Board also had a reputation for having confronted the central administration on earlier issues.

> I think the Board is very responsible, and if they don't think the president is doing something right they speak up on it. There might be the odd specific thing where there has been no agreement, but I don't think I'd like to go into that. Certainly, the Board hasn't been reluctant to say "no" to the president and the administration, "and here's why." That message has been communicated. (Board member)

Many people at UBC believed that had the administration been unwilling to take action on program elimination, the Board might have acted unilaterally, invoking financial exigency and the restraint legislation introduced by the provincial government. The *University Act* was unclear about the role of the Board of Governors in closing programs: it only stipulated that the Senate had the power to recommend to the Board "the establishment and discontinuance of any faculty, department or course" (p. 11). It did not say whether, in the absence of any such recommendation, the Board could act alone.

In summary, the cutbacks at the University of British Columbia were the result of the central administration's attempts to balance the competing demands of the deans, the Board, the government, the Senate, the SBC, and faculty members. The willingness to engage in program closure and dismiss tenured faculty was influenced by pressure from the Board and the government. The implementation of that response was then shaped by the Senate, the SBC, the deans, and the faculty association. The fact that the president *pro-tem* would shortly be leaving to occupy a post in Australia may have increased the willingness to take action: he did not feel pressure to maintain longer-term popularity in the university community.

THE AFTERMATH

While the termination of tenured faculty may have increased UBC's credibility in the eyes of the government, it did cause some internal problems.

> UBC was wise in that it demonstrated to the government and the public that it was prepared to take tough and difficult decisions; it was unwise because they [fired tenured faculty] in isolation and damaged their reputation. Because there were so few, it didn't do a lot of good and probably did a lot of harm. (Representative of the Universities Council)

> I don't think the government realizes what a black mark it has left on this institution, which we will be paying for a long time. UBC now has a reputation of being controlled by [the provincial government]. (Dean)

> This is still a good university, but it's not as good as it used to be. (Dean)

The program closures also damaged relations between the administration and the faculty association. In July 1985, the association passed a vote of no-confidence in the Board, the president *pro-tem*, and the acting vice-president (academic). Members of the university community were depressed about salaries, the hostile relationship with the government, and the possibility that more layoffs might occur.

> People were pretty edgy, [fearing] that the terminations were an open door by which it could happen again. (Central administrator)

NEW LEADERSHIP

A new president appointed in 1985 introduced a number of changes. He negotiated settlements with those affected by program closures and came to an agreement with the faculty association on a policy for declaring financial exigency; he also prepared a mission statement.

> The university has never had a plan of where it's going because of the tradition of administrators. UBC has been under-administered and badly administered, so there was no one with the time and the ability to sit back and say, "Maybe we should get out of those areas." UBC had no priorities except to do everything. (Faculty association representative)

Control of budget allocations was centralized.

Right now, most of the budget planning is in the hands of central administration. (Dean)

The university has to figure out how it is spending its money. The system isn't quite working yet but yes, in principle, they have to do it. (Faculty association representative)

A new centralized accounting system was introduced.

The new vice-president (finance) is a breath of fresh air because he represented centralization of the budget and centralization of control. He's being fought tooth and nail by the peripheral system. He's trying to avoid waste, avoid duplication, do the types of things only central administration should do, and reduce administrative costs. If you've got that peripheral nonsense, you never know what the hell is going on. Now we are much more accountable, to the chagrin of some people who liked the freedom to spend money on any damn thing they pleased. (Dean)

The president also demanded more information from the deans.

UBC has not been run with a wide, open sharing of information. We are now putting out information on the budget, financial statements at the end of the year – [and] publishing them in the campus newspaper. That is putting a lot of pressure on some people because suddenly decisions are being made with an openness of information. It means you can't make your decisions arbitrarily – you have to be able to defend them. We're trying to make department heads much more aware of university issues, we're trying to make them more accountable. All this puts everyone on the line. (Central administrator)

The role of central administrators was enhanced.

The role of the vice-president (academic) has to be strengthened. More has to be done with him, rather than the president, who has to do more external things. (Central administrator)

The vice-president (academic) was also named provost; a new vice-president for student services was appointed; and a budget committee consisting of the vice-presidents was being considered. These moves to increase central controls had been started by earlier presidents.

Since the mid 1970s there have been a number of factors that have forced a degree of centralization that is not traditional at UBC ... This centralization has in recent years existed to a greater degree than the culture is prepared to acknowledge. The previous president was regarded as centralizing things in a way that his predecessor did not. When he left, perhaps people breathed a sigh of relief and thought that things would go back to normal – reasserting the sovereignty of the deans and their fiefdoms. When that didn't happen, there was a substantial uneasiness because people were forced to acknowledge that there were conditions outside and inside the institution which were not [linked to] a single individual, but which had to do with a context in which we are living and the need to make priorities and so on. (Central administrator)

The presence of the faculty association had led to centralized bargaining over salaries – by far the largest part of the budget – and reduced the discretion of the deans.

The fact that you have a collective agreement and the fact that you negotiate salaries is itself the primary centralizer because the main item of the budget is salaries. As soon as you negotiate salaries across the university, you have immediately made a major financial decision as a central [administration], and everything else has to follow from that. (Central administrator)

Scarce resources reinforced these trends by concentrating power into the hands of the central administrators because they, rather than the deans, made the choices about where cost reductions were to be made and where new positions should be located.

Unwittingly, the deans are forcing centralization because they are saying, "You ought to take the cuts from somewhere else." As soon as they say that, they are, in effect, saying, "*You* make the cuts." (Central administrator)

The measures introduced by the new president effectively reduced the power of the deans. For example, they restricted access to the president.

The resistance to the new vice-president [of student services] is not so much [to] the portfolio as [to] having another vice-president. I think the issue is [that] we are really creating a layer of vice-presidents rather than having a single route to get through to the president. (Central administrator)

[The establishment of additional positions in the central administration] has created the impression in the minds of the deans that they are being circumvented. (Dean)

The new measures also forced deans to share information and operate in a more open environment.

> It's a moot point. Is that centralization or isn't it? I would say it's greater and wider awareness of, and involvement in, the decision-making process, but you can't have this autonomy without real accountability. Some people find this very difficult because they have not operated in an open environment in the past. (Central administrator)

Not all the deans were happy with these changes, in particular those in the larger faculties who had previously been extremely powerful.

> The centralization is causing the biggest instability among those used to the periphery and [to] the fight [against the centre]. (Dean)

> Now there is not necessarily automatic acceptance of the dean as the ultimate authority over what should happen to his faculty. The deans, especially those who have been deans for a long time, find it disturbing, and I think there's discontent. (Dean)

The deans saw the new appointments and the introduction of new systems as a waste of money in an environment characterized by fiscal restraint.

> Some deans are appalled at the increase in administration, which they think is at the expense of their faculties. (Dean)

> There is a feeling among the deans that the paperwork is being pushed downward while resources are being pulled upward, and there's no time to think anymore. Everyone seems to be looking over their shoulder and defending what they have. If the centralization had happened at another time, another place, it would be different, but here some people view it very negatively. (Dean)

Many of the deans expressed little interest in centralized planning and were suspicious of the president's desire to formulate a new mission statement.

> Mission statements rarely have a continuing impact and are a heck of a lot of work without any resources. (Dean)

The centralization thus ran the risk of alienating the deans at a time when their support was needed to endorse the changes.

> To make radical reallocations, [the] central administration is going to have to handle the deans, and I'm not sure that any of them want to do that. (Senate member)

Opposition from the deans had been quoted as one of the reasons for the departure of the previous president.

> If a significant number of the deans are alienated, then he's going to have a tough time. This is what happened with the previous president. Basically, he got a vote of no-confidence from the deans. It's hard to govern UBC if the deans are against you. (Dean)

The new president did, however, have some advantages. First of all, there was a honeymoon period.

> At some stage, you have to trust the president's judgment: that's why you hired him. (Faculty association representative)

There was a willingness in the university community to "give him a try," in the words of a faculty association representative. There had also been a number of new decanal appointments, as the majority of the deans in office in 1986 had been appointed since 1983. These newer deans appeared to be far more receptive to the changes that were being made. Finally, the new president provided reassurances that he would not engage in such dramatic retrenchment again, notwithstanding any recommendations that the SBC might make.

> Today, the SBC is saying that we should be making another retrenchment. The president's office is saying we haven't recovered from the last one. It's really a traumatic experience for the president's office, because they have to take the final decision. They wanted to do the least possible. (SBC member)

> We would be foolish to be optimistic, but the president has privately said that the way to go is retirements and resignations. (Faculty association representative)

On the other hand, the president's emphasis on his external role – dealing with business and with the government – worked against him. Traditionally, UBC presidents had spent most of their time on internal matters, and there was little indication that the university community supported the need to rebuild government and business relationships. The previous president had been the object of a considerable amount of criticism for not spending enough time on campus. The new president ran into similar objections.

> He's paying a price internally for all the good things he's doing externally. I think some of the deans feel neglected – I do. All the deans feel neglected, but the funny thing is they all feel he's talking to someone else. I haven't found out who that someone else is. (Dean)

> I feel that the president should be directly involved. The arrangement of having the president as an external ambassador is very contrary to the tradition here. Our presidents in the past twenty years have essentially been internal presidents. So much so that the external community is not very aware of what is happening here, but it did mean that the deans were recognized as being involved. (Dean)

> The president has not established a strong presence on campus [or] close relationships with anybody. (Faculty association representative)

In summary, the new administration faced a challenging task. The previous retrenchment exercise had left the faculty relatively demoralized. The difficult financial and political environment required a great deal of external activity on the part of the president; yet the community expected him to play an internal role. Moves to centralize the institution in preparation for new initiatives had alienated some of the deans, and without their support, UBC would be difficult to administer. This politicized context was difficult to manage and was cited as having contributed to the early departure of the previous president.

> The previous president alienated all the constituencies. He had alienated the Board because of his public criticism of the government; the deans were unhappy because he had taken away power from them; and the faculty wanted him on campus more. (Senate member)

CONCLUSIONS

Power at the University of British Columbia was widely dispersed among a number of influential interest groups that were often at odds: the deans were a powerful but disunited group; the Senate had to approve program closures; the Senate Budget Committee was a relatively active group; the faculty association opposed the central administration on the matter of redundancies; the government appeared to be hostile to the university sector; and the Board of Governors had a reputation for being confrontational in its relations with the central administration. In this respect, of the six institutions of higher learning surveyed in the present study, UBC was the most politicized.

The university's response to funding constraints can be interpreted in the light of these conflicting pressures. The previous administration appeared to have decided to terminate tenured faculty in an attempt to reassure and placate the provincial government. Internally, the need to involve the SBC, obtain Senate approval, and maintain the deans' support shaped the form that the cutbacks actually took. The price the university paid can be seen in the difficult relations between the faculty association and the administration.

This situation also placed considerable demands on the new president. He was faced with a particularly difficult task in that he had to protect and buffer the institution from a hostile external environment in a university community that demanded a chief executive who would play an active role within the university itself.

> We wanted someone from the academic community who could command some respect, who also knew how to run a business, and who was politically astute – you know, someone who could walk on water. (Board member)

His strategy appeared to be one of strengthening a relatively weak administration. Yet, that in itself was incurring resistance, particularly from the deans, some of whom saw themselves as losing power to the centre.

CHAPTER SEVEN

Simon Fraser University

Simon Fraser University (SFU), named after the fur trader who explored the Fraser River in 1808, opened its doors to 2,500 students in 1965, two years after the publication of a report that recommended the creation of a new university in British Columbia. By 1984 SFU had some 450 faculty and 12,000 students, of whom almost half were part-time and about 1,500 were at the graduate level. The budget was nearly $70 million, in addition to which over $7 million was obtained through research grants. The university's administrative structure is outlined in Figure 7.1. As we shall see, the strategy adopted by Simon Fraser University in response to the provincial government's 1983 restraint legislation was very different from that followed by the University of British Columbia.

In some respects, SFU had always considered itself underfunded. As a hurriedly constructed and rapidly growing university, it often lacked badly needed resources. In an attempt to overcome these difficulties, past presidents had undertaken reviews of resource allocation and made cutbacks. A university review committee in 1977 had looked at work loads and performance in the different areas but had not led to substantial change. Some cutbacks had been carried out in 1981–82, mainly on an across-the-board basis.

The university's financial problems intensified considerably, however, when the Bennett government (Social Credit) was re-elected in 1983, on the basis of a promise to control public spending, and the British Columbia legislature adopted the *Public Sector Restraint Act* (see chapter six). The government froze operating grants to universities in 1983–84 and instituted a 5 percent decrease in those grants for each of the next two years.

Almost as soon as he took up his position in 1983, it became clear to the incoming president that the university's financial situation would

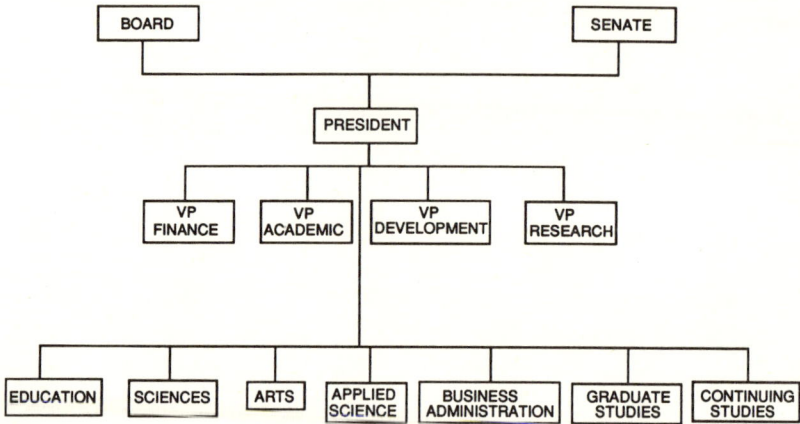

Figure 7.1
Simon Fraser University: Simplified Organization Chart (ca 1986)

be difficult, and he set about finding ways of cutting costs. The objective underlying the choice of strategy was to achieve a balance between applying cost-saving measures and maintaining morale within the university. The new administration did not want to maintain a policy of across-the-board cuts, nor did it want to undertake more drastic action if that risked alienating the employees.

> The strategy was to pull the cuts off and still keep the university – not have it fragment around us politically. (Dean)

The first step was the establishment of the Presidential Advisory Committee on University Priorities (PACUP), which consisted of five senior academics from different areas of the university. The committee carried out a review by inviting briefs, holding meetings, and conducting interviews. Based on the information that it gathered and analysed, PACUP made a number of recommendations to the president.

Following the submission of the PACUP report, the president proposed a plan (known as "The President's Plan" or the "September 20th Speech") that included the discontinuance of programs in German and Russian; a reduction in the Centre of Arts budget by one third; the dissolution of the faculty of Interdisciplinary Studies and the transfer of its departments to other faculties; and the establishment of a new faculty of Applied Science. These changes were subsequently approved by the SFU Senate and put into effect.

THE REASONS BEHIND THE
RETRENCHMENT STRATEGY

As a result of the restraint legislation, relations with the government had become strained.

> It was a poisoned atmosphere [between the government and the universities]. I couldn't believe how bad it was. (Central administrator)

It was felt that politicians had little respect or support for higher education.

> Many ministers have never been to a university. We are a frontier province. They are not very sophisticated culturally. The government should take a look at what they are doing to us. (Dean)

There was fear that the government might want to intervene actively in university affairs.

> Some people felt that the government just wanted blood on the floor and wouldn't be satisfied until faculty were dismissed. That was the route UBC was perceived to have gone. (Professor)

SFU's willingness to create a new faculty of Applied Science was part of an effort to win favour with the government by showing it was responding to community needs.

> It is clear that a lot of those decisions were political: "What can we do to increase the visibility of the university as a contributor to the province?" We did it by [establishing the faculty of Applied Science] and riding pretty hard over groups in Arts. (Board member)

> The Engineering Science program, which was new and small, was bolstered by Computer Science and converted into the faculty of Applied Science. Politically, in terms of our relations with the community, getting a new building – which we now have – and joint ventures with business, it would have much more impact. (Central administrator)

The dissolution of a faculty was also a political response – in the same way that the University of British Columbia had terminated tenured faculty, the administration of Simon Fraser University chose a highly visible action to demonstrate that it was serious in its attempts to lower its costs.

The university would do something, and wait and see what the reaction was. Was it enough? (Dean)

We are trying to demonstrate responsibility and accountability. We have done our belt-tightening like any other university. (Central administrator)

SFU's strategy thus included an external component designed to placate a government that appeared to be increasingly disenchanted with higher education.

SFU made these changes relatively quickly and with little dissension from the university community. What enabled it to do so? The answer lies in the timing of these changes, the decision-making context in which they were introduced, and the process used to implement them.

TIMING

The timing of the actions taken by the administration was significant for two reasons. First, the measures taken by the provincial government, by both threatening tenure and reducing funding more dramatically than in any other province, created a perception that a crisis existed. There was, as a result, a recognition that some distasteful decisions would be necessary if the university was to survive these attacks.

The external situation was so bleak that the community was more accepting of the need for action. I don't think we could have done it in Ontario, where changes had been slow. (Central administrator)

There's always talk about tough times, but no one believes it and no one believed it here in the 1970s. Now people are sensitized to the idea that there are some very real budget problems. Some of the agreements we've made with some of the employee groups we could never have reached had there not been the realization that [there was] a problem. (Central administrator)

Second, it would have been difficult to dismiss the president's proposals so soon after his appointment.

The president was a new boy then. He was still on his honeymoon and so was able to get a lot of support from his executive. (Dean)

The feeling was, "If we don't do it what is the president's future here?" This was his major program. There was a feeling of, "Give the man a chance." (Senate member)

DECISION-MAKING

The timing alone, however, does not explain why SFU was able to take the actions it did. The actions of the various interest groups were also important.

The Central Administration

Power was relatively centralized at Simon Fraser University. The president was a highly active internal (and external) administrator. He was "very much involved in the academic governance of this university" (in the words of one dean) and believed that he had an important role to play in shaping the organizational climate. He met with the deans and vice-presidents once every two weeks, with the president of the faculty association every month, and with department heads once a semester. He had even been accused of being too active and "trying to do the job of the vice-president (academic)," as one central administrator saw it.

The president believed in a relatively high degree of centralization, and tight control over the budget was a key mechanism in this approach. All budget items were categorized down to the departmental level, and it was difficult to move funds between categories. For example, as one administrator explained, replacing a typewriter with a word processor would require central approval, since office equipment and computers fell under different categories.

> We don't have much room for making decisions. We almost have a line-by-line budget. It's very tight. I certainly admire the dean who has a one-line budget. (Dean)

Working with the president was a powerful group of vice-presidents. Three positions had been established at that level since 1982 – development, finance, and research and information systems. The position of vice-president (administration) had been phased out, but it was argued that the executive director of administration acted much like a vice-president anyway. As a result of these changes, a clearly defined administrative layer had been created at the central level.

> Now I think there are more vice-presidents than deans: there's a cabinet of vice-presidents. (Professor)

There was considerable intervention by the vice-president (finance). An example was cited where faculty had received $1,000 in research grants, against which they could claim research expenses. One interviewee said that in some circumstances, the vice-president (finance) had made unjustifiable judgments about what did and did not constitute academic expenses.

This tightly managed financial situation had existed for a number of years at SFU and was unlikely to change, given the continued problem of funding restrictions. The administration had a conservative financial policy and believed that strict financial controls enabled the university to demonstrate fiscal responsibility and accountability to the public and to the government.

> I like to think that if we can show responsible financial management – realism. We can also show the fundamental importance of higher education. (Central administrator)

A second reason for this financial control was the personality and power of the vice-president (finance). The president relied on him for financial information.

> The president really depends on the vice-president (finance). He [the president] really doesn't know much about the university budget. He's not very good at numbers, especially in the last three years, when we have been in deep trouble. He's not at all eager to change the relationship he has with him. (Central administrator)

Finally, with government support uncertain and unpredictable, central administrators were reluctant to loosen their control.

> The budget process is highly centralized, with some frustration on the part of the deans. We are committed to reducing it, but recently we've been in a crisis and chasing our tails. Everything militates against rational planning, long-term planning, committee advice, etc. until we have a longer-time horizon and we know the budget in advance of the fiscal year. (Central administrator)

The three other vice-presidents had been deans of three important faculties – Education, which because of its innovative teaching and research focus was a strong area; Continuing Studies, powerful because half of the university's students were part-time; and Interdisciplinary Studies, one of SFU's early innovations to create and nurture new areas.

> The current vice-presidents were good deans: the cream has risen to the top. (Dean)

In the 1970s, the deans of these faculties and the dean of Arts – a faculty that employed 65 percent of the academic staff – had been important decision-makers at both the faculty and the university levels. With the rise of three of these deans to the central administration, decision-making had become more centralized.

> The deans [used to be] a small group who were clearly an integral part of the policy-making team, and all major decisions and policy questions went before the committee of deans. It wasn't that they were tremendously powerful – it was just that nothing concerning institutional policy went through without their being involved. Added to which Senate had put all deans on all its major committees. (Central administrator)

So, once-powerful deans were now powerful vice-presidents.

> The existence of new vice-presidents has dramatically changed decision-making. It has shifted power away from the deans. The first ten years I was a dean, the deans had a lot of power. (Dean)

> When that group [of central administrators] were deans, they wanted to keep decision-making at that level; now they are vice-presidents, they want to be vice-presidents and deans too. (Dean)

The Role of the Deans

The changes discussed above affected the role of the deans. They complained about their lack of autonomy in budgetary matters. According to one dean, the line budget was "one of the main frustrations of the deans."

> We have a rigid financial structure. It takes a lot of effort to make changes. I would think a lot of the bitches that the deans have start with the finance department. (Central administrator)

This restrictive stance was coupled with a high degree of bureaucracy.

> SFU is a twenty-year-old institution with a 200-year-old bureaucracy. (Professor)

> When I came, I was a builder; now, I'm a bureaucrat. (Dean)

> At SFU there is a paranoic attention to detail, structure – who approves what. (Central administrator)

The deans perceived themselves to have lost power to the group of vice-presidents.

> The deans, five years ago, had a more vital role in the administration of the university. (Dean)

> Here it's paternalistic: the administration decides for you. We are sheep. There is not much regard for the blood that circulates in the veins of the university. I don't think that we're particularly consulted on what position the university should take. (Dean)

These feelings were partly the result of the new layer of vice-presidents, who were knowledgeable and experienced members of the university. They had an awareness both of individual faculties and of a broader institutional perspective. Most of the deans, on the other hand, were more recent appointments. Four of them had been in their posts less than two years, and only one had held his position more than five years. They were, as a result, a relatively inexperienced group.

The inability of this new group of deans to form a united front had also contributed to the diminution of their power. Some personality differences had been introduced into the group with the arrival of new individuals.

> The deans at one point were very clubby, but now there are a couple of new club members. (Professor)

> I don't think there's the same relationship between the deans. I think there's been a decline in the quality of the deans. (Dean)

Scarce resources had exacerbated this conflict.

> I need three positions, and frankly I don't give a damn what positions are needed in other departments. (Dean)

> It's much more difficult to have an institutional perspective with scarce resources. (Dean)

The deans felt they had been frozen out of the policy-making executive. They complained that they rarely interacted with the central administration; they seldom saw the vice-presidents except for the vice-president (academic) or the president, apart from formal meetings that, in the words of one dean, "didn't work very well."

The deans did, however, have the *potential* to exert a considerable amount of influence on university decision-making.

> The power has shifted from the deans to the vice-presidents, and that has happened because some of the deans have become vice-presidents and they were reasonably strong deans. But I don't think the deans have used the power they have. They have become more competitive and are not so collegial now because of the personalities ... They don't work as a force together. (Central administrator)

The deans were all members of the university's Senate, and most of them sat on the two key committees, dealing with the undergraduate curriculum and with academic planning. If they voted together, they could influence the outcome of central initiatives, particularly at the committee stage. Together, they represented a large percentage of the votes and could also influence other Senate and committee members.

> The administration is very powerful on Senate. All the deans are there, although Senate does outvote the administration. The deans are also on the committees. They don't outvote the other members, but if they turn out and vote *en bloc*, they would probably win on any given day; and the deans do sway other votes. It is in the committee structures that the deans are very powerful, but they don't feel that it gives them much authority. (Central administrator)

While the Senate was seen as relatively powerless – a "gutless wonder" – its committees did have influence. It was here that proposals were discussed and the likelihood of opposition was ascertained. Significant resistance at the committee stage had led the central administration to withdraw proposals.

> Senate meetings don't result in very controversial decision-making. On the floor, Senate doesn't act very much as a shaping mechanism, but Senate has a number of committees where business does get conducted, and Senate members do have some influence. You don't do certain things because you know you won't get away with it, and that is an influence. Senate functions more subtly than visibly. (Dean)

> Senate was influential because one has to consider its reaction to anything that is proposed, and some things are not carried forward because of the feeling that they would not be passed. So, not many things get turned down but not everything is put forward. (Dean)

In one case, the opposition of the deans helped to ensure that a proposal to elect two vice-presidents to the Senate was never brought to the latter body. The administration withdrew the proposal when it became clear the deans would not support it. This type of action was the exception rather than the rule, however. Only rarely did the deans act in unison to challenge the central administration.

Other Interest Groups

As indicated above, the Senate was not very influential, particularly in budgetary matters. As one faculty association representative put it, it was simply a "university curriculum committee" – a view shared by many.

> Senate has no responsibility in budget matters. Apparently that's the way it's supposed to be. (Dean)

Senate opposition to central initiatives was therefore unlikely.

The Senate Committee on the University Budget (SCUB) acted as advisor to the president on budgetary matters. This body, provided for in the *University Act*, was thus equivalent to the Senate Budget Committee at the University of British Columbia, but unlike the SBC, SCUB played virtually no role in deciding resource allocation. Because it was often staffed by the more "activist" professors, the administration was reluctant to invite SCUB to examine contentious issues or provide revealing information.

> SCUB has not been used very wisely by any of the presidents. Everything gets vetoed [from being submitted to the committee] because no one wants some of the members looking at it. We're trying to keep the political fires down. (Central administrator)

> The university only plays lip service to [SCUB]. We only get the information after decisions have been made. (SCUB member)

The SFU Board of Governors appeared to be less confrontational that its UBC counterpart. Having just appointed the president, it was unlikely to oppose him. In the words of a central administrator, the governors were "prepared to be guided by the president."

> The Board is good and the people dedicated, but the limitation is that they have no real insight into the institution. They can't have [any]: their information comes from the administration. (Board member)

I often think that the real role of the Board is community relations. They pretty well pass everything that is put before them. Part of the problem is knowing what information to ask for. It's always struck me how little the Board is involved in the day-to-day affairs of the university. (Board member)

Occasionally, in the past, the Board had overruled the administration. For example, it had refused to increase fees for student residences. As a result, the administration was careful to involve Board members and to secure their support before it put forth a proposal.

The Board doesn't just rubber-stamp. They debate and may ask for more information, but on the whole they are supportive. We work very hard at involving them so there are no surprises. (Central administrator)

The faculty association rarely confronted the central administration. Relations between them had been cordial in recent years.

I cherish the collegial relationship we have created between the faculty association and the central administration. It's a very, very good relationship; unlimited credit must go to the people who work here. Given what we've faced, I think we've come through it with flying colours. (Central administrator)

At UBC, because of the way they [carried out program closures], the faculty association turned on the administration. Here, we've never forgotten that there's a common enemy [the government]. (Faculty association representative)

Regular meetings had been instituted by a previous president and continued under the current administration. The president of the faculty association met with the vice-president (academic) "as often as I need to," had regular meetings with the central administrative group, and lunched with the president every four to six weeks.

The current president has created the impression of being open, accessible, and willing to listen, if not always willing to agree. You felt that at least you had a chance by talking to him. (Faculty association representative)

In summary, Simon Fraser University can be described as a relatively centralized institution because of strict budgetary control and the power of central administrators. The Board, the Senate, and the faculty association were not particularly influential in university decision-making. Nor did the deans "run" SFU as they had in the past. Key individuals had moved up in the hierarchy, taking their power with them. The deans had failed to capitalize on their power. They could have used their domination of the Senate as a mechanism to counter central initiatives, but they were prevented from doing so by their inability to work closely together. The deans at SFU seemed to be in limbo – neither part of the policy-making executive, since that function had been taken over by the vice-presidents; nor effective CEOs of their own faculties because of the considerable constraints placed on them by the bureaucracy.

THE PACUP PROCESS

Although the university had a relatively centralized structure, the deans did pose a potential threat to any initiatives launched by the president because they could oppose the central administration through the Senate. Since they would clearly be affected by any changes, their support was crucial. How did the PACUP process enable the president to implement the changes while avoiding any resistance from the deans or other groups?

PACUP served a number of purposes. First, the president's recent appointment meant that, as an outsider, he knew relatively little about the university. As a result, it was difficult for him to know where and how to cut, and PACUP gave him some useful information in this area.

> The overwhelming feeling I had was that I had to act decisively. There was no time to sit and reflect. Secondly, as a newcomer I didn't know the institution at all. (President)

Both the committee's analysis and its recommendations highlighted the areas that could be eliminated or reorganized.

Second, PACUP's analysis made the whole university community aware of the difficulty of the situation, adding to the sense of crisis and to the belief that something had to be done.

> The overt reason [for PACUP] was to generate information for the president to make priorities in a scarce-resource situation. The less acknowledged reason was to communicate to the university that indeed there was a problem by looking at ourselves in the light of the problem. (Central administrator)

Third, PACUP appeared to be a highly representative committee with no particular axe to grind. It held hearings and interviews with different faculty representatives and helped to ensure that the eventual changes had some faculty involvement. It legitimized the process and helped to ensure its acceptance in the university community.

> Everyone understood that something had to be done. It was better to have these things done by faculty than administrators. So PACUP lent some credibility to the process. (Dean)

There was a risk, however, that PACUP might make recommendations that would alienate the deans and that this might prompt them to mount a concerted opposition. The president took a number of precautions to avoid this situation. First, the committee's mandate was made advisory: it could make recommendations but the president was under no obligation to accept them.

> There was always concern about what PACUP might come up with, but we understood that they would only be recommendations and they would always be brought back to us – recommendations to the president on which he may or may not choose to take action. (Dean)

Second, there was a considerable amount of dialogue between the president and the committee during the review to ensure that it was going in the right direction.

> The process was set up so that they were supposed to consult from time to time with the president, so that a real difference of opinion would not occur. (Central administrator)

Third, the deans were actively involved in the change process. For example, they made recommendations concerning the membership of the committee.

> The members of PACUP were chosen for their wisdom or perhaps their socialization. (Dean)

And last, the deans were involved in the discussion of the final recommendations.

> It was clear to us [deans] from the beginning that there was no binding legislation [in PACUP]. (Dean)

The involvement of the deans secured their support for the president's plan. This included those who were most directly affected – the dean of Interdisciplinary Studies, a program that was to be dissolved; and the dean of Arts, whose faculty would receive many of the constituent parts of the abolished faculty. The presence of a united administration effectively ruled out the possibility of Senate opposition.

The chances of opposition from the faculty association were reduced by PACUP's consultation process and by the president's promise to avoid enforced layoffs.

> The president said very clearly (and he deserves a lot of credit for this), "I do not want to cut faculty positions. If we can put through this program, I can guarantee that there will be no cuts in tenure-stream faculty." So no one felt there was an axe hanging over their heads. (Faculty association representative)

There was no attempt to negotiate a financial-exigency plan, and the association volunteered to take a 1.8 percent salary reduction in 1983–84, while an early retirement policy was used to reduce numbers.

> We didn't actually lay anybody off, but we sure bought a lot of people off. (Dean)

In summary, PACUP was an integral part of the implementation process. It reduced the likelihood of opposition from the various interest groups and made recommendations about where changes could be made. The presence of the committee created a context in which change could be made by helping to shape a process that would be acceptable to the university community and by influencing the content of the eventual changes through the identification of some of the possible options. It was also clear that the cutbacks did not derive solely from PACUP.

> I wish to emphasize that the initiatives I am about to propose, while respectful of PACUP's analysis, originate also out of my own institutional and pedagogical views and out of the shared perceptions and combined commitment of the university's vice-presidents and deans. (SFU president, in his "September 20th speech")

> The recommendations in the president's famous speech were constructed to appear to come from PACUP, but I think they originated primarily from him in the context of having read the report. The two documents were not that closely related. (Dean)

Thus the changes instituted by SFU were a product of the interactions of a number of groups, including the president, the vice-presidents, the deans, and PACUP.

PACUP didn't really give us that much direction. What it did do was give the president a rationale for moving. He did consult, [and] senior faculty were involved, but in the end it was essentially the plan that emerged from his own views of the university and discussions with the vice-presidents and the deans. (Central administrator)

CONCLUSIONS

Simon Fraser University was a relatively centralized university, in which the president and vice-presidents held a considerable amount of power. The central administration adopted a highly visible retrenchment strategy – a move intended to show the government that the university was a responsible corporate citizen. This group also wanted to avoid internal conflict and rejected the option of dismissals as a way of reassuring the university community. The PACUP process also helped to legitimize the changes in the eyes of faculty members by involving professorial representatives. The potential power of the deans meant that they were also part of these changes.

Expenditures were reduced at SFU primarily through the reduction of positions. It is not clear, however, how much of a saving was achieved in this way.

I suppose there was money saved – but not much, I suspect. I think we got rid of a dean but gained a vice-president. (Professor)

Nevertheless, administrators balanced the budget and considered the strategy a success.

Because we made some major changes, I think we have weathered the cuts better than other institutions. We're collegial, open, and have strong leadership from the president. We've come out of it reasonably intact – we're still a pretty good institution, but there are some strains around. (Central administrator)

Simon Fraser University thus responded to government restraint with the same rationale as the University of British Columbia – a perceived need to make visible and dramatic cost reductions. The strategy it employed was, however, very different, as we shall see in greater detail in the next chapter.

CHAPTER EIGHT

Comparison: The University of British Columbia and Simon Fraser University

Whereas the comparison between McGill University and the University of Montreal shows that similar strategies were implemented in different ways, a comparison of the University of British Columbia with Simon Fraser University reveals that quite different retrenchment strategies were adopted in response to the same external pressures (Hardy 1992). SFU explicitly ruled out the termination of tenured faculty, while UBC engaged in program closures that resulted in nine tenured faculty members losing their jobs. The UBC/SFU comparison suggests that differences in institutional contexts played a role in shaping the choice of strategy. It also shows how both universities attempted to defend themselves against a government that was becoming increasingly unsupportive of the university sector.

While the cost reductions implemented in British Columbia do not compare with the cutbacks experienced in some U.S. and U.K. universities, they nevertheless represent relatively severe financial problems in the Canadian context. The universities in British Columbia relied on government funding for 85 percent of their operating revenues, and thus the cuts here were more severe and dramatic than in other provinces, particularly in the light of the government threat to eliminate tenure.

THE INSTITUTIONAL CONTEXTS

Simon Fraser University was a relatively centralized institution, with central administrators holding a considerable amount of power. A key mechanism of this centralization was the budget, which was highly restrictive: all budget items were categorized, and deans found it difficult to move funds between categories. A significant amount of bureaucratic control provided other means of centralizing power. In addition, the appointment of several deans to vice-presidential positions increased the power of the central administration. In the 1970s, these deans had been important decision-makers in both their faculties and the university as a whole. As they were elevated, the locus of power shifted correspondingly. The president's personal power was enhanced by the fact that he had only recently been appointed and thus enjoyed the freedom afforded by a "honeymoon" period.

The greater degree of centralization reduced the power of the deans. They were also hampered by a lack of cohesiveness that resulted from personality differences introduced by the appointment of new deans and the greater scarcity of resources. This fragmentation prevented the deans from joining forces to influence the central administration. They rarely used the power they had as opinion leaders in the university's Senate, preferring to side with the central administration on most matters and rendering the Senate a "gutless wonder," as it was affectionately known. The Board of Governors played a relatively passive role in the internal administration of the university and, on the whole, supported the president's proposals. The faculty association also tended to support the central administration.

In contrast, the political context at the University of British Columbia was characterized by a central administration that was traditionally weak relative to the deans, who were powerful, independent "sovereigns" of their particular faculties. While the deans were not part of any formal policy-making team for the university as a whole, individually they had a great deal of influence on decisions taken by central administrators. Moreover, they retained control over many functions – such as budgeting and purchasing – which, central administrators argued, would have been carried out centrally in many other universities. This decentralization meant that the deans controlled the information about the operation of their faculties, which they kept to themselves rather than share it with the central administration. They also maintained their independence by remaining separate from each other. The result was, many argued, the development of a faculty perspective among the deans rather than an identification with the institution.

The Senate Budget Committee, which played a role in program closures, had some influence on the Senate, which ultimately had to approve these measures. As a result, the SBC was consulted by the central administration, even though its advice was not always followed. It was far more influential than SCUB, its counterpart at Simon Fraser University, which played no role in the cutbacks or, for that matter, in the budgetary process in general.

Relations between the faculty association and the central administration at UBC could hardly be described as cordial, particularly on the matter of proposed redundancies. Repeated attempts to establish agreement on the criteria for the declaration of financial exigency and redundancy procedures had failed. An agreement was reached in 1984 between the central administration and the association's executive but was not ratified by the membership until the following year.

Finally, UBC's Board of Governors had a reputation for challenging the central administration and was considered, by members of both the academic community and the administration, to be highly supportive of the policies of the provincial government and to share its concern about inefficiency in the university. The statutes were unclear about the Board's role in program closure, and many people thought the Board could – and would – act unilaterally if the administration did not take steps to reduce costs.

THE SHAPING OF RETRENCHMENT

The high degree of centralization at Simon Fraser University afforded the president a margin for manœuvre in deciding how to respond to the new financial situation. His power was further augmented by the fact that he had just recently been appointed and by the crisis caused by the government's restraint program. Thus the president had a clear mandate for action, and his proposals emphasized highly visible changes, with an emphasis on high-tech aspects. The adoption of these proposals by the university was prompted by the desire to show the government that the SFU was "paying its dues" by making cutbacks and by providing the province with important expertise and skills training. The president made it clear that he was committed to avoiding the dismissal of tenured faculty, a stance that undoubtedly predisposed the union to agree to a salary cut – which, in turn, gave the central administration added flexibility. The retrenchment strategy thus reflected a desire to show the external community that the university was acting responsibly and to reassure the internal community that jobs were not threatened.

Since the proposals would have to be approved by the Senate, the work undertaken by PACUP played an important role in legitimizing them. PACUP helped to create an awareness that a problem existed, and it represented an independent mechanism through which the faculty would be consulted. It would be unfair, however, to suggest that the creation of this committee was a purely political move. As a newcomer to SFU, the president knew relatively little about the institution, and PACUP gave him important information. There was a risk in relying on PACUP, however: if the committee arrived at conclusions that were unacceptable to the deans, they might be prompted to block the proposals in the Senate. To avoid this situation, PACUP's mandate was restricted to an advisory one, and the deans were involved in the decision-making process.

At the University of British Columbia, the decision to terminate tenured faculty was also a highly visible strategy chosen by the central administration to placate the government. In reality, however, the dismissals saved only a small amount of money, and attrition was the more important mechanism for reducing expenditures. The work done by the Senate Budget Committee on core and noncore programs appeared to play an important part in formulating the closure proposals presented to the Senate. There were other influences, however. The proposals were also shaped by the ideas of the president *pro-tem*, who, in his previous capacity as vice-president (academic), had chaired the 1984 study into cutbacks. Another influence was that of the deans. Both the SBC and the central administration were forced to rely on their information about where cuts should be carried out. As opinion leaders in the Senate, the deans also had the power to inhibit the implementation of any proposals by persuading the other members to vote against them.

The actual recommendations that went to the Senate were not, therefore, a simple regurgitation of the SBC's suggestions, nor were they a straightforward implementation of the president's plan: they were also a reflection of the deans' willingness and ability to negotiate. The central administration wanted to avoid acting on proposals that would produce outright opposition. Thus the deans of some faculties faced percentage budget reductions rather than specific cuts because they threatened resistance. The failure of the Senate to approve the proposal to close the Landscape Architecture program was further testimony to the strength of the deans. The SBC's participation in the retrenchment exercise, much like PACUP's, was as important in legitimizing the proposals as in formulating them. It incorporated faculty representation into the decision process and helped secure the Senate's approval. The power of the deans, however, meant that some of the SBC's recommendations were politically infeasible and, as a result, were not presented to the Senate.

Thus UBC's retrenchment strategy would appear to represent a delicate balance by central administrators in accommodating competing interest groups. Given the complexity of their situation, it is perhaps difficult to understand how they managed to make any sort of cutbacks at all, but the sense of crisis that prevailed in British Columbia at that time undoubtedly prompted them to act. That same reason helps to explain why the deans, who had also become aware of an institutional problem, agreed to at least some form of cutback.

CONCLUSIONS

This analysis has indicated that, while the provincial government's restraint policy was putting pressure on both institutions, that pressure was felt more keenly at the University of British Columbia, possibly because as the larger, "elite" institution, it had more visibility. This helps to explain why UBC used program closure to signal to the government that it was taking restraint seriously. At Simon Fraser University, administrators chose to avoid dismissals in order to protect relations with the faculty association. They had some additional flexibility to do so because, first, as a smaller institution with an apparently more supportive Board, SFU was less susceptible to government scrutiny and, second, the faculty volunteered a pay cut that offered additional financial leeway.

Internally, the central administration at UBC had to contend with powerful deans, a more active Senate, a less supportive Board, and a faculty association with which it was unable to secure agreement on redundancy procedures. The cost reductions that were implemented thus represented a delicate juggling act between these groups. Even though the central administration at SFU appeared to have more power, it still took care to accommodate both deans and faculty members. PACUP helped to engage professorial representation, but its limited terms of reference afforded the president sufficient flexibility in the event that its recommendations alienated the deans. The power to act in both universities was enhanced by a perception of crisis, as well as by the new president's "honeymoon" period in the case of SFU and the imminent departure of the president *pro-tem* at UBC.

Another important finding concerns the symbolic aspects of the retrenchment strategies. As with McGill University and the University of Montreal, the UBC and SFU strategies were adopted as much for their symbolic component as for their cost-saving impact. While the strategies of the two Quebec universities were directed at the internal community, those of the British Columbia institutions were important for their external impact. Both SFU and UBC adopted strategies that clearly indicated to the government that they were serious in responding to provincial concerns – a new faculty in the case of the former, program closure in the case of the latter. Internally, these strategies had to be "sold" to the community. Both PACUP and the SBC played an important symbolic role in legitimizing the decisions in the eyes of the professoriate.

CHAPTER NINE

The University of Toronto

The University of Toronto (UT), which received its charter in 1827, is the largest university in Canada. In 1984, it operated under the 1971 *University of Toronto Act* and had 15 faculties, six colleges, and three campuses – at Toronto (the focus of this chapter), Scarborough, and Erindale. It had over 50,000 students, of whom nearly one fifth were graduates; over 2,000 professors; and a budget that exceeded $500 million (including over $100 million in research grants).

The University of Toronto had two structural characteristics that differentiated it from the other universities examined in this study (Figure 9.1). First, its hierarchy was highly elaborate, with a vice-provostial level. And second, the university had a unicameral governance system, in which the functions of board and senate were combined under the Governing Council. These two features had important implications for the decision-making process.

DECISION-MAKING AT THE UNIVERSITY OF TORONTO

Formal Structure

The University of Toronto had a relatively complex hierarchy. There was a layer of vice-provosts between the vice-presidential level and the deans, separating the faculties into three broad divisions – professional, health sciences, and arts and science – each headed by a vice-provost. Within the first two divisions, the deans reported to their vice-provost, who then reported to the provost, whereas the dean of Arts and Science reported directly to the provost. The hierarchy had been reinforced by the introduction of new procedures by the president, who had been appointed in 1984. He had standardized budget allocation procedures

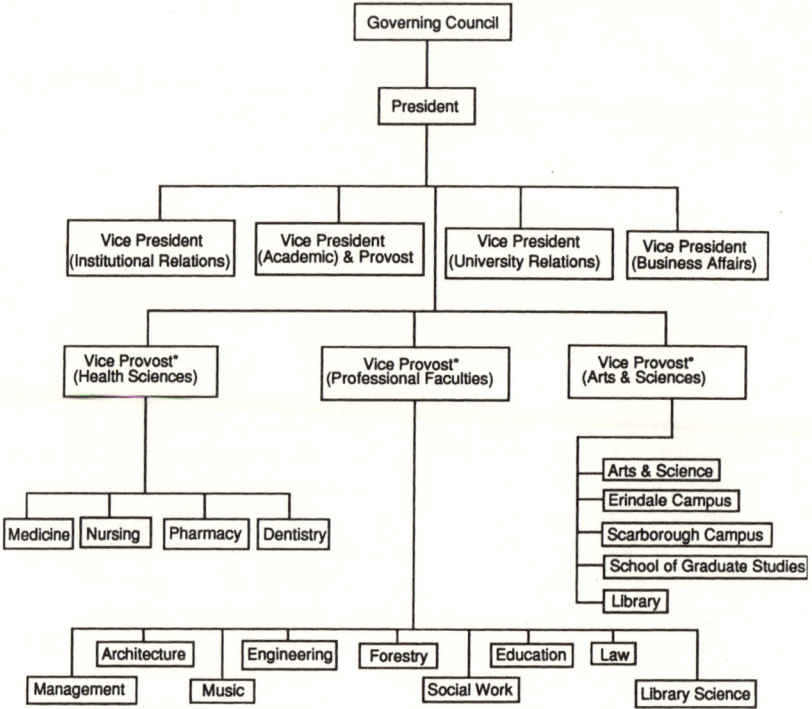

Figure 9.1
University of Toronto: Simplified Organization Chart (ca 1986)

* Please note the deans formally report to the Provost directly on certain matters

at the central level; developed criteria to allocate resources on the basis of quality, institutional role, and feasibility; and increased central planning.

> Our greatest need is for a new planning paradigm to influence strategic direction of the university as a whole. (Central administrator)

A central information bank had been created to support this planning effort.

> The Budget Planning Secretariat has been created. [Its] purpose is to provide [us] with information to make decisions. (Central administrator)

The president had also centralized the resource allocation process. Instead of the original budget committee of vice-presidents and vice-provosts, decisions were taken by the president and vice-presidents alone. Once the budget was determined for each portfolio, the vice-president had full autonomy to decide how it was to be spent.

These changes had been made with a view to strengthening the vice-presidents' roles; reducing the time spent on the budget; and making the budgetary process more consistent and less political, so as to increase confidence in it.

> Some of the wrangling that used to go on over the budget was divisive. It was seen as the forum in which there were winners and losers, and there were grievances. Arbitration between the vice-presidents is the president's job. We should be able to sort them out harmoniously rather than lump them together all in a room where they tear each other apart. (Central administrator)

> We've always had guidelines but they differed from year to year. They led to some pretty unproductive games-playing. You would cut the things you knew no one wanted you to cut. You presented a political or polemical plan aimed at scaring the living daylights out of senior administration. The budget system was highly politicized. Some years some people won, other years others won. It was taking more of the senior administrators' time than it was worth. The budget process has been more stable in the last two years: the president calls the shots regarding budget cuts. He's naturally inclined towards a systematic process, towards a deliberate chain of command. (Central administrator)

According to one dean, the president had a "a strict hierarchical notion of administration. He believed in a line structure."

> The president has a strong sense of organization, planning and hierarchy. He believes that decisions should be taken through channels. It's very structured. (Dean)

Deans reported to the president via the vice-provost and provost.

> [The president] introduced line authority. Everything is handled at the vice-provostial level, not the presidential level. (Dean)

> It's virtually impossible to approach the president directly. You have to go through channels. (Dean)

The University of Toronto had a unicameral governance system in which financial and academic responsibilities were combined in the Governing Council, which had fifty members from a number of different constituencies. Among the members were the chancellor and the president (both *ex officio*), two presidential appointments, sixteen government appointments, eight alumni, twelve teaching staff, two administrative staff, and eight students. The Governing Council had a number of committees and subcommittees – including the executive committee, which had fourteen members.

The unicameral system had been the subject of a considerable amount of criticism since its inception by provincial statute. A review in 1973 had recommended changes, but these were not acted on by the provincial legislature. The 1975 Dunphy study had argued that unicameralism resulted in a lesser role for deans, principals, and faculty, and it introduced some changes to increase their input. A review under J.B. MacDonald in 1977 had modified the Governing Council so that only the president could initiate proposals, while the Council was to restrict itself to approving, rejecting, or referring them back to the administration. A study carried out in 1986 also uncovered considerable criticism of the system among faculty members.

The university's structure and governance system contributed to perceptions of a high degree of bureaucracy. Moves to formalize and rationalize decision-making had introduced more bureaucratic procedures, and the complex committee structure associated with the Governing Council involved, in many people's eyes, a considerable amount of red tape. Line authority further distanced the university community from the central administration.

The Role of the Deans

The deans had a limited role in university policy-making for three reasons: they were separated from the centre by the hierarchy; they did not exert influence as a group; and their influence on the university community was circumscribed by that of the Governing Council.

The hierarchy served to distance the deans from the central administration. They were physically separated from the president, since they reported to their vice-provosts, and rarely met with him.

> Other than committees, I only see the president once a year. From the planning point of view, it makes sense. It doesn't make sense from a people point of view. People feel distanced, people feel alienated, people feel an aloofness. A place like this demands more collegiality. The idea would be to communicate a strong sense of collegiality but a strong sense of hierarchy in actually taking decisions. I think the president would be wiser to see the deans much more frequently. (Dean)

The deans did not feel that they were able to exert much influence through the various committees of which they were members. For example, one of the main communication mechanisms between central and faculty administrators was the Committee of Principals, Deans, Directors and Chairmen, which was convened once a month. However, this committee consisted of *all* deans and department heads, as well as heads of administrative units – nearly 200 individuals. It was seen as providing an information session "for dealing out the party line" (in the words of a vice-provost) rather than as a vehicle for the deans' active participation in university affairs.

> These are clearly information-giving sessions; there is a very small opportunity for dialogue. (Dean)

The deans also felt excluded from the budget allocation process because it was centralized.

> How is the budget decided? A good question. The budget is basically a decision of the provost's office. There is a budget committee supposedly, which none of the deans of the major faculties are on, which makes very global sorts of decisions. There is a lot of interaction between the vice-provost and the dean's office, and the provost as well. That I certainly can't complain about, but if one doesn't understand the details of the discussions at the more global level, one feels there must be a better way. (Dean)

The changes introduced to streamline the process and ensure consistency had also reduced the amount of participation by deans in resource allocation.

> I think the critical thing now is not participation but formal protocols that people understand and know are being followed. They don't have to participate if they know who's doing what. Budgeting has too many problems, is too complex to have a high degree of participation. (Central administrator)

Within the three major divisions, budgets were determined primarily by the vice-provost, with limited input from individual deans.

> There are no discussions of any consequence before your budget allocation. Any discussions we have are purely for information. They are not structured in such a way to elicit participation in decision-making. The personal contact is absolutely minimal. (Dean)

> The deans don't propose a budget to us. We tell them what their base budget is going to be. (Vice-provost)

The hierarchy also served to isolate the deans from each other by dividing them into three separate portfolios that rarely interacted. There was no forum in which the deans met together to form a closely knit group. There was a Provost's Advisory Group that reviewed budget strategy, but it included only the deans of Arts and Science, Law, Graduate Studies, Dentistry, Engineering, and Medicine, as did the Presidential Advisory Committee, which reviewed broader institutional issues. So, while these groups enabled some deans to discuss issues with central administrators, they isolated them from the remaining faculties. The result of this lack of lateral communication was a series of self-contained territories.

> There are several empires and I don't think communication is great between them. (Dean)

Horizontal communication was limited even within the divisions. Deans tended to interact with their vice-provost rather than with each other.

> I have the feeling that a lot of lobbying goes on in the vice-provost's office by the individual deans. (Dean)

There were few regular divisional meetings of deans. The professional faculties met most regularly, but they were hampered by a lack of commonality since they represented highly diverse interests. There had been an attempt to meet more often in the health sciences division, but it was described as "sporadic and infrequent."

> We are [still] trying to draw the health sciences together to have health sciences function as a division rather than as a collection of faculties. (Vice-provost)

This compartmentalization prevented the deans from forming a united group that could pressure and influence the central administration.

> The deans are not cohesive or competitive. My inclination would be for cohesion, my experience has been isolation. We've not formed a lobby group. We've not formed a pressure group. We tend to work in isolation. It's for budgetary convenience that we're groups, not for cohesion potential – and that's why we don't have it. (Dean)

I don't phone the deans to conspire. I'm much more likely to get something by conspiring with my vice-provost against the other deans than I am by getting the deans to conspire against the vice-provost. (Dean)

A third distinguishing feature of the deans' role in academic policy-making was linked to the unicameral system. Deans were not normally members of the Governing Council, which meant that there was no forum, like a senate, in which deans could play an active role in shaping academic policy.

We made the mistake of opting for a unicameral system. It's been a disaster. When we had a senate, if you were a dean you thought you had a definite role in the academic governance of the university. There is no longer any role in this university for deans other than as glorified department heads. You have no role in the academic governance of the university. There is no way deans can communicate directly with Governing Council. A dean is someone, God knows why, who agrees to take on the headaches of a faculty with a limited budget, with no prestige, who can only take instruction from the provost and deal with the departmental budgets. (Dean)

It's a major weakness that the major deans with major budgetary responsibilities are not heard by the governors of the university. They don't have the opportunity to make their case, to participate and debate. (Dean)

Deans in the other universities in the study were able to exercise considerable influence through the university senate. They represented important opinion leaders and a sizable voting minority in the smaller institutions. In some cases, they were also members of key senate committees. Thus these deans had a number of avenues through which they could influence university policy. At the University of Toronto, on the other hand, deans had little impact on decision-making at the institutional level because they were distanced from the central administration, separated from each other, and isolated from the broader university community because of the Governing Council.

The result was that the deans turned their attention towards their individual faculty. They saw themselves as faculty CEOs rather than as part of the university's management team.

The only way to keep morale and keep the place operating in difficult times is if the chairmen see the dean is working for them. The central administration in this university is typically viewed as being aloof and distant. It would not be constructive if I added myself to that group. (Dean)

This role was reinforced by the budgetary autonomy of the deans. Faculty budgets were global envelopes and, subject to approval for new appointments and salary commitments, items were not categorized. Deficits and surpluses could be carried over, and only the creation of tenure-stream positions had to be approved centrally. Thus the deans had considerable power within the context of their own faculty.

> Once the deans accept the budget process – or become resigned to it, [since] I would say they don't have much influence on the amount they get – there's a fair trade-off. We say to the deans, "You may not like what you get, but we are not going to muck about in your affairs once you get it." (Central administrator)

Departmental budgets were allocated largely at the discretion of the dean. For example, the budget for teaching assistants in Arts and Science had recently been centralized and administered by the dean rather than by individual departments.

> Within their budget, they can pretty well do what they want. Each department will have its budget, but the dean decides the budget. (Vice-provost)

Many deans described themselves as autocratic managers. They considered resource allocation a decision for them to take – not a matter for faculty participation.

> If [budget decisions] are taken through faculty discussion, I could see no decision being made because everyone would become territorial and self-serving, and that isn't in the best interests of the faculty. (Dean)

> I have a top-down management style. Consultation can factionalize, and committees result in an uneasy compromise of preserving the status quo. (Dean)

In summary, the deans at the University of Toronto were compartmentalized. They did not identify with either other deans or the central administration, and the Governing Council circumscribed their influence over the academic community. Their power revolved around their faculties.

The Role of the Central Administration

The hierarchical structure also had implications for the role of the central administration. It resulted in a considerable amount of distance between the administration and the university community at large.

> The president has made it clear that he's not part of the academic community. Deans cannot communicate directly with him. (Dean)

> The president is more structured, hierarchical, and delegates better. The faculty get disquieted because they don't see enough of him. (Vice-provost)

The University of Toronto's central administration was seen as an "enormous central bureaucracy." Although some in the administration argued that the number of central administrators at the university was average, the existence of the vice-provosts and the red tape associated with the Governing Council gave rise to perceptions of a top-heavy system.

> I think it's a pretty common perception that the university is top-heavy administratively and that there are heavy financial commitments with that system. I've never seen such long memoranda in my life – everyone is writing a novel. (Dean)

> There is a highly centralized, bureaucratized central administration which controls everything. It is said in this university that deans cannot see the president. (Faculty association representative)

The central administration had a considerable amount of power, as the centralized resource-allocation process has already shown. The unicameral system also centralized power: the Governing Council could not initiate proposals but could only respond to those made by the president.

> Within this system, administration has a lot of power: Governing Council can reject things or send them back, but it cannot initiate policy, which an academic senate can. (Vice-provost)

The Governing Council consisted of representatives from a number of diverse interest groups. Consequently, there was considerable potential for conflict amongst its members, which inhibited the Council's ability to counter central initiatives because of the difficulties in mobilizing a united opposition. As a result, it rarely overturned recommendations made by the president.

> Governing Council is a rubber-stamping committee, because everything is so well thought out before it goes through so many committees that there's generally very little discussion. (Dean)

Because the University of Toronto was a large and complex university, detailed knowledge of its operations was difficult for the governors to acquire. That information was possessed only by the full-time administrators, making it relatively easy to "manage" the Governing Council.

> We involve governors, but not in the true sense as you might with a board. At the moment, we can't afford to have them involved in decision-making, so we carry out a delicate ballet dance. The decision is really made by the president and vice-presidents. (Central administrator)

While this aspect of the university's governance did serve to concentrate power in the hands of the central administration, the Council also acted as a brake on administrative initiatives.

> Governing Council doesn't really make decisions but it prevents decisions from being made. You have to go through so many levels to get to Governing Council. The bureaucracy has a function to slow things up. (Dean)

Major changes had to be approved by the Council, but the diversity of the various interest groups represented in it made it difficult for the administrators to orchestrate a consensus in support of radical change.

> Governing Council is a mix of rational, hard-headed business types, dewy-eyed students, and pious faculty that generates a confusion I find hard to fathom. (Vice-provost)

> The weakness of the structure is that it is always a crapshoot. You can't predict how it will turn out. You don't know who's going to be away; who's going to turn up; or what the politics of that particular issue are. (Central administrator)

In summary, the University of Toronto was characterized by a bureaucratic structure – the result of size, hierarchy, governance, and administrative style. Within that structure, it was the central administrators who had the major influence over institutional decision-making. Deans had considerable power in their own faculties but were not part of the policy-making executive of the university. If power lay anywhere in a structure as large and diverse as the University of Toronto, it was with the central administration: while constrained to a certain extent by the complexity of the unicameral system, the administration was also empowered by it.

RESOURCE ALLOCATION AND FINANCIAL RESTRICTIONS

How did the decision-making context described above influence the way in which the University of Toronto responded to financial restrictions? The university had experienced a gradual accumulation of budgetary restrictions in the 1970s that had created a significant concern by the 1980s.

> Cutbacks were not an issue until the mid-1970s. Luckily, prior to that, budgets had been built up to a point that there was some capability of responding to budget reductions without seriously embarrassing important programs ... By the 1980s, budget reductions had a major impact. (Vice-provost)

For the most part, interviewees felt that there had been no major attempt to establish priorities or make differential funding allocations.

> We have never had the debate and resolution in this university that more money should go to engineering and the sciences and less to the social sciences and humanities. That's a very difficult debate to have when contracting. (Dean)

> I don't know whether you could talk of criteria [in allocating the budget] so much as a round-table discussion. We might say on paper that academic priorities might have to come first, but it's not necessarily how it appears afterwards. On the whole, in recent years, we've made even cuts between the three major portfolios. We're not going to make hard choices, and when we try to, we just get into serious trouble. I don't like discriminating in my portfolio. Last year, I made a certain judgment of what I think different units can absorb, but this year they can't absorb these cuts, so I deal with them even-handedly. (Vice-provost)

Financial allocations were based largely on the previous year's budget.

> With minor exceptions budgets have been allocated roughly in proportion to the existing distribution. (Vice-provost)

Some differential decisions had occurred where significant changes in student enrolments had occurred. For example, the faculty of Education had sustained a large reduction in resources as the demand for teachers had fallen and the number of bachelor-level students had declined from 1,700 in 1976 to 800 in 1985.

> There has been a very deliberate decision to reduce the size of the faculty of Education for obvious reasons: there are no longer as many students. There has been an attempt to shift resources from departments which are viewed as overstaffed to newly developing or popular areas. (Faculty association representative)

The main cutback mechanism was the nonreplacement of vacant positions, which were reallocated to growing areas such as Law and Engineering.

> The dean of Engineering has been extraordinarily successful in protecting his faculty. The vice-provost only likes Engineering and Law. Engineering and Law have a mutual understanding; among the others there is resignation, if not acceptance. (Dean)

These changes were, however, happening slowly, and there was no indication of a radical reallocation of resources.

> I think the university believes that its strategy must include differential cuts. I believe it is happening. However, I think there is a qualitative difference between a closure and a slow budgetary extraction. I admire the attempt to cut units, but I think politically it's extraordinarily difficult both in the outside world and internally. I wouldn't be optimistic that there will be a lot of such decisions. (Dean)

THE FACULTY OF ARCHITECTURE

The university did take steps to try to close one faculty – Architecture. It was a complicated issue that was related to program quality and internal politics, as well as scarce resources. The faculty was politicized and factionalized. The underlying problem was a form of "internecine warfare" that had been waged among faculty members for years and had made it impossible to hire a dean. As a result of these internal problems, criticism had grown that the faculty had become ungovernable and teaching standards were falling (Eastman 1986).

The attempt to close the faculty was interpreted in a number of very different ways. Some interviewees saw it as a purely internal affair – an act of frustration on the part of a central administration that had become irritated by an "ungovernable" faculty.

> I think the administration felt they had to make a symbolic gesture. It had been irritated for years by internecine warfare within the faculty which had become ungovernable. The administration has contributed to the ungovernability. [With the closure] they were responding to political problems. (Professor)

Others, on the other hand, argued that the closure had become necessary because scarce resources meant that insufficient funds were available the rectify the problem. Architecture was not being closed for financial reasons *per se*, but because the university could not afford the money necessary to bring about a turnaround.

> Architecture is not an academic problem. It's a financial problem coupled with a people problem in the faculty, which the university simply doesn't have to resources to solve. (Dean)

These people saw the proposed closure as an attempt to establish priorities and allocate resources differentially.

> There comes a time when a university faced with declining resources has to establish for itself what its priorities are, what programs it will protect, what programs it will not protect. The faculty of Architecture, for a variety of reasons, has placed itself in a difficult position at a time when the university has to make judgments. It was a responsible view to adopt. (Vice-provost)

In some quarters, the attempted closure was interpreted as a gesture intended to draw the attention of government officials to the university's financial problems.

> It was believed it wasn't a bad issue on which to make a symbolic gesture and publicize its financial problems. (Professor)

If this had been the intent, the government was not impressed.

What was resented by the minister and some others in government was that every time the president mentioned that issue [Architecture] and funding in the same breath, it was deemed to be a deliberate and machiavellian attack on the government and underfunding. It wasn't seen as sincere ... since the university was covering up for several years of mismanagement and the blame was really on the administration for screwing up. The government felt it shouldn't be splashed with any mud whatsoever. (Ministry representative)

The proposed closure was never carried out, however. A report prepared by the vice-provost advocated the closure of Architecture, but two committees of the Governing Council held hearings, during which it became clear that approval by the Council was unlikely. As a result, the proposal was withdrawn, and an advisory committee was struck to consider the possibility of establishing an affiliated college that would operate with a separate budget but whose degrees would be administered by the university. Central administrators explained this change of plan as a rational response to community concern.

In the debate that ensued [around Architecture], the concept of an affiliated college was put forward by interested professional groups. We thought it would be derelict on our part to ignore that choice. We were never trying to save money; what we were saving was the opportunity cost of improving it. (Vice-provost)

Others saw this move as a retreat in the face of concerted opposition from the Governing Council.

It was ill-advised – it did not give the administration much credibility. They are now exactly where they were six months ago. The Architecture issue represents the first time Governing Council challenged the administration. I don't think any other decision has been overturned by Governing Council. (Professor)

There are a number of factors, discussed in some detail below, that help to explain why the proposal to close the Architecture faculty failed.

The Decision-Making Context

The inertia inherent in the University of Toronto's bureaucracy mitigated against radical change. Any large bureaucracy is difficult to change, and this university was no exception.

> Universities are inherently resistant to change and in some cases rightly so, but there's been a more than normal institutional paralysis here. (Central administrator)

This inertia may have been greater because of the climate of financial restrictions.

> If you don't fight, you are going to end up like Architecture. As budgets get tighter, anyone who is vulnerable is going to get whacked. You can't afford to be passive. Because decisions are not made by a senate, they are made by individuals and, consequently, lobbying power is very strong. (Dean)

Scarce resources can provoke change if funding cuts are dramatic enough to give rise to perceptions of a crisis. In this case, the idea that something needs to be done allows administrators to take radical and rapid action. At the University of Toronto, however, fiscal restraint had been implemented only gradually. There was no sense of crisis in the university community and, therefore, no perceived need for major change.

> We need a greater sense that there is a problem. I don't think the university as a whole perceives a problem. (Dean)

The governance system compounded the problem because contentious decisions provided something around which otherwise diverse groups could coalesce in a struggle against the administration. The usual "divide and conquer" rule no longer prevailed. If the administration was to secure the safe passage of its proposal, it would have to construct an effective coalition to support it.

> The structure makes some strategic decisions more difficult because there are more actors involved, which makes it harder to bring about full discussion and consensus. So you do tend to have a harder time of it if you are trying to coordinate things for a broad university response. (Vice-provost)

The Role of the Deans

The central administration also suffered from the lack of visible advocates for the closure of Architecture, particularly among the deans. Few of them expressed any direct interest in the issue. They did not appear to be familiar with the details – one dean referred to the problem of the Architecture faculty as a "mysterious area" – and were reluctant to take a stand.

> I kept out of the Architecture issue. I had nothing to win. If I agreed with it, I had little to add; and if I disagreed, it would put me into conflict with a guy I have to work with [the vice-provost]. (Dean)

> When I came into this job I asked myself, What was my role? Was it [as an] advocate of the departments or [as the] central administration's representative in the faculty. I chose the former. Given that point of view, I am not going to initiate a recommendation to close a particular area in the faculty. That can only happen as part of a broad look at the university. I think that has to be a central initiative and responsibility. The central administrators are the ones who are going to have to answer the question, How is the university going to cope with further budget cuts? It cannot be simply more of the same. (Dean)

Their exclusion from the senior management team turned the deans' allegiances towards their own faculties. They tended to adopt a parochial view rather than an institutional one. They had neither the motivation nor the interest in actively supporting the central administration in its attempt to close the faculty of Architecture. Even if they had chosen to do so, the governance system would have deprived them of a forum in which they could have influenced the wider academic community.

> There is nowhere to go with academic problems – to have them discussed in a body that somehow brings everyone together. In a senate, I would at least have had the whole university understanding the problem. They don't have to agree with you. It's the one place where the university comes together. We don't have that right now. What you want is not simply to "get approval but to get understanding. It's very difficult to communicate now. (Vice-provost)

Central administrators in some of the other universities in the study were able to use their deans as opinion leaders in the wider university community. Those deans had voting rights in the senate, often monop-olized key academic policy-making committees, and had the ability to influence other senators. A united coalition of both central adminis-trators and deans carried a considerable amount of weight. At the University of Toronto, in contrast, the central administration, already distanced from the university community, was unable to use the active support of the deans to help champion the closure.

The Process

For a variety of reasons, then, the university's structure and decision-making style were not conducive to radical change. In the case of Architecture, the central administrators also made some errors in managing the process. In particular, consultation was felt to be inadequate in an institution where the administration was already perceived to be distanced from the university community.

> The president has a hierarchical way of dealing with the rest of the administration. I'm not sure it's working as well as it might for him in terms of getting the community behind him. (Vice-provost)

Decisions were perceived to be taken by a small group of central administrators, considered immune to the views of the university community at large.

> Some major decisions are being made that have an impact on the whole university but very few people are making those decisions. There's no mechanism for discussing them. There's a mechanism where you can go and vent your spleen about it, you have a tirade, everyone listens but that is the end of it. Architecture was a decision made in Simcoe Hall [where the offices of the central administration are located], and now they are trying to justify it. (Dean)

> If you had consultation and faculty felt they were involved in things, you would get their consent to a greater rate of change. If faculty perceive themselves to be frozen out of the entire decision-making process, then they are not going to welcome change. [The] administration has a much better chance of change if the faculty is behind them rather than against them. (Faculty association representative)

The administration compounded these problem by creating a situation where it appeared that the decision had already been taken and "consultation" was undertaken only to justify it. The report examining the faculty was entitled "Recommendation for *Closure* of the Faculty of Architecture and Landscape Architecture" (emphasis added). Alternatives were not considered until the end of the report, and they were restricted to a large-scale reallocation of resources from other programs. The possibility of establishing an affiliated college was not considered, giving the impression that the central administrators had already made up their minds.

> Was it responsible for the university to adopt as an opening gambit the recommendation that the faculty should close? I don't know. I think the question could be asked whether the university carefully explored the alternatives. (Vice-provost)

A second problem concerned the timing of the report. An announcement was made that a decision had been taken to close Architecture on 23 January 1986. The report, however, was not released until 19 February, again contributing to the view that the outcome was a foregone conclusion.

In summary, there were a number of forces working against the proposal to close the faculty of Architecture. First, contracting resources is nearly always a painful process that arouses conflict and dissension. Second, the situation in Ontario had not been dramatic enough for the university community to provide its administration with a mandate for change. Third, the structure did not encourage change. Fourth, the central administration was unable to find champions for its plans among the deans. Fifth, the administration was distanced from the grass roots and found it difficult to mobilize support. The consultation process not only failed to reassure faculty but it cast doubt on the validity of the recommendation. It is, of course, impossible to say whether a different handling of the issue would have enabled the administration to close Architecture. The discussion above does, however, outline a number of factors that contributed to the failure.

The Outcome

What were the outcomes of the University of Toronto's response to funding cuts and to the other changes introduced by the president? Interviews indicated that the attempt to close Architecture may have led to some concerns among the university community.

> This year it's Architecture, next year it might be us. (Professor)

> University morale is low because the cuts keep coming and the professors are getting older. The university has to find some way of turning it around. The closure threat [against the faculty of Architecture] must have put the fear of God into everyone else. (Dean)

Some of the other changes instigated by the president were, however, relatively well received by some central administrators. These senior administrators were pleased with the advent of a more systematic approach to budget allocation and decision-making.

> The president has tried to reduce the games-playing that went on before and the song and dance about justifications, because we are only talking about a small amount of money. In my first year I found the process very debilitating and very competitive. I think it is now less competitive and we are working together better. We are wasting less time. (Central administrator)

On the other hand, with greater emphasis being placed on planning, other administrators felt alienated and complained that this new requirement demanded too much time and effort in a system already beset with heavy paperwork demands from the Governing Council.

> It's extremely difficult to find the time to do planning. Any planning I do has to take place during the summer: once Governing Council meets, we are back on the treadmill. (Central administrator)

There were few rewards for engaging in the planning process, particularly in the light of the scarcity of resources and of the possibility of program closure.

> Ever since I became dean I've been told to plan, plan, plan – but if you do produce a plan, it can be wiped away at a moment's notice because of a budgetary situation over which you have no control. Nobody examines your plan then. There's also evidence that the university itself doesn't plan. (Dean)

> Planning here ran out of steam because of budgetary constraints, which attenuated the incentives to effect comprehensive planning. (Central administrator)

The lack of resources made it difficult to use the budget as a mechanism for change. There was insufficient money to fund new developments in any way other than incremental.

> My objective has been to downplay the budget. I think it has caused far too much concern and attracted too much attention, time, and effort relative to its importance. We haven't been in times in which very large allocations can take place. The budget *reflects* change rather than being its cutting edge. (Central administrator)

The University of Toronto had initiated an institutional renewal exercise to rebuild morale.

> It's a little bit of rebuilding of pride – standing up and fighting back a bit. (Central administrator)

It involved planning new initiatives that could be launched in spite of the scarcity of resources.

> The renewal process is to redefine [the] mission and find objectives from that mission, so that you can put your money where your mouth is. (Central administrator)

The first phase involved consultations with over 400 faculty, administrators, staff, students, and alumni concerning a strategy for change. The report from these discussions was published in March 1987. Its main recommendations dealt with redesigning the undergraduate program in Arts and Science, introducing independent planning at the Erindale and Scarborough campuses, and building research strengths in line with government priorities. The next phase involved the development of consensus around how these changes should be made.

It was clear, however, that the university community was ambivalent about these initiatives. On the one hand, people raised doubts as to whether the renewal exercise would produce any fundamental changes.

> I think the university will undergo a self-analysis. What is doubtful is whether anything will change. I think it's unfortunate that universities have become as preoccupied as they have with budgets. When you have this review, I think there will be a tendency to focus exclusively on what do you do about budget cuts, which will reinforce inertia. It's not an environment in which you think about radical change. If there's no change, the exercise isn't really worth the investment. (Central administrator)

These people criticized the process for being *too* participative and demanded more direction and leadership.

> I don't think a grass-roots, bottom-up kind of study will get us very far. We need a more top-down, action-oriented, leadership-directed strategic plan from the president, saying, "This is where we are going, this is where I am taking you – and if you don't like it, get off." Build a consensus around the leadership and go for it. We also need senior leadership to announce a plan which will include substantial decentral-

ization. We can't ask every group where to go – we won't ever move. I think strong leadership in any kind of structure can make the place grow. We need a lot of leadership and courage. (Dean)

We don't understand what [the president is] talking about. There are no specific changes. He doesn't actually say what the problem is other than financial, which we all know about. It's hard to give approval for demands for change or renewal if you don't know what they are. He's trying to lead without suggesting where he's going to go – as if he's trying to lead from behind. He's trying to introduce a consultative process, but there's no mechanism for one. I know he's got a lot of problems, but I don't think this renewal thing is very constructive. (Faculty association representative)

On the other hand, even while individuals advocated more central direction, they did not seem to favour major changes.

If this is the way the universities are going to have to live for another decade, I doubt that we can cut little bits uniformly without very serious damage being done. I am not, on the other hand, advocating the excision model. (Dean)

The fact of life is, you can't use the budget in a highly discriminatory way. You might have heard people say they would like to see much more decisive allocations of budget, but that's theoretical only. (Central administrator)

I see the university preferring to take the tough decisions, but I have low confidence in their ability to do so. I would prefer the continuation of across-the-board cuts – at least we'd all survive, and we'd all survive together. (Dean)

CONCLUSIONS

The University of Toronto faced a difficult time in dealing with the scarcity of resources. It is clear that its size and structure alone made the implementation of change problematic by distancing the central administration from the university community and making it difficult to mobilize faculty support. Senior administrators contributed to this problem by not engaging in sufficient consultation. The governance system precluded the use of the deans as advocates for change. The central administration had been aware of the problems with the present governance arrangements but had been unable to overcome them.

Moreover, many of its decisions and much of its administrative style had, albeit inadvertently, reinforced the existing pressures.

The result seemed to be a university community that had become ambivalent about what it wanted – a more planned, selective approach to resource allocation, with new initiatives being undertaken in priority areas, or the continuation of a more low-key, egalitarian approach. This ambivalence further complicated matters for the administration, which was caught between the proverbial rock and hard place: there was considerable criticism of the central administration's previous policies, but no clear mandate for any change.

CHAPTER TEN

Comparison: The University of British Columbia and the University of Toronto

A comparison of the University of British Columbia and the University of Toronto reveals that there were differences in the ability their respective central administrators to neutralize potentially rebellious interest groups. It shows that administrators at UBC were far more successful in dealing with resistance and implementing their intended retrenchment strategy.

As seen in chapter eight, the context at UBC was relatively decentralized, with the deans enjoying a substantial degree of power. In comparison, the University of Toronto was more centralized: there was a larger and more clearly defined hierarchy, and the central administration had far greater control over budgeting and other procedures than its counterpart at UBC. The presence of the Governing Council also led to a greater concentration of power in the hands of central administrators since its mandate was restricted to approving, rejecting, or sending back proposals from the president. Normally, the Governing Council did not initiate matters. Most decisions were, in effect, taken by the central administration and automatically approved by the Council, particularly those involving the complex finances and operations of the university.

Some issues, however, polarized the diverse interests on the Governing Council. Unlike at UBC, where financial matters were judged by a relatively small group dominated by government appointees while academic decisions were made separately by a group of academics, at the University of Toronto both financial and academic decisions were ultimately approved or rejected by the Governing Council. Because of its heterogeneous composition, when contentious issues did arise it became difficult to reach consensus.

The University of Toronto deans were similar to their UBC counterparts in some ways, They were independent faculty administrators and, although they did not participate in global budget decisions, they had considerable freedom once the budget had been allocated. They were also fragmented and did not form a united pressure group. Unlike what happened at UBC, however, this fragmentation did not manifest itself in competition either amongst themselves or with the central administration. While the UBC deans might be described as politicized, those at the University of Toronto were relatively more quiescent and kept to their own territory. They also lacked an important source of power: whereas the UBC deans were members of the Senate, their Toronto counterparts were not members of the Governing Council. As a result, there was no arena in which the deans could appeal to and influence the wider university community.

In summary, power appears to have been more centralized at the University of Toronto than at the University of British Columbia. The central administration's role in decision-making was clearly institutionalized; the deans were less confrontational; and there was no evidence that the faculty association was particularly militant. The Governing Council further centralized power, although it was clear that consensus might be more difficult to obtain with contentious issues than would be the case with a senate or a board.

From the analysis so far, we might expect the University of Toronto to have been more successful than UBC in implementing its retrenchment plans, but in fact the reverse was true. To understand why this was so, we must also examine the effectiveness of central administrators in managing their respective situations. As Pettigrew (1985a, 1985b) has argued, organizational context can be managed: it is not only a barrier to action, it is also a source of power that can be mobilized to bring about change. Sizer (1988a, 1988b) has shown how institutional leaders create "on switches" that help to build commitment to change, as opposed to "off switches," which lead organizational members fight the idea of change.

MANAGING THE CONTEXT

Consultation at the University of Toronto differed from that at the University of British Columbia in a number of ways. Administrators did not use a committee like the Senate Budget Committee to involve faculty members. The committee that proposed the closure of the faculty of Architecture was comprised of administrators and presented closure as the only feasible option. The only alternative it considered was a large-scale reallocation of resources from other programs to upgrade Architecture; and that option was not considered until the very end of the report. The possibility of establishing an affiliated college was not even mentioned. Another problem concerned the timing of the report: the decision to close the faculty was announced on 23 January 1986 but the report of the committee was not released until 19 February. This created the impression that central administrators had already made up their minds about the closure and that no real consultation had occurred. Consultation was an important issue in an institution as large as the University of Toronto, where the administration was already perceived as being distanced from the university community, making it difficult to mobilize grassroots support.

The University of Toronto also failed to use its deans as advocates of the closure. The deans at UBC were powerful and, in some cases, clearly opposed to program closure. The nature of the proposals that were presented to the Senate, however, effectively neutralized the opposition (apart from the case of the Landscape Architecture program), and the deans were seen as giving their tacit support to the administration's plans. While the deans at the University of Toronto did not oppose the closure, they did not lend any support. They disassociated themselves from the problem, leaving it in the hands of the central administration.

CONCLUSIONS

Central administrators at both universities faced a difficult situation because of the interest groups they had to contend with. The University of British Columbia was more successful at neutralizing the opposition of the deans and converting it into tacit support during the debate in the Senate. The Senate Budget Committee also helped to legitimize the proposals by involving an independent analysis by a group of faculty members. In contrast, the lack of consultation prior to the announcement of the decision to eliminate the faculty of Architecture and the disassociation of the deans at the University of Toronto helped to create the impression that the closure proposal was solely the work of the central administration, which had not fully investigated the options open to it. The University of Toronto faced another disadvantage – the lack of a perceived crisis to create a mandate for change. The gradual cutbacks in Ontario and the relatively supportive attitude of the new Liberal government had none of the drama present in the UBC situation.

It is impossible to say that, had they used more extensive consultation and had they been able to create perceptions of a crisis and to mobilize the deans, the University of Toronto's administrators would have been successful in implementing their plans. This chapter had nonetheless provided some indication of why they failed to carry out the proposed closure while those at UBC were able to terminate all but one of the programs that had been marked for closure. It also shows that the institutional context is not an impenetrable barrier to change but can be managed and mobilized in ways that allow change.

CHAPTER ELEVEN

Carleton University

Carleton University was founded in the 1940s. In 1984, the university had an annual budget of $95 million and another $10 million in research grants. There were some 16,000 students (excluding those registered for the summer session), of whom one third were part-time and slightly over one tenth were in graduate programs. The university employed over 600 faculty members. The administrative structure of the university is outlined in Figure 11.1. The Board of Governors had thirty members in addition to the chancellor and president. Most were appointed by the Board, but three were elected by the Senate, and two by the students. The Senate had over sixty members, about half of whom were elected by the faculties.

One distinguishing feature of Carleton University was its commitment to accessibility rather than the "elitist" admissions policies of other institutions.

> The president has been at odds with other university presidents [in Ontario] for refusing to play the elitist game. The university is committed to accessibility. (Dean)

> [Carleton] is a bit of a maverick regarding accessibility. The Big Five [universities in Ontario] would say, "Quality first, and you may have to trim accessibility around the edges." (Ministry representative)

Carleton University had first experienced financial problems in the 1970s, and this influenced the way the institution responded to financial restrictions during the following decade. Carleton's first brush with financial restraint occurred when the president threatened a large number of layoffs in the mid-1970s in an attempt to avoid a predicted deficit. In the fall of 1974, the Senate began to consider

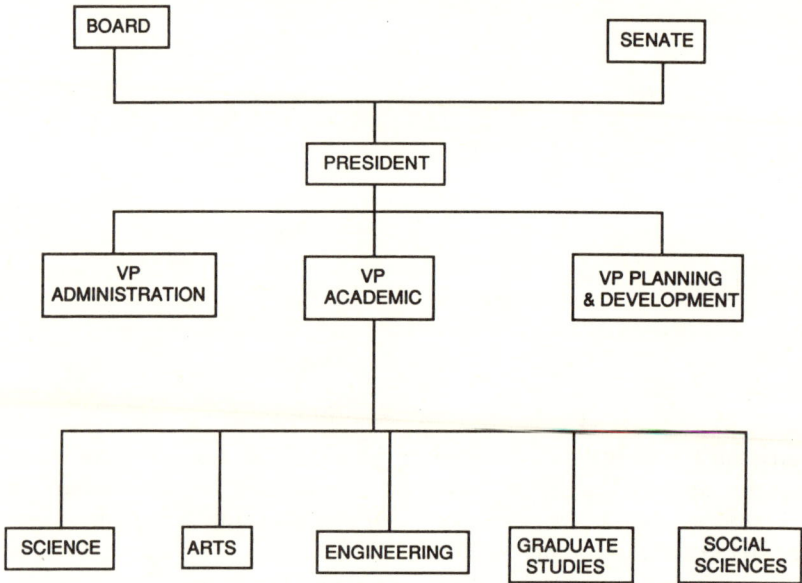

Figure 11.1
Carleton University: Simplified Organization Chart (ca 1986)

layoff procedures. The president, however, maintained that the administration – not the Senate – would determine how the layoffs would be made. He established two presidential advisory bodies that held closed deliberations. Even though the layoffs never took place, the university experienced considerable turmoil as a result of this threat.

Financial problems began to emerge again at the end of the 1970s. In 1979, an accumulated operating deficit of $1.3 million on a $55 million budget was predicted. Although relatively small (certainly compared with corresponding figures in the Quebec system), this deficit led to fears of bankruptcy and concern that the university might be forced to close. Some studies of the Ontario university system had recommended that it be rationalized, and there were some at Carleton who feared that their university might be a candidate for closure because it was a young institution without the research record of some of the older schools, and with financial difficulties.

> Carleton was perceived in the system as the most vulnerable. I think there was a time when Queen's, McMaster's, the University of Toronto, and Western felt relatively invulnerable to these pressures. If a sacrificial lamb could be found then everything would be o.k. I guess this university was elected. (Dean)

People were beginning to predict that Carleton would go under – would go bankrupt and close. (Dean)

THE UNIVERSITY CONTEXT

Carleton faced these difficulties with a president who had taken up his position in 1979. The vice-president (academic) and most of the incumbent deans had been appointed between 1978 and 1981. The vice-president (planning) – a director in the earlier administration – had been appointed to this new position by the president; in 1985, his portfolio was broadened to include development.

The new administration changed the management style at the senior levels. It incorporated the deans into the university's "management team" by increasing their autonomy and the degree of collegiality between them.

The Autonomy of the Deans

During the early 1980s, the deans had received greater autonomy with respect to the management of faculty budgets. Budgets were determined as a result of discussions between individual deans and the vice-president (planning). While formal budget planning began during the Fall term, it was a continuous process shaped during weekly meetings with the deans. It was described by one central administrator as a process of "osmosis – a continuous and continual process of data gathering," of which formal meetings were just one part. Once the vice-president (planning) and a faculty's dean had finalized that faculty's budget, it was approved by the president, and a preliminary budget plan was presented to the Board in December or January. A final budget was presented as soon as information on government funding became available, and the Board's approval was given by the end of April.

Once the deans received their budget, they had a fair degree of flexibility in spending it. Over the previous twelve years, the university had moved towards more global budgets.

> We have moved away from line budgets. The deans have complete freedom within categories. Certain areas are guidelined, not policy-controlled. (Central administrator)

Appointments still had to be approved by the central administration, but in other matters funds could easily be moved between categories. Consequently, the power of the deans to manage their faculties independently had increased.

The president gives you your job, and away you go and do it. (Dean)

Such autonomy would have caused problems had the deans adopted a territorial view and taken actions exclusively intended to benefit their respective faculty rather than the university as a whole, especially in an era of funding constraints and competition for limited resources. To ensure that this situation did not arise, some formal controls were maintained: deans were not allowed to run deficits, and the retention of surpluses had to be negotiated. The budget process itself was an exercise in control. Budgeting occurred on an annual basis, and deans who did not live up to their commitments would find negotiating for funds the following year a difficult process.

> We expect that at the end of the year, we will be able to analyse and see a fairly close fit between the plans and the patterns of expenditure. During the year, they have complete freedom to spend their money as they see fit. The reckoning only comes at the end of the year, and it forms the basis of next year's budget. (Central administrator)

As a result, deans knew that it was important to make feasible plans for their faculties, to submit realistic budget requests based on these plans, and to adhere to their commitments.

> I would be in trouble if I didn't do what I said I would. (Dean)

> I do what I say I will with my money, otherwise my credibility will be shot. (Dean)

Thus the increase in autonomy was offset by a variety of controls. There was, however, another important reason why deans remained committed to an institutional perspective – the collegial relations that had been established both among the deans themselves and between them and the central administration.

Collegiality

A conscious attempt had been made by the incoming administration to change the management culture at Carleton. In the opinion of many observers on campus, the previous president had overreacted to the threat of budget cuts in the 1970s. This had had a harmful effect on the morale of the university, resulting in acrimonious relations between faculty and administration, and in the subsequent unionization of the faculty (Axelrod 1982).

> The previous president was not trusted by the faculty, and the deans probably didn't trust one another. Everyone was at loggerheads. (Dean)

The new administration, in contrast, wanted to promote more collegial relationships among administrators and with the university community at large.

> [There is now] a community orientation – a culture change via conscious leadership concerning management style. Instead of offering edicts, you have to evoke cooperation. (Professor)

The first step in this process was the selection of a new group of deans, since the previous group had been not been particularly cohesive.

> We've been in a period over the last six years of a remarkably collegial group of deans. In the 1970s, they were promoters of their own empires and didn't get on so well. (Professor)

At least one incumbent dean sat on the committee searching for a new dean, and he or she knew the type of person the central administration was looking for.

> We do more than nurture collegiality. There is a dean from another faculty on every search committee, and you can be certain that we talk to that dean about what names we want to see on the final list. It's too important to let it happen by itself. (Central administrator)

If the president did not agree with the committee's recommendation, he did not have to accept it, since the committee had only advisory status. The president could then ask the committee to try again or he could simply appoint his preferred candidate.

Having appointed a group of like-minded individuals, the central administration sought to foster collegiality by increasing the number of meetings.

> We are a close-knit – we like each other – working group. It wasn't always like that. We changed it by changing the individuals and the way we have developed the informal networks. (Central administrator)

Deans and central administrators met regularly, within either the Long Range Planning Committee or the Deans Committee, which met on alternate weeks. The former was chaired by the vice-president (planning), and involved the deans and vice-president (academic). The latter consisted of all the vice-presidents, deans, and directors, and was chaired by the president. Weekend retreats for the deans had also been instituted. Informal meetings revolved around the "deans' lunch," held every Friday.

The aim of the meetings was to increase communication between the deans and to provide a forum for more intensive consultation. This degree of openness in the administration prevented complaints and criticism from festering. Differences of opinion were aired and discussed.

> We never have the opportunity to build up any grievances: they are always resolved. (Dean)

The fact that the deans got on well together and understood each other's problems through communication made consensus relatively easy to achieve.

> There's a collective decision-making process. It's usually easy to arrive at consensus because it's a close working relationship. We operate on a solidarity basis. (Dean)

The integration of the two levels led the deans to adopt an institutional perspective. They were attuned to university-wide issues rather than to a more limited faculty viewpoint. These attitudes may have been easier to foster because of the threat to Carleton's existence during the 1970s. These attacks from the outside made it easier to band together.

> Whatever financial difficulties we would run into, we would run into them as a university. I think as an administrative group we are committed to the university. We helped build the university, and we'll be damned if anyone is going to take it apart – even us. (Dean)

> It was commonly accepted that if we were to go down, we would go with all flags flying rather than commit suicide. (Dean)

These protective feelings had endured. The fact that the institution was relatively small also helped to protect collegiality: whereas the larger institutions in reviewed in this study had twelve or more deans from highly diversified backgrounds with which to contend, Carleton University had only three vice-presidents and five deans.

At Carleton, the deans were thus integrated into the central policy-making group. They identified as much with the university as with their particular faculty.

We have a very collegial operation here – in faculties, between faculties, and with the vice-presidents. Earlier, the deans were unhappy with each other or with the central administration. Now the deans feel part of the central administration. (Dean)

This identification was important because of the deans' involvement in institutional decision-making: the university would be unable to function if they were divided and parochial.

It has been a great source of pleasure in the management of this university to experience the amount of cooperation, cohesiveness, and teamwork that has gone on among the deans. It's amazing how they work together as part of the management team. (Central administrator)

Deans could argue their own case in private, but they had to be prepared to promote the group's decision, whether or not they agreed with it.

The deans' job is somewhat schizophrenic. When they are in the committee of deans, they can disagree all they want but, after that meeting is over and we have decided on a policy, the dean is to speak for it even if [he or she] fought [against it earlier]. (Central administrator)

In summary, by increasing autonomy and enhancing collegiality, Carleton University had moved from a system that coerced the deans through budget restrictions and centralized power to one in which they were, in effect, selected for their ability to identify with the institution as a whole. Direct controls had been replaced by more subtle controls.

DECISION-MAKING

The deans were clearly part of the senior decision-making group at Carleton. According to one dean, "there is nothing within this university that is considered outside the prerogative of a dean." The group also included the vice-presidents and president. Within it, two vice-presidents were particularly influential.

The decisions are formally taken by the president, but the vice-president (planning) and vice-president (academic) really take the decisions. The president tends to take their recommendations. (Dean)

If I had to choose the most powerful individuals, I'd start with the two vice-presidents – planning and academic. They choose not to work in a confrontational mode. (Dean)

It was a highly effective coalition: the vice-president (academic) had ultimate control over academic issues, while the vice-president (planning) had control over the budget. The latter was particularly powerful.

> Of those two individuals, I would attach great importance to the vice-president (planning) because he is the fiscal wizard, he's had the longest tenure in office – he was doing the job before it was defined as a vice-president's. (Dean)

He also had more detailed information about the university than any other single individual.

> The vice-president (planning) deserves a lot of credit. He has lots of statistics and information so no one could bamboozle him. He's a whiz. (Professor)

The vice-president (planning) was a key proponent of, and player in, the move to increase the collegiality of the deans. He chaired the Long Range Planning Committee and sat on the Deans' Committee.

Outside this group of administrators, others had only limited influence over resource allocation. The Senate had responsibility for curricula but little influence over the budget: it only reviewed the previous year's allocation.

> Anything to do with resources, the Senate has nothing to do with it. It's a management decision – the president, vice-presidents, and deans. (Senate member)

It lacked the necessary authority and information to intervene in the resource allocation process.

> Senate is largely ineffectual. It appears to have no policy-making authority at all. Senate is playing a game that the administration is quite willing to let them play. (Faculty association representative)

Even future academic plans were not an matter into which the Senate had a great deal of input.

> Senate doesn't have jurisdiction over the academic plans for the university as some of our sister institutions love to do. I'm afraid I am glad we don't do it their way. We chose not to proceed along that route. (Central administrator)

The Board of Governors was supportive of the president and took a relatively passive role.

> The Board of Governors may have questions and an issue may take more than one meeting, but there is no conflict [with the central administration]. (Board member)

> The president and the vice-presidents have managed the board well. They have kept them very passive – perhaps too passive. (Dean)

The Board was mainly concerned with the size of the deficit or surplus and did not intervene in operational matters. As with many university boards, it operated on the basis of information provided by the administration and did not have a detailed knowledge or understanding of the university.

> [The Board of Governors] can only ask questions in relation to what they know was spent last year because they don't know, they don't get enough information. We try to second-guess those questions in our budget presentation by giving a detailed rundown on how we arrived at our figures. (Central administrator)

Carleton's faculty members formed a union in the mid-1970s as a result of the threat of layoffs. Despite this inauspicious beginning, there was no return of the adversarial mode that had led to the formation of the union, nor had the latter "handicapped the university financially." (Dean)

> The union hasn't had a direct effect. The threat of a union was more of an issue than the union itself. (Dean)

If anything, the existence of the union had further concentrated power in the hands of the central administration. It had formalized relations through the collective agreement and had created a coherent and clearly defined management structure.

> Unionization gives us a discipline in management. You know what you're dealing with. It clarifies the process of decision-making wonderfully. Sitting there at two a.m., wondering if they are going to strike in the morning, concentrates the mind. (Central administrator)

> I don't think such a complicated agreement is needed but, once you learn it and have experience with it, it's no different from any other –

with [the] one possible exception that it's more predictable. (Central administrator)

In summary, decision-making at Carleton might be described as relatively centralized from the decanal level upward. The vice-president (planning), in particular, wielded a considerable amount of power. The group was highly collegial, and the deans adopted an institutional perspective. Other interest groups had little influence over university decision-making. The Senate's role was limited to curriculum; the Board of Governors was highly supportive of the central administration; and the union's main influence was through salary negotiations.

> The Senate has absolutely nothing to do regarding resource allocation. The student newspaper looked at the power distribution in the university. They looked at the formal structure and got it wrong. The Senate has binding authority over academic matters, but it is discursive rather than decision-making. They have curriculum responsibility, but there is no real change these days. Resources are a managerial prerogative subject to contracts. There is not much important business for the Senate. The union created management. We didn't really have a coherent management structure before. (Dean)

THE CUTBACK STRATEGY

The president's office and the deans thus represented the key group of decision-makers. How did they deal with financial restrictions? The university's previous experience had not provided a particularly harmonious background. Widespread layoffs had been proposed in the 1970s, which had generated confusion and uncertainty, and alarmed the faculty. This had led to the formation of the faculty union and to the adoption of a particularly complex clause on layoff procedures in the collective agreement, known as "Article 17."

> There's no doubt in my mind that when the [previous] president began to talk about fiscal crisis, the faculty began to be aware of deficits. The board was alarmed, the faculty was alarmed, and the faculty hastened to unionize as a way to ensure they were well represented in terms of salaries and benefits. The current president has regenerated confidence in the fiscal management of the university. (Dean)

The current administration decided to have a "no layoff" policy, for two reasons. One was the complexity of Article 17, which effectively precluded redundancies.

> Article 17 is a joke. It would never be used because it is such a cumbersome procedure. By the time you implemented it, you'd be broke. (Central administrator)

The second reason was to avoid the problems encountered earlier by assuring faculty that their jobs were not under threat.

> What was explicit was that if we did it [lay off tenured staff], we did it under Article 17. Have you read Article 17? ... Firing a full-time tenured professor was not on. If you start with that, you can go a long way. (Dean)

Instead, a voluntary severance package was used to reduce faculty staff, offering up to two years' pay as an incentive.

The earlier brush with financial problems did prove beneficial in one way: it served as "a dry run," as one dean expressed it. The 1970s scare meant that various cost-cutting options had been explored and, in some cases, implemented.

> We were leaders in conservation, taking out every other light bulb, sharing phones. (Central administrator)

> I think this university perceived earlier than most the logic of our situation and adjusted to it by maximizing the use of our resources. (Dean)

Expenditures had already been lowered by reducing the number of sessional lecturers and by such measures as energy savings, larger classes, reduced maintenance, cuts to the libraries, etc.

> A second important feature of the cutback process was its differential nature.

> If resource allocation isn't differential, then I don't think you are doing a good job. The world isn't that way round. (Central administrator)

For example, the Arts faculty bore the brunt of the cuts, with the number of teaching staff decreasing from 220 in 1978 to 202 in 1986, while Social Sciences increased its establishment by thirty. Other well-protected areas included Engineering and, in particular, Computer Science. The administration established priority areas and continued to fund them at the expense of some other faculties. Another priority was a building program. Deans agreed to make additional cuts in their operating revenue and to transfer the savings to a maintenance fund, which was used to redress some of the maintenance problems that had arisen during the years of restraint.

These decisions were influenced by the style of the administration. The involvement of the deans in the decision-making process and, in particular, their collegial relationship resulted in a better understanding of the financial situation.

> All policy with respect to budget limits, budget control, and budget constraint is based to a large measure on discussion and negotiation that goes on in the committee of deans. (Central administrator)

As senior policy-makers, the deans were aware of, and committed to, the need for the differential cutbacks.

> We have incredibly good innovative deans who work in a consensual mode. They are the senior managers of the university and not just CEOs of their faculty. Therefore, there has to be a real willingness to under-stand and recognize the difficulties of the different faculties and to accept differential rates of change and agreed-upon privileges. (Central admin-istrator)

> There is a consensus among the deans – a social contract. The deans accept the social-science growth area. (Dean)

The involvement of the deans also enabled a "strategic planning" initiative to be developed. Formal planning involved a number of elements at Carleton University. Each budget plan included a five-year forecast and contained establishment (number of faculty positions) plans, so that faculties and departments knew in advance the number of positions that would be available to them.

The Long Range Planning Committee looked at the broader issue of making Carleton a "bigger and better place" over the following ten years. This process was more complex. Broad objectives emerged from discussions with the deans, while details were worked out on a more incremental basis. They depended "on the politically expedient thing to do at the time," as one central administrator put it. This process also involved securing commitment and cooperation. Many issues were worked out in the Long Range Planning Committee before they were publicized and formally approved by the Board of Governors. The result was that by the time initiatives such as capital and building campaigns were announced, all parties were fully committed to their execution.

Strategic planning is to keep reminding people in the midst of all the other things that are happening what we've *got* to do and engaging in the political process of maintaining cohesiveness and cooperation. (Central administrator)

Carleton University was the only institution covered in this study where interviewees believed that meaningful planning was being carried out.

[Strategic planning] is vitally necessary, and it's done every two weeks at the deans' meeting and on a regular and continuous basis by board. [It means that] every time a department says, "I want a tenure track slot," the questions are, "Where's this department going to be in fifteen years from now? How does it fit into your existing programs? How does it deal with present research? How does it relate to the international development in that area? How does it fit with present degree programs? How does it fit into our organization?" (Dean)

We've been in a planning mode for quite some time now and not only have we determined priorities, but [we've] had them approved [by the Board]. (Dean)

Planning was seen not as a mechanical procedure but as a process whereby valid ideas were operationalized.

It hasn't led to mechanistic planning, it meant that there was a disciplined way of discussing [resource allocation ... The central administration] was too smart to engage in mechanistic planning – there were too many social scientists around for that. (Professor)

The analysis of Carleton's response to budget cuts shows that it was shaped by both the historical and current context of the university. Earlier experiences with financial restraint precluded some options, such as laying off faculty, but they also provided some experience with different cost-cutting measures. The integration of the deans into the senior policy-making team enabled differential cuts to be carried out and new initiatives to be implemented.

EXTERNAL FUNDING

Carleton University launched a stronger initiative to raise external funds so as to help offset government funding restraints. Part of this strategy involved forging a stronger relationship with business in order to augment private funding – a resource that is becoming increasingly important in today's environment of financial scarcity. Carleton began to lay the foundations for a capital campaign. The goal was to raise $30 million and to increase private donations to 4 percent of operating revenue by 1995. Consultants were hired, the vice-president (planning) took on a new development portfolio, and the public relations office was revitalized with some new appointments.

While people were optimistic about the campaign, some frustration was expressed concerning the university's lack of "appeal."

> We have to blow our own horn more. We've not done a good job of selling ourselves. We've got to turn that around. (Central administrator)

Carleton had not always been very effective in its handling of public relations.

> P.R. is not just damage control, it should be promotion. What you have to do is promote all the things that relate to the central mission. (Dean)

This deficiency was attributed to a number of causes. In the eyes of some, the resources devoted to the public relations function were inadequate. Others suggested that internal changes had occurred at the expense of external strategies.

> We have let external relations slide because we have been preoccupied with internal problems. We have been lax in firming up ties with the local community. We don't convey the excellent things we do here. (Dean)

The board also received some criticism for not being a strong advocate on behalf of the university.

> [The Board of Governors] has a community-service mentality. They "do" Carleton as they might "do" a hospital. (Board member)

> The Board of Governors didn't have a sense of the university. They saw themselves as trustees of the public interest and were never with us in our enthusiasm for the university. (Dean)

The attempt to secure external funds also suffered from the lack of a clearly defined constituency. Carleton did not have the well-established networks of business and political alumni upon which older and larger universities can call.

Carleton is neither old and rich, nor new and relevant in a technological sense; nor does it have a strong sense of community. (Board member)

CONCLUSIONS

In summary, Carleton University's retrenchment strategy revolved around the incorporation of the deans into the senior policy-making team. This effectively secured their commitment to an institutional view and preempted parochial, territorial behaviour. With this consensus among senior administrators, it became relatively easy to make some differential cuts and to secure commitment to initiatives such as the building fund, the capital campaign, and long-term planning.

The deans and central administrators were clearly pleased with their approach to cutbacks.

> We anticipated these financial constraints [in the late 1970s], adapted to them, and lived with them. There's a grudging respect for that [from the outside], but I believe that people are surprised that we survived. There was a fear of closure some years ago. We felt we were seen as a redundant university, but we've proved that we're not. (Dean)

> Carleton has really turned around. We are one of the few universities in the province building new buildings – and that's a revelation. (Dean)

Opinions concerning the effect of cutbacks on the quality of education were more ambivalent. Interviewees complained that larger classes had resulted from an influx of students at a time of constrained resources. This situation also inhibited the ability to respond to new demands – for example, there were only 100 Computer Science places for 1,800 applications, and only 280 places for 2,000 Engineering candidates. While there were some questions concerning the quality of the teaching, administrators were uncertain about the scope of the problem. The issue of declining quality was discussed only in a long-term perspective or in very philosophical terms.

> Underfunding has meant that for every extra student, the richness of the experience is diminished. (Dean)

> I believe that the quality of undergraduate education for an individual in a class of 200 is less for the same individual in a class of 30, but I don't *know* that – and I would have one hell of a time proving it. (Central administrator)

From a political perspective, a decline in quality is difficult to admit, particularly in a university whose commitment to accessibility had already been interpreted in some quarters as a lack of concern with quality.

> It's very difficult for a university president to say that quality has gone down from ten years ago; and if you do you, can get into a lot of trouble. (Professor)

> It's a dilemma we haven't solved yet. How do you admit, how do you even show that quality isn't what it was? How do you psychologically put yourself in the situation of saying our graduates aren't as good as they were? Some of them are. Who's going to say it? Have Carleton say it and the others deny it? That's suicide. (Dean)

Thus broadcasting the downgrading effects of underfunding can be a double-edged sword.

CHAPTER TWELVE

Understanding
the Institutional Context

The retrenchment policies adopted by a number of Canadian universities in the early 1980s were shaped by the internal context of each institution, as we have seen in the preceding chapters. It has been argued that these differences in context, which stemmed from variations in access to, and the use of, power by university actors, played some role in influencing choices concerning both retrenchment strategies and methods of implementation. The comparative chapters focused on three particular examples. The first (chapter five) showed that the institutional context helps to explain why the two Montreal universities examined in this study chose very different methods to implement similar cutback strategies. The second (chapter eight) argued that contextual factors also helped to account for differences in the choice of quite different retrenchment strategies in British Columbia. The third (chapter ten) moved from a static analysis to illustrate how administrators can manage their contexts in order to improve the chances of implementing cutback plans. In this regard, the University of British Columbia appeared to more successful than the University of Toronto.

The concept of institutional context is analysed in greater detail in the present chapter, which begins with a discussion of the existing theory on university governance and decision-making. For the purposes of this discussion, governance refers to the process of making academic decisions – that is, to the reality of decision-making rather than simply to the official distribution of policy-making authority. Some of the basic models that have been used to analyse university decision-making will be presented – the bureaucracy, collegium, political-organization, and organized-anarchy models. This is followed by a look at how the universities in this study compare to these archetypes and at the links between context and strategy. It will be argued that understanding the context in which one operates is crucial to the management not only of retrenchment but of all types of change. For it is in the institutional context that the sources of power are embedded.

THE PROFESSIONAL-
BUREAUCRACY MODEL

Research on the bureaucratic elements of universities can be traced back to the increase in size and complexity of many academic institutions that occurred during the 1950s and 1960s, which drew attention to the need for administrative structures to provide coordination and direction (e.g., Kerr 1964). Stroup (1966) noted that certain characteristics of the bureaucratic model described by Weber were present in universities: coordination through the division of labour; standardization of activities; use of impersonal criteria; an administrative hierarchy; and formal rules and regulations (Baldridge 1971; Blau 1973). It was also pointed out that other bureaucratic features were absent: direct supervision of work; detailed operating rules; and a high degree of centralization (Platt and Parsons 1968; Baldridge 1971; Blau 1973). Blau drew attention to the inherent contradictions between the rigidity and discipline present in a bureaucracy and the flexibility and innovation required of scholarship, and between authority based on position and authority based on expertise and knowledge. He argued that bureaucratic and academic features coexisted in a decentralized bureaucracy.

Satow (1975) identified a gap in Weber's theory of bureaucracy that accommodated the professional organization. In the traditional bureaucracy, obedience is secured by formal rules that are grounded in rational/legal authority, and members are committed to the organization's goals. Professional obedience takes the form of allegiance to a profession or discipline rather than to an organization, and is secured through that profession's values and norms. Coordination is achieved by the standardization of skills, and commitment by socialization, both of which are acquired through professional training (Schein 1968; Van Maanen and Schein 1979; Van Maanen 1983). This organization differs markedly from the traditional bureaucracy since power and responsibility are decentralized, not centralized: "It hires duly trained and indoctrinated specialists – professionals – for the operating core, and then gives them considerable control over their work" (Mintzberg 1988: 639). The existence of professional values thus makes "self-government" possible.

In this professional bureaucracy (Mintzberg 1979a), the professional and the bureaucratic coexist in a number of ways. First, there is considerable standardization of the skills, procedures, and programs used to carry out the work. Clients are categorized and placed into predetermined programs, within which a standardized set of procedures are invoked. For example, students seeking a Law degree will take a relatively predetermined program of courses, while Medical students will face different, but equally standardized, options. Although these skills, procedures, and programs are regulated by the profession (rather than by the organization, as in a traditional bureaucracy), they nevertheless remain standardized, formalized, and difficult to change – in other words, they are bureaucratic.

A second bureaucratic characteristic derives from the presence of autonomous, loosely coupled subunits within the larger organization (Weick 1976). As anyone who has worked in a university is only too aware, the type of democracy and decentralization associated with this structure requires a considerable amount of red tape and is characterized by a hierarchical structure and by procedures that are extensive and pervasive. The approval routes for programs, promotion, tenure, and recruitment are standardized, predetermined, and run the length of the hierarchy.

The third way in which the bureaucratic and academic organizations overlap pertains to the support staff. While the professional side of the university may be characterized by autonomy and academic freedom, the support staff are typically arranged in a traditional, top-down bureaucracy (Corson 1960; Eztioni 1964; Holdaway et al. 1975; Mintzberg 1979a).

Thus the analysis of the bureaucratic nature of the university has uncovered an organization in which both professional and bureaucratic features are to be found. Professionals develop a wide array of techniques to standardize their product, and the integration of autonomous subunits requires a bureaucratic structure. Universities typically encompass a decentralized, but bureaucratic, academic community that coexists with a bureaucratized nonacademic one.

THE COLLEGIAL MODEL

The concept of collegiality stems from two main sources. First, it has been linked to professional authority based on competence rather than position and to a flatter hierarchy (Baldridge 1971; Childers 1981). Second, it refers to a community of scholars (Goodman 1962) in which decisions are a matter of consensus (Millett 1962). Collegiality has thus been viewed as either a decentralized structure or a consensual decision-making process.

The Collegial Structure

The work of Beyer and colleagues (Lodahl and Gordon 1972, 1973; Beyer and Lodahl 1976; Beyer 1982) has focused on whether university departments are collegial or bureaucratic, terms that are seen as mutually exclusive. Collegiality is defined as decentralization within the subunit, with a high degree of influence being exerted over decision-making by faculty members, while bureaucracy is viewed as centralization, characterized by a low degree of faculty influence relative to that of the department head.

> The terms "collegial" vs "bureaucratic" were adapted to apply to relatively decentralized and centralized decision making within the university subunit. (Beyer and Lodahl 1976: 109)

The authors also study what they argue is a second dimension – decentralization *vs* centralization – defined in terms of subunit autonomy from the influence of central administration.

> A university was considered decentralized if it was divided into subunits that exercise substantial control over a range of decisions relevant to their own functioning. (Beyer and Lodahl 1976: 109)

The authors argue that a department can operate in a centralized manner, under an influential central administration or, if autonomous, in a decentralized way. Decision-making in the subunit can be collegial, with influential faculty, or bureaucratic, with a strong department head. The use of two continua is justified on the grounds that decentralization can exist without collegiality – as in Germany, where professors have total control over their departments. This use of two dimensions is somewhat misleading, however, since the authors are not measuring two different phenomena but one (Hardy 1990e). They are, in effect, examining different degrees of decentralization – to the level of department head or to faculty members. The authors themselves imply that one dimension is an extension of the other.

> Decentralization of authority to departments and collegial decision making within departments can be viewed as successive steps in the same process. (Beyer and Lodahl 1976: 109)

Beyer and Lodahl are not really referring to either collegial or bureaucratic *processes*: their work focuses on one aspect of formal *structure*. The terminology implies that their study has something to say about how decisions are made and influence is exerted, but it completely ignores any element of process. For example, as Beyer (1982: 174–5) points out, department heads can influence decision-making bureaucratically as agents of the central administration, or collegially as faculty leaders. Beyer (1982) assumes the latter, but all she can conclude is that the department head exerted influence: the study does not show the way in which that influence was exerted. Similarly, while a high degree of faculty influence is assumed to reflect collegiality, it could also indicate political activity where faculty members are fighting each other for personal gain.

Collegiality and Consensus

While collegiality has been repeatedly presented as the traditional view of university governance, there has been little work explicitly dealing with decision-making by consensus. However, this topic is implicit in Clark's work (1970, 1971, 1972) on the saga – or institutional mission – typical of institutions where the loyalty and commitment of members bind them to the organization's goals. As a result, one would expect consensus decision-making. Such a situation is characterized by shared responsibility and shared premises about organizational purpose; alternatives that are generated by different specializations; and decisions that occur as a result of consensus-building processes to which participants are willing to contribute the necessary time, effort, and information (Chaffee 1983a). It is also implicit in Satow's (1975) work, where allegiance to professional values represents an ideology that integrates members (also see Dill 1982).

Recent interest in the cultural and symbolic aspects of university life has indirectly examined collegiality (Dill 1982; Chaffee 1984; Masland 1985; Tierney 1987, 1988, 1989; Chaffee and Tierney 1988; Gumport 1988). This body of work has drawn attention to the role of administrators as symbolic managers of meaning, able to create a *de facto* saga, and emphasized the importance of nurturing culture in order to foster identification with the institution, protect the university community from external threats, and enhance effectiveness (e.g., Dill 1982; Bess 1988).

In summary, research on collegiality has focused on either decentralized decision-making structures or culture. The former has little to say about decision-making *processes* because these studies measure only the degree of decentralization – not whether actors use their influence in a political, collegial, or bureaucratic way. In effect, this body of research relates closely to the concept of professional bureaucracy, in which the centralized power of position is juxtapositioned against the decentralized power of expertise and knowledge. Collegiality, according to the work of Satow and Clark, is more than just structure; it is a *gestalt* that pervades all aspects of university life and is reflected in structure, process, behaviour, and attitudes. This work on culture focuses on how leaders create an environment in which consensus is the norm, although it rarely examines how consensus can be created around specific decisions. In other words, it illustrates the creation of collegial institutions rather than of collegial processes *within* institutions.

THE POLITICAL MODEL

Baldridge (1971) dismissed the collegial view as unrealistic and utopian, and substituted a model of political decision-making. Other writers, such as Pfeffer and colleagues, have also studied the use of power. Like Beyer, they have tended to ignore process and to concentrate on the structural arrangements that provide actors with power.

The Political Process

Writers such as Hill and French (1967) and Darkenwald (1971) were among the first to examine the political dimensions of university life, but it was Baldridge who fully explicated the political model of university administration. He lamented the absence of a political model in organization theory although, in fact, a body of literature had begun to emerge by the 1970s (Burns 1961; Cyert and March 1963; Crozier 1964; French and Raven 1968). Baldridge did not refer to this literature but used theories of conflict, community power, and interest groups to develop a framework for political analysis. He claimed that his model included consensual and bureaucratic processes, but it presented an intensely political view of university life.

> We see neither the rigid formal aspects of bureaucracy nor the calm, consensus-directed elements of an academic collegium. On the contrary, if student riots cripple the campus, if professors form unions and strike, if administrators defend their traditional positions, and if external interest groups and irate governors invade the academic halls, all these acts must be seen as political (Baldridge 1971: 19–20).

It is difficult to see how an institution could function for very long in the midst of such conflict, however, and Baldridge toned down the political rhetoric in his later work.

> Many decisions are made not in the heat of political controversy but because standard operating procedures dominate in most organizations ... The political model developed from that [earlier] study probably overstresses the role of conflict, bargaining, and negotiating. (Baldridge et al. 1978: 42)

Unfortunately, these additional assumptions result in considerable ambiguity about the centrality of conflict and the degree of political activity. For example, Baldridge et al. (1978) argue that inactivity prevails on the part of most people, but at the same time, they also suggest that policy decisions inevitably mobilize political interests. Second, participation is said to be fluid, even though it is argued elsewhere in the book that people are active in decision-making and political elites often dominate. Third, the authors maintain that fragmented interest groups normally coexist harmoniously except when resources are scarce; yet they go on to insist that conflict is normal. In effect, the authors seem unclear whether universities are characterized by endemic, ubiquitous conflict or by occasional, sporadic upheavals. Instead of trying to resolve this confusion by discussing the conditions that might make politics and conflict more likely, the authors try to incorporate a variety of models under the rubric of one framework.

> There is a subtle mix of bureaucratic factors, collegial and professional influences, and political dynamics at work in academic institutions. These confusing organizational situations [are called] organized anarchies. (Baldridge et al. 1978: 70)

One reason for the confusion may lie in the lack of reference to the organizational literature on power and politics that had emerged by the late 1970s. The 1971 model was grounded in theoretical developments from other areas of study, and the exclusion of the relevant work from organizational theory was understandable since it was relatively new. By 1978, however, a much larger body of work had accumulated (including, for example, Allison 1971; Hickson et al. 1971; Pettigrew 1973; Pfeffer and Salancik 1974). Yet this literature was ignored by Baldridge, who added only the theory of organized anarchy to his later work.

Political Structures

Pfeffer and colleagues conducted a series of studies on the relationship between power and decision outcomes. They argued that a department's share of the budget was predicted more accurately by its power (as

defined by other department heads and by the extent of its representation on committees) than by its size or reputation (Salancik and
Pfeffer 1974); that the ability to obtain outside grants influenced the
ability to obtain internal funding (Pfeffer and Salancik 1974); that the
relationship between the panel members who judged grant applications
and grant recipients affected grant allocations (Pfeffer et al. 1976); and
that the turnover of department heads was a political process, particularly where the underlying paradigm of the academic field was not
well developed (Pfeffer and Moore 1980). In other words, it was argued
that, first, resource allocation was best explained by power (defined
primarily as the ability to attract highly valued external resources); and
second, where there was no clear consensus in an academic field,
decisions were resolved by politics.

This work is highly quantitative and involves a more systematic
analysis than Baldridge's work. It focuses on measurable, structural
factors that, according to the authors, indicate the possession of power
sources, which in turn determine decision outcomes. The research
design has its limitations, however. First, a process in which those
departments which secure highly valued research grants, have high
prestige, or have large graduate enrolments receive a larger share of
the budget, is not necessarily political. Rewarding such areas of strength
could equally be interpreted as rational! Second, the research design
allows the authors to say little about process. It implies that the mere
possession of power is sufficient to influence decision outcomes and
fails to show *how* power is mobilized. Third, by assuming that the
dissensus associated with an underdeveloped disciplinary paradigm
automatically results in political behaviour, the authors rule out the
ability to *create* consensus, making the analysis highly deterministic.

In summary, the work on power and politics has examined both
structure and process, but not within the same study. One stream of
research has focused on the decision-making process but in a way that
makes it difficult to draw conclusions about the conditions under
which politics is likely to emerge. The second stream has adopted a
more systematic approach to the antecedents of power but, in so doing,
has ignored the process by which power is put to use (Hardy 1990e).

THE ORGANIZED-ANARCHY MODEL

The "garbage can" model, in which universities are viewed as organized anarchies (Cohen and March 1974; March and Olsen 1976)
is different from both the bureaucratic and the political approaches
in that it assumes that behaviour is not goal-driven. It argues that

decisions are not the result of intention but are made by default or by accident (Chaffee 1983a). Problems exist all the time and are not necessarily resolved by choice; solutions are answers actively looking for questions; choice opportunities occur when the organization is expected to make decisions, and those decisions are often made by oversight and flight; participants come and go; issues often have a low salience; there is a weak information base; and the total system has high inertia. This situation arises when there is goal ambiguity, problematic technology, and fluid participation (March and Olsen 1976). Other conditions were added by Baldridge et al. (1978) – client service, a high degree of professionalism, and environmental vulnerability.

This model has been contested (Musselin 1987), especially in the context of important decisions and scarce organizational resources. It has been argued that issues may become too important to be left in the "garbage can" and that the model is best suited to peripheral matters, to be replaced by another style of decision-making when issues become salient (Hardy et al. 1983). Even its proponents point out that the model applies only to situations of slack resources (Cohen and March 1974). The authors are also unclear regarding the role of leadership: the true organized anarchy, one would assume, would be unmanageable, yet these writers argue that leaders can influence the organization (Cohen and March 1974). They recommend a number of strategies: publicly soliciting a consensus; managing agendas; expending time, energy, and persistence, since they are scarce resources; collecting information; coopting opposition parties; overloading the system with information; providing garbage cans in which to dump issues (for example, creating a committee to deflect attention); managing unobtrusively; selectively interpreting history; and writing minutes after meetings have been forgotten.

All these recommendations sound remarkably political: people are mobilizing their power to influence decisions. Such action is purposeful, directed, and focused, in which case participation will not be fluid nor will individual goals be unclear. As Lutz (1982) points out, when Padgett (1980) talks about "managing the garbage can," he is no longer talking about the garbage can. In other words, organized anarchy may exist in certain circumstances and peripheral decisions may get made in the garbage can, but once issues become salient, the system becomes a political arena.

MIXED MODELS

Allison's (1971) application of mixed metaphors to government decision-making was copied in the work on university governance. The bureaucratic and academic dimensions continued to attract attention (Helsabeck 1973; Kort-Krieger and Schmidt 1982; Bresser 1984; Hendrickson and Bartkovich 1986), although other studies emphasized a mix of bureaucratic, collegial, political, and, sometimes, garbage-can characteristics (e.g., Davies and Morgan 1982; Ellstrom 1983; Taylor 1983; Bess 1988; Birnbaum 1988). Childers (1981) attempted to identify the relationship between bureaucratic, collegial, and political models. Her definition of collegiality is a continuation of Beyer's work – a structural phenomenon involving decentralization. Her findings reaffirm the earlier work suggesting that both bureaucratic and professional elements are integrated into the professional bureaucracy in the form of a structural continuum between the traditional (centralized) bureaucracy and the professional (decentralized) bureaucracy. Universities display elements of both, approaching one extreme or the other, depending on such factors as size, prestige, traditions, and leadership.

In turning to process, Childers argued that there is only one model to explain how decisions are made – politics – and continued the trend of neglecting collegial *processes*.

> Political decision making in the literature usually refers to competitive strategies rather than mediation strategies aimed toward establishing mutual agreement or cooperative-collaborative strategies. (Childers 1981: 43)

Collegiality is the reverse side of the political coin: separate groups with disparate goals exist as a result of specialization and loose coupling. In the political model, self-interest prevails; in the collegial model, the disparate goals are integrated by a process of consensus-building.

At this point, it is useful to jettison the term collegial as a description of a decentralized structure and reserve it, instead, to convey a *process* where there is agreement on an organizational purpose even though alternatives are generated through specialization. Decisions are made as a result of consensus-building efforts (Chaffee 1983a).

> The concept of community presupposes an organization in which functions are differentiated and in which specialization must be brought together, or the coordination if you will is achieved not through a structure of superordination and subordination of persons and groups but through a dynamic of consensus. (Millett 1962: 234–5)

Collegiality does not preclude conflict; it just means that the conflict is resolved. Hardy et al. (1983) expand on this theme when they discuss common interest and self-interest. The former refers to consensus-building associated with collegiality; the latter, to the political model where actions are undertaken for personal gain. The two can, in fact, look very similar as politicians cloak their actions in the garb of the common good; alternatively, genuine differences of opinion about the common good can generate conflict. Thus there is a need to explore both politics and collegiality more carefully.

Models of Institutional Context

What conclusions can be drawn from the analysis, synthesis, and critique of the work on university decision-making and governance? The following is a summary of the different models that can be derived from the literature.

The professional bureaucracy appears to be the basic building block of universities. It is, however, a structural component. It describes the formal organizational arrangements and says more about what the university looks like than about how it operates (Chaffee 1983b). It can, in effect, be overlaid with one or more of a number of different decision-making models. The three most commonly cited are: political; "garbage can"; and collegial.

The political model is, broadly speaking, characterized by the pursuit of self-interest, in which each actor attempts to influence decision-making in order to protect or further his or her own position. In contrast, the garbage can refers to a situation in which anarchic influences, reflected in the fluidity of participation and complexity of decision-making processes, result in decisions being made by default and by chance. The collegial model can be described as being motivated by the common interest, where actions are taken and decisions made by actors to benefit the larger institution rather than parochial agendas.

There has been a tendency, in the existing literature, to confound rational and bureaucratic processes (e.g., Birnbaum 1988), but there are significant differences between them (Chaffee 1983a, 1983b; Hardy 1988, 1990e, 1991b). A bureaucratic-process model assumes that routines and procedures are used to resolve decisions. The focus is on efficiency: goals may relate more to means than to ends; the search for alternatives is limited and routine; the criteria used are historical; and the process is largely predictable (Chaffee 1983a). Rational decision-making, in contrast, is more concerned with optimal effectiveness: goals are clear; alternatives are considered; information is procured and analysed; criteria are clearly explicated; the optimal outcome is selected; and resources are channelled towards it (Chaffee 1983b). While limits to cognition, information, and time may bound rationality

174 The Politics of Collegiality

(Simon 1955), there is nevertheless a substantive difference between bureaucratic and rational decision-making.

Rationality and efficiency have often been equated, following Weber's model of rational/legal authority (Gerth and Wright Mills 1946; Weiss 1983). It has been argued, however, that Weber disassociated efficiency from administrative rationality, where actors try to influence decisions on the basis of scientific knowledge and rational thinking.

> Such rational organizations, although they often aim at the increase of organizational efficiency, do not necessarily achieve this goal. This rational determination not to let things go by themselves (the effort towards conscious control of organizational evolution) is not necessarily accompanied by the existence of strict procedural rules. (Mouzelis 1967: 52–3)

Accordingly, we can differentiate between the bureaucratic and the rational-analytic university. The former relates to popular conceptions of bureaucracy where organizations, geared towards efficiency based on functional or material rationality, largely ignore the purpose and meaning of behaviour (Mouzelis 1967; Weiss 1983). The latter is based on substantive or formal rationality, in which experts (or technocrats – see Mintzberg 1979a) apply intellectually analysable rules to decisions; and the act of thought reveals intelligent insight into the interrelations of events (Mouzelis 1967; Weiss 1983).

In summary, then, we can distinguish five "ideal types" of institutional context – political; anarchic (garbage can); collegial; bureaucratic; and technocratic (rational-analytic) – that may overlay the professional bureaucratic structure. It is important to note that these categories represent an extremely broad brush with which to capture the innumerable nuances of complex organizations. The intention here is not to suggest that by understanding institutional context at this level, we are delving into the complex, hidden, underlying values and assumptions that comprise organizational culture. Comprehending culture is a far more intense, complex, and lengthy process (e.g., Schein 1985). Nevertheless, the examination of institutional context offers a useful way to understand the dynamics of retrenchment; and, as the following chapter goes on to discuss, it represents the basic building block on which the ability to use power rests.

INSTITUTIONAL CONTEXT AND RETRENCHMENT STRATEGY

In light of the foregoing review of the literature on bureaucratic models, we now turn to the institutional contexts at each of the six universities covered in the present study and establish some links between these contexts and the different retrenchment strategies and methods of implementation that were adopted (also see Hardy 1990f). It is important to note that these governance models do not comprise systematic criteria that researchers can use to apply them. The identification of institutional context is an inherently subjective process where researchers attempt to draw meaningful patterns out of the information they uncover (e.g., Chaffee and Tierney 1988). This analysis rests on the examination of the access to and use of power by the main interest groups. While it was made on the basis of far more data than were provided in the case-study chapters, readers should nonetheless be able to draw similar conclusions concerning the link between the earlier pictures of the six universities and the classification below.

The Decentralized Collegium

McGill was a relatively decentralized, collegial university (Arnold 1981). "McGill University enjoys at present a collegial model, or probably as close as it is possible to come" (Thompson 1977: 44). The president played a primarily external role, delegating operational matters to the vice-president (academic), who formed a highly effective coalition with the vice-president (finance). The budget was decentralized to the level of department heads in the form of global budgets. Accordingly, the deans at McGill played a middle-management role, not because power was centralized above them but because it was decentralized *below* them through the departmental budgets. As a result, deans were unable to move resources between departments. They were, nevertheless, a very cohesive group that displayed an institutional perspective and identified closely with the central administration. The Senate played a relatively active role in university decision-making. In the 1960s, McGill had changed from a "one-man benevolent autocracy" into a democratically governed institution (Frost 1984) by streamlining the Senate and increasing its influence in university decision-making (Thompson 1977). The Board of Governors was supportive of the administration, and the faculty association offered to give up salary increases to help the university make budget cuts.

McGill University's response to budget restraints was designed to protect the existing degree of decentralization and nurture the collegial atmosphere. Resource allocation was determined by an apparently "objective" formula that did not overtly differentiate between departments and faculties. The administration thus tried to avoid provoking conflict by distributing cutbacks in an equitable manner instead of making selective cuts. The discretionary fund did not create conflict, since the deans appealed individually to the central administration for these funds and did not compete for them in an open forum. The implementation of cost reductions was decentralized to department heads and deans through global budgets.

The Centralized Collegium

Carleton University was also collegial but, unlike McGill University, it was relatively centralized. It was the only university in which the deans played an active role in a highly collegial policy-making executive. The vice-president (planning) had helped to create and nurture this situation. The deans were "senior managers of the university, and not just CEOs of their faculty," according to a central administrator. All the deans were members of two key committees that met on alternate weeks. They also met informally every week for lunch. The result was a highly cohesive group in which the deans were integrated with the central administration to form a team committed to an institutional perspective. This central executive was very powerful, with the Senate, the Board of Governors, and the faculty association all playing relatively passive roles.

Carleton University had ruled out enforced dismissals because of the problems it had encountered during the 1970s. Instead, it relied on attrition and voluntary early retirement. The university was able to allocate its resources differentially because of the collegiality among the deans, their ability to adopt an institutional perspective, and their integration into the decision- making executive of the university. It was also able to initiate a building campaign, which involved deans giving up some of their operating grants to fund new building projects.

The Bureaucratic Collegium

Simon Fraser University had elements of not only of collegiality but also of bureaucracy. Power was centralized in the cabinet of the president and vice-presidents, which had been recently formed with the establishment of three new vice-presidential positions. Since three of the four vice-presidents had previously been deans of strong faculties, they possessed expertise, information, and credibility, as well as formal authority. The remaining vice-president was also powerful as a result of the highly centralized financial system. The use of formal controls and procedures resulted in a very bureaucratic institution. Thus SFU was characterized by a cabinet in terms of formal authority, financial controls, and informal power. Many relationships, however, were collegial, and the Senate, Board of Governors, and faculty association were supportive of the central administration. The deans occasionally worked in unison to challenge the central administration through the Senate, where they were important opinion leaders. For example, the proposal to make two vice-presidents members of the Senate was withdrawn by the central administration as a result of opposition from the group of deans. Such action was the exception rather than the rule, however, indicating a relatively collegial atmosphere.

As at the University of British Columbia, SFU administrators maintained that their choice of retrenchment strategy was designed to pacify external groups. They created a new faculty of Applied Sciences to show the government and community that the university was responsive to societal needs. In contrast to UBC, however, SFU avoided tenured dismissals. It was aided by an offer by the faculty association to accept a pay cut. Also, the centralization of power in the president's position and his recent appointment appeared to provide him with sufficient room for manœuvre to carry out the structural changes he wanted. These changes were proposed following a study by the President's Advisory Committee on University Priorities – a group of five senior scholars that examined the various units and made recommendations. PACUP informed the new president of the situation and at the same time, contributed to the perception that consultation had taken place. The final decision also involved the participation of the deans in order to ensure the Senate's approval. The united front of central administrators and deans, coupled with consultation through PACUP, thus helped to secure success.

If we compare the three collegial institutions, we can make a number of observations. McGill University is perhaps closest to the classic example of collegiality by virtue of the decentralized nature of its decision-making, reflecting the concepts of academic freedom and professorial autonomy that are traditionally associated with universities. Both Carleton University and Simon Fraser University were considerably more centralized than McGill. SFU was centralized through its bureaucracy, while Carleton's centralization was a result of the way in which the deans were, in effect, drafted into the central administration rather than regulated through centralized rules. Both bureaucracy and centralization would appear to be at odds with collegiality. The reason why they were able to coexist here may lie with the small size of these two institutions. Centralization and bureaucracy may be far less alienating in an institution where virtually everyone knows everyone else than in a larger, more impersonal institution.

The Technocratic Institution

The University of Montreal was a more centralized university, run by a cabinet of president and vice-presidents. The deans were relatively powerless to influence institutional decisions because of the centralization of decision-making. Their power over faculty decision-making was increased, in theory, with the introduction of global budgets, but since the move occurred at a time when budget cuts were being implemented, the lack of funds left them with little real autonomy. The deans were also fragmented: they tended to concentrate on their own "territory," and there was no evidence that they formed a united group seeking to challenge the decisions of the administration. The decentralization of the budget stopped at the level of the deans, and department heads did not have their own budgets. Other groups were also relatively powerless in comparison with the central administration: the division of academic responsibilities between the Assembly and the Commission weakened both of these faculty arenas; the Council tended to act as a rubber-stamp for the recommendations of the central administration; and the faculty, although unionized, was rarely confrontational and, in fact, offered to give up part of a pay increase to save jobs.

The cutbacks were determined by the central administration, which developed the productivity formulae. The University of Montreal has thus been described as a technocratic institution because analysts in the central administration engaged in the production of quantitative data to determine priority areas based on productivity, and allocated resources accordingly (Hardy 1988). In addition to the two committees that developed the productivity criteria, there were studies on priorities in teaching and research and on administrative services in 1981; a study on the costs and benefits of closing all units in the university in 1983; and a major study comparing each unit within the University of Montreal with similar units in eleven other major universities in Canada in 1985. McGill University, in contrast, only published two reports on the cutbacks, neither of which contained any statistical or quantitative analyses (Hardy 1987b).

The Federal Bureaucracy

The University of Toronto was a relatively centralized and highly bureaucratic university as a result of its size, hierarchy, and governance structure. The president operated the university through a powerful cabinet of vice-presidents. In many respects, bureaucratic processes were encouraged by the president, who emphasized the use of line authority and hierarchy, and who had attempted to standardize resource allocation procedures. Academic and financial responsibilities at the university were combined in the Governing Council – a diverse body of often conflicting interests, representing government, professors, alumni, students, and administrators. The presence of this body contributed to both bureaucracy and centralization. First, the reporting relationships associated with the Governing Council involved a considerable amount of red tape. Second, in its day-to-day operations, the Council tended to support the central administration because it did not have the knowledge and information necessary to understand the operations of such a large and complex institution. It also robbed the deans of an academic arena in which they could exercise influence since, unlike a senate, they were not members, which curtailed their impact on institutional matters.

The large size of the University of Toronto, however, meant that some power had to be delegated to the deans. The university has been described as a federal bureaucracy to indicate that the decanal level had access to considerable sources of faculty power. The distance between the deans, and between them and the central administration, the presence of the Governing Council, the emphasis on line authority, and the lack of meetings created a group of loosely federated states within the larger institution.

If we compare the University of Toronto and the University of Montreal, we can see the difference between the bureaucratic and the technocratic institution. The University of Montreal attempted to use analysis generated by the technocracy, in the central administration and in the Office of Institutional Research, to allocate resources on a selective basis in favour of the more productive units. It incorporated a rational-analytic component: goals were known and articulated; alternatives were considered; information was collected and analysed; criteria were used to evaluate alternatives; and there was a link between resource allocation and decision processes (Hardy 1988). The University of Toronto, on the other hand, used bureaucratic routines to allocate resources rather than employ criteria to evaluate different options. For example, the report that recommended the closure of the faculty of Architecture had none of the type of analysis found in the University of Montreal's studies, nor did it consider any alternatives until the final conclusion.

The failure to close the faculty of Architecture is partially explained by the compartmentalization that characterized the university: deans were separated from each other and had little contact with the president; the central administration was distanced from the academic community; and the deans were excluded from the Governing Council. *Only* the bureaucracy served to tie these disparate parts of the university together; there was little consultation and face-to-face communication. When the proposal to close the faculty of Architecture came to the fore, the governance structure proved to be inadequate for the implementation of the central administration's plans. On this contentious matter, the Governing Council became a highly politicized arena that the central administration found difficult to influence, especially in the absence of consultation. Other members of the university community also complained of inadequate consultation. The Architecture decision was perceived as a *fait accompli*; and the report, as justification after the fact. The deans distanced themselves from the issue: they considered it to be none of their business and were unwilling to act as champions for the closure. Thus it was difficult to secure any broad base of support for the closure, and the actions of the administrators exacerbated rather than resolved the situation.

The Political University

Despite attempts to strengthen the president's office, much of the power at the University of British Columbia continued to lie with the deans, many of whom continued to identify with the interests of their particular faculty rather than those of the institution as a whole. They were a fragmented group but, unlike their counterparts at the University of Toronto, whose fragmentation rendered them relatively quiescent, UBC deans were far more politicized. They used their power to confront each other, as well as the central administration. Although they did not form part of a policy-making executive, their support was essential to the president.

Other interest groups were also powerful. The Senate had to approve program closures, making it a key actor in the context of retrenchment. The faculty association was confrontational, as witnessed by the failure of repeated attempts to negotiate redundancy and financial-exigency agreements. The dismissal of tenured faculty provoked fierce opposition from the association, which initiated an arbitration procedure and only withdrew it when a settlement was negotiated with the staff concerned. It also passed a vote of no-confidence in the Board of Governors and in the acting president and vice-president. UBC's Board, which consisted primarily of government appointees, reflected the prevailing government opinion and had a reputation for confrontation. Its powers with regard to program closure were unclear, and many people thought that if the university failed to act in keeping with the government's restraint legislation, the Board would take the matter into its own hands and unilaterally impose cuts. As a result, UBC was the most politicized university, and the central administration had to select and manage its retrenchment strategy in a way that enabled it to balance the conflicting demands of these interest groups.

The reason for choosing to dismiss tenured faculty stemmed, according to UBC administrators, from a need to accommodate the demands of the Board of Governors and of the government for a "tougher" approach. The proposals for elimination that went to the Senate matched those of the Senate Budget Committee, which had devised a framework for assessing priority and nonpriority programs except those where the central administration could not guarantee the dean's support. So, for example, Arts and Medicine received global reductions rather than targeted cuts. The Senate approved all of the proposals except the one opposed by the dean concerned. It is, in part, the ability to juggle these interest groups that distinguishes the University of British Columbia from the University of Toronto and helps to account for the implementation of all but one of the program closures.

CONCLUSIONS

In exploring the institutional contexts of the six universities during the early to mid-1980s, we sought to flesh out the governance models found in the literature. In this regard, we find evidence for political and collegial contexts and can see how these characteristics might manifest themselves in university life. We also find evidence to distinguish the bureaucratic from the technocratic institution. Finally, it is clear that mixed models exist, such as a combination of bureaucracy and collegiality; and variations on a theme can arise, such as a centralized collegium, instead of the traditional decentralized version. The one model notable by its absence is the "garbage can" (which has been found in elsewhere – see Hardy 1990c), which is not particularly surprising in the context of funding restrictions. The absence of slack resources reduces the likelihood of decision-making by default. Cutback decisions are, to put it simply, too important to be left in the garbage can.

The institutional contexts identified here are obviously not the only ones that exist in universities. Nonetheless, the basic models of university governance would appear to be a useful way in which to make sense of organizational complexity. It is important to note that this classification process rests on a discussion of *ideal types* – broadly based models that have been applied to complex university settings. There is no suggestion that this categorization can in any way capture the entirety of organization life; nor does it deny that subcultures may exist in different parts of the university that are at odds with the larger picture. Nevertheless, examining the interest groups and their access to and use of power represents an effective starting point from which to assess the nature of a particular institution. In this way, context becomes a pragmatic surrogate for culture. It trades off complexity and depth for a quicker, easier assessment of institutional characteristics that nonetheless provide a useful way to understand how a particular university operates.

The aim is not just to classify different institutional contexts, but also to show how they relate to the decisions and actions taken regarding retrenchment. There is no intention to suggest that context is the *only* influence on the choice and implementation of retrenchment strategy. Other factors, including the extent of funding restrictions, perceptions of crisis in the community, and government legislation and regulations, undoubtedly play a role in shaping retrenchment. The aim here is to provide evidence that context is one – an important one – of those influences.

Accordingly, the analysis is this chapter has deliberately been a subjective affair. There are no quantitative measures or clearly defined criteria that can be used to categorize universities. Nor can causation between context and strategy be proven. In fact, it is the intent of this book neither to "measure" context nor to "prove" causation. Rather, it seeks to provide evidence from an in-depth study of six universities to give a persuasive account of differences in institutional context and to suggest that these contexts, mediated by administrative action, influenced the choice, implementation, and outcomes of retrenchment strategies. In so doing, the aim is to provide university actors with a way of seeing patterns that will help them to make sense of the complexity in which they operate. In doing so, a sensitivity can be developed that helps actors to better understand how they can *mobilize* context and the power embedded within it to influence outcomes in a particular institution.

CHAPTER THIRTEEN

The Politics of Collegiality

In the rhetoric of higher education, universities are often assumed to be collegial organizations, even though collegiality is usually associated with loyalty to a professional group and overrides commitment to the institution (Gaff and Wilson 1971; Satow 1975; Becher 1981; Clark 1983). Collegiality can, however, operate at the institutional level as well. Clark (1970, 1971, 1972) was among the first to propound the concept of a collegial institution in which individuals are bound together by the "saga" or institutional mission. The recent literature on university cultures shows how shared beliefs and ideologies commit members to the organization and motivate them to work towards collective goals (Dill 1982; Masland 1985). A parallel can be seen in the business world, where "strong" cultures have been linked to success (e.g., Ouchi 1981; Deal and Kennedy 1982; Peters and Waterman 1982).

It is argued here that institutional collegiality is an important mechanism in managing the competing pressures currently facing universities. On the one hand, constraints on government funding, the scarcity of resources, and increased demands for accountability have pushed administrators towards planning mechanisms, increased controls, and centralized strategic decisions. On the other hand, the need to be responsive to market forces and societal developments, and to spearhead technological innovation and development implies a reliance on creativity and innovation, which are less easily planned and require autonomy among researchers and teachers. Institutional collegiality helps to overcome this dilemma. It motivates diverse members of the community to participate in strategic initiatives and support a shared conception of the organizational mission (Dill and Helm 1989). Individuals are more willing to make the sacrifices that may be necessary to support strategic choices, and that, in turn, helps to offset the more debilitating effects of financial restraint (Dill 1982). It also reduces the amount of counterproductive conflict that occurs over territorial boundaries, helping to foster the multidisciplinary research that is crucial to innovation and market responsiveness.

Thus institutional loyalty is more conducive to meeting the challenges currently facing higher education than the parochial allegiances associated with affiliations to individual disciplines. The only problem is that university actors have little guidance on how to create and sustain collegiality, particularly in the light of the increasing emphasis on managerialist techniques, which largely ignore these matters. How, then, can collegiality be managed? In seeking to answer that question, we highlight the role that power can play in creating collegiality by changing attitudes and legitimizing actions, thereby leading to agreement and to an avoidance of opposition and conflict. By illustrating how the sources of power are deeply embedded in the institutional context (dealt with in chapter twelve), we also show that actors need to understand the context in which they operate. Finally, we show how power can be used to create an inclusive, collective form of strategy-making that not only reinforces collegiality but also helps to realize change.

POWER AND COLLEGIALITY

Institutional collegiality can be defined as a situation characterized by agreement around organizational purpose; by the exercise of alternative courses of action that are generated by different specializations; and by decision outcomes that occur as a result of consensus-building efforts to which participants are willing to contribute the necessary time and effort (Chaffee 1983a). In other words, collegiality is identified as collaboration between actors who are motivated by their conceptions of the common interest. Such collaboration is not automatic, however, because allegiances to different disciplines tend to produce departmental subcultures rather than identification to the institution (Dill 1982). Institutional collegiality has to be *created*, and the diversity of opinion produced by the loosely coupled (Weick 1976) and fragmented (Friedberg and Musselin 1989) nature of universities has to be counteracted. This requires that certain behaviours, cultures, and structures serve to counteract the fissures inherent in universities and to reinforce a commitment to common goals (Bess 1988). The use of power is thus integral to collegiality: power is as important in securing collaboration as it is in defeating opposition. To understand the link between power and collegiality, we need a relatively sophisticated view of power – not just power over another individual or group but also the ability to achieve a collaborative outcome.

Much of the work on power in the higher-education literature, however, associates it solely with actions taken in response to opposition (Clark 1983). These studies are premised on the definition of power seen as the ability of A to make B do something B would not otherwise do (Dahl 1961). This model assumes that individuals act on their grievances and engage in an overt struggle over decisions. The concept of nondecision-making was subsequently developed by Bachrach and Baratz (1962), who pointed out that powerful actors are able to exclude threatening issues and individuals from the decision-making process. While this work presented a less visible use of power, it continued to assume that power is employed only in the face of conflict (Lukes 1974; Ranson et al. 1980).

A number of writers have questioned this assumption, however. It was pointed out that power could be used to *prevent* opposition by "shaping perceptions, cognitions, and preferences in such a way that they accept their role in the existing order of things, either because they can see or imagine no alternative to it, or because they view it as natural and unchangeable, or because they value it as divinely ordained and beneficial" (Lukes 1974: 24). Rather than risk defeat in open conflict, dominant groups avoid challenge by sectioning off spheres of influence where they are deemed legitimate (Ranson et al. 1980).

> Stable organizing power requires legitimation. To be sure, men can be made to work and do obey commands through coercion, but the coercive use of power engenders resistance and sometimes active opposition ... Effective operations necessitate ... that members do not exhibit resistance in discharging their daily duties but perform them and comply with directives *willingly*. (Blauner 1964: 199–200)

Researchers thus began to consider the possibility that the absence of conflict could be the result of the exercise of power (e.g., Gaventa 1980; Hardy 1985a, 1985b). In other words, power is not just used to defeat opposition but also to prevent it from occurring altogether.

Once we allow that power can be used to prevent opposition and conflict from arising, it becomes clear that it can also be used to secure collaboration. This view relates to the "power to" achieve common goals (Parsons 1967) rather than to "power over" other groups (Knights and Willmott 1985). It rests on the management of meaning, which is "a process of symbol construction and value use designed both to create legitimacy for one's own demands and to 'delegitimize'

INSTRUMENTAL POWER   SYMBOLIC POWER

Management of Dependencies   Management of Meaning

Behaviour ◄———————————————— Attitudes

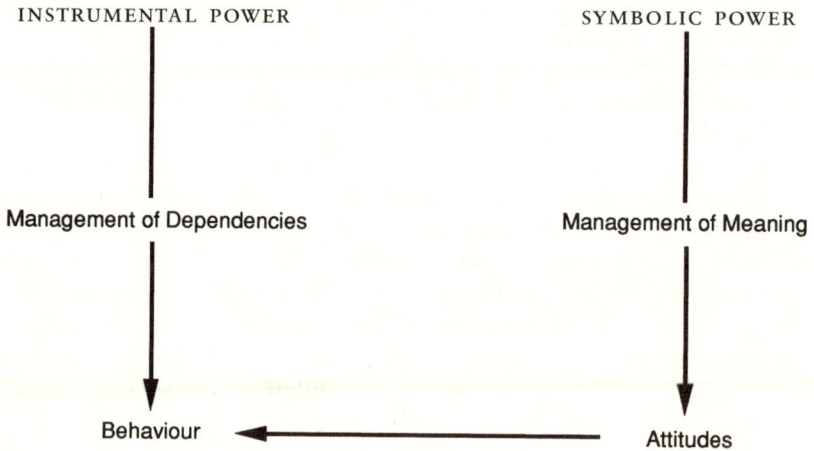

Figure 13.1
Instrumental and Symbolic Power

the demands of others" (Pettigrew 1977: 85). In this way, agreement
to actions and decisions is secured.

> The point is that political and symbolic language can have real conse-
> quences. Actors respond on the basis of perceptions and sentiments even
> when these perceptions and sentiments have been produced through
> evocative symbolic language ... Symbolic language may serve to mollify
> groups that are dissatisfied with the organization, thereby ensuring their
> continued support of the organization and diminishing opposition and
> conflict. (Pfeffer 1981a: 206)

Accordingly, two forms of power – instrumental and symbolic (Figure
13.1) – can be distinguished (Clegg 1975; Pfeffer, 1981b; Hardy 1985a,
1985b; Frost and Egri 1991).

Instrumental power (Pfeffer 1981b) is conferred by control over
scarce, valued resources on which others are dependent. The objective
is to influence behaviour directly: what people think about the use of
this power is not taken into consideration, as long as their behaviour
is affected in the desired way. As a result, this form of power is usually
visible. Certain sources of instrumental power are available to university administrators – line authority and hierarchy; the centralization
of information; centralized budgets and procedures. At the University
of Toronto, for example, the president increased the use of line authority, enhanced the power of the vice-presidents, and instituted a number
of centralized procedures regarding resource allocation. As a result,

institutional decision-making was confined to the central administration, and the deans played virtually no role in this domain, although they did have considerable power over their faculties. Many of the central controls were duplicated at the faculty level, where deans played a relatively authoritarian role. Formal controls were also used at the University of British Columbia in attempts to wrestle some of the power away from the deans by centralizing information and budget procedures, and by establishing a new vice-presidential post and a central budget committee.

It seems, however, that instrumental power can have an alienating effect as deans and faculty members rail against the restrictions imposed on them. In addition, formal controls are often limited in university settings: budgets may be determined primarily by the government; most of the funds are tied up in salary commitments; and the options for raising additional revenues are limited. University presidents cannot fire employees and close units when faced with financial problems in the way that private sector managers do. Even if funding is not a problem, decisions concerning hiring, promotion, teaching, and research are often a matter for individual departments and the committee structure – not the central administration. To put it simply, rewards and resources do not constitute a major source of power for university administrators because they have little control over them. Administrators (and other actors) do, however, have access to other sources of power.

Symbolic power is used unobtrusively (see Hardy 1985a, 1985b) to influence attitudes. It helps to secure agreement, prevent opposition, and elicit collaboration where differences of opinion might otherwise occur. It relies heavily on the use of symbols – myths, rites, language – to manage meaning and shape the attitudes and perceptions of others and, thereby, influence behaviour. More specifically, symbolic acts and political language are used to legitimize one's actions (or delegitimize those of others) and render them acceptable to the broader university community, thereby producing agreement and avoiding opposition and conflict. Because of the focus on attitudes and the prevention of conflict, this form of power is much less visible, and members of the organization may be totally unaware of it. In fact, those who are on the receiving end of this unobtrusive use of power may only become aware of it when it fails and they see through the symbols and political rhetoric (see Hardy 1994).

What constitutes an effective use of symbolism or language can vary from the choice of a global strategy that encompasses a series of interconnected decisions to a specific, self-contained gesture or statement. For example, administrators at McGill University explicitly adopted a general response to the financial restrictions in order to minimize the chances of conflict. They applied the cuts across the board so that no individual area was singled out for major "surgery." More specific actions can also be used. McGill's discretionary fund, which distributed some resources in response to deans' requests, helped to demonstrate that, within the context of across-the-board cuts, some resources were being reallocated on the basis of quality or of the need for new developments. The gesture was largely symbolic, since the fund represented no more than 4 percent of the operating budget.

When the University of Montreal implemented its cutbacks, financial decisions were decentralized to the level of the deans. This move was designed to create legitimacy for the actions of the central administration by devolving power. It constituted a symbolic act because, at a time when deans gained more latitude in distributing resources, they had little money to allocate. Nevertheless, it did reassure at least some of them that they had more control over resource decisions. Some of the university's actions, however, had a negative symbolic effect. For example, the press articles concerning the rector's personal chauffeur at a time when junior faculty risked losing their jobs helped to discredit both the administration and its approach to cutbacks. Similarly, confining membership of the committees that developed the criteria for selective cuts to the "technocrats" produced suspicion, whereas the study commissioned by the Assembly appeared to have far more impact in justifying a differential approach to retrenchment.

Other gestures can be used to build support and legitimacy. Changing language – for example, from "units" to "departments," from "union" to "faculty," from "planning" to "priorities" – emphasizes a particular direction. Signing memos with the first name only and visiting people in their offices can be used to promote a more egalitarian culture and bridge the gap between the administration and the university community. Meetings with nonacademic staff or allowing them access to the Faculty Club can signify that nonacademic personnel represent an important of the university community in the eyes of the administration. Creating a new post that reports directly to the president or upgrading a position to the vice-presidential level are ways of demonstrating the importance of particular initiatives. External consultants can be used to convey neutrality and objectivity in a politically charged situation.

Representative committees are a particularly important legitimating device in universities because they represent a widely accepted symbol through which consultation is signified. The University of British Columbia used its Senate Budget Committee to consult the professorial community on the matter of program closures, while Simon Fraser

University established a special committee – the Presidential Advisory Committee on University Priorities (PACUP) – with designated professors for a similar purpose. Both committees were partly symbolic, since they could act only in response to requests by the president and their recommendations were ignored in cases where deans objected. In other words, both committees were as important in signalling to the university community that a consultation process was taking place as they were in providing concrete solutions to financial problems.

Consultative meetings appear to be an integral part of administering a university – one to which considerable time must be devoted. Cutting or circumventing meetings is often widely perceived as a counter-collegial move and can lead to dissatisfaction. On the other hand, by conducting meetings, allowing other groups to set the agenda, or holding a mixture of formal, informal, off-the-record, individual, and collective meetings, actors can manage meaning and send a variety of signals to the university community, thus legitimating their actions.

Administrators may be wary of meetings for fear they will be railroaded by malcontents. Although direct control over the process and outcomes of consultative bodies is limited, administrators can control committees through membership and agendas. While both the University of British Columbia and Simon Fraser University had a Senate Budget Committee, as required by provincial legislation, only at UBC did it play a prominent (if not always influential) role; at SFU, it played a negligible role, and PACUP was far more visible. SFU administrators viewed the Senate Budget Committee as being comprised of militants, and as a result, they restricted its access to information and limited its mandate. In effect, the budget committee was frozen out of the budget process and its role was preempted by PACUP, over which central administrators had far more power because of their control over its membership and terms of reference. Thus it is clear that using power in a symbolic, unobtrusive way does not constitute a *loss* of power but a *different use* of power.

SYMBOLIC POWER AND INSTITUTIONAL CONTEXT

At this point it becomes possible to link symbolic power to the concept of institutional context examined in chapter twelve. As the foregoing discussion indicates, there are many different ways of exerting using power to legitimize actions and decisions. The question of *which* sources should be used has to do with the institutional context in which the relevant symbols are embedded. For example, both McGill University and the University of Montreal used formulae to allocate cutbacks, but these formulae were quite different. McGill's formula, based on student enrolments, symbolized a "fair" and "objective" way of distributing funding reductions, consistent with an institutional context in which equality had a great deal of credibility and central intervention had little legitimacy. The formula applied at the University of Montreal, on the other hand, measured the productivity of departments' research and teaching. This formula, too, represented objectivity and fairness, although those two notions were understood differently at the two universities. Despite some cynicism at the University of Montreal concerning the central administration's virtual monopoly over the committees, resource decisions were often linked to statistical studies; performance measures were a common way of legitimating decisions; and centralization had long been a feature of university life.

The two formulae, while apparently very different, produced similar results in terms of resource allocation. Their main contribution to the cutback process was that they reassured the university community that resources were being allocated on legitimate grounds. Thus the impact was symbolic rather than substantive, and the fact that their outward appearance differed can be explained by the different contexts that existed at the two institutions. To put it simply, what was symbolically effective at one would have lacked credibility at the other.

So far, we have mainly discussed the symbolic impact of actions and language. We must also consider the matter of structure. Structures do not only form a system of power relations, they also constitute systems of meaning (Giddens 1984). The creation of vice-presidential posts, a change in the allocation of portfolios, the establishment of nonstatutory advisory groups are instances of structural decisions that can be used to signify change. For example, a president can emphasize academic priorities by adding provostial duties to the portfolio of the academic vice-president; establishing a new position of vice-president for development may serve to signal a new emphasis on fund-raising; the appointment of a new vice-president for student services may indicate a renewed focus on undergraduate education; the creation of a position within the central administration to deal with women's affairs that reports directly to the president may demonstrate a move towards equal opportunity; placing a postgraduate student on the board may indicate that greater emphasis is being placed on graduate programs. The choice of particular individuals to fill positions also sends messages: the appointment of a renowned "people person" or of an ex-member of the faculty association may reveal that the administration is concerned with faculty relations.

Thus structural change has symbolic implications that cannot be ignored. It will be assigned meanings by members of the organization that depend on the context of the individual institution. For example, firing (or securing the resignations of) old-guard administrators may signal long-awaited change in one institution and be seen as evidence of tyrannical leadership in another. A president's decision to establish an advisory committee of senior administrators may be perfectly acceptable in one university but may be viewed as a ploy to exclude faculty participation in another.

Managing collegiality, whether through symbolic behaviours, language, or structures, requires an understanding of the context in order to identify the levers of change.

> A CEO creating strategic change has to recognize that a key element of the politics of organizational change relates to how the context of strategy can be mobilized to legitimate the content and process of any strategic adjustment. He [sic] who understands the political and cultural system of his organization, and the impact of changing economic and social trends on the emergence and dissolution of old issues, values, and priorities, and the rise of new rationalities and priorities is at least beyond the starting gate in formulating, packaging and influencing the direction of organizational change. (Pettigrew 1985b: 70–1)

The "embeddedness" of symbolic power lies in the interconnected nature of the behavioural, structural, and cultural components of collegiality (Bess 1988). We cannot talk about behaviour or structure *without* taking into account their symbolic impact in the particular setting in question. Thus the management of collegiality depends upon an understanding of institutional context in a way that enables actors to assess accurately the symbolic impact of particular structures and behaviours, and upon the ability to use that symbolic impact to legitimate decisions and actions with regard to both retrenchment strategies and change in general.

COLLECTIVE STRATEGY-MAKING: COLLEGIALITY AND CHANGE

By understanding institutional context and deploying symbolic power, actors can engage in collective strategy-making. This approach to strategy-making is not only consistent with collegiality, it is a mechanism for realizing change. It represents a move towards what has been termed "empowerment" in the business literature (Leiba and Hardy 1994).

One important component of collegiality is the involvement of the broader community in decision-making. The archetypal collegial model includes extensive decentralization. This was true of McGill University, where the departments retained a considerable degree of power, and Carleton University, where the deans were heavily involved. It was somewhat less true of Simon Fraser University although, even here, the deans and PACUP members were important players in decisions relating to the cutbacks.

The benefits of collegiality or empowerment have started to attract attention in the business world, where empowerment has been seen as a factor in strategic success.

> The term "collegiality" evokes images of warm, supportive relationships and teamwork. Collegial organizations have communal tendencies in the form of coherent social rules and common identities. Highly successful organizations such as Honda derive much of their magic from collegial networks. (Pascale 1990: 12)

Wider involvement in strategy-making has many advantages: it brings more extensive knowledge and expertise to bear on the process of forming strategic intentions and, at the same time, helps to increase the chances of successfully realizing those strategic intentions.

Westley (1990) has examined collective strategy-making in the context of the involvement of middle management in strategic "conversations." Much of the existing work on strategy-making advocates the confinement of strategic activity to senior echelons on the grounds of efficiency. But as Westley has pointed out, because they have the power to ignore strategic initiatives and impede their implementation, the exclusion of middle managers from the strategy-making process can inhibit successful results. Westley has argued that middle managers should be included in strategy-making and should be provided with an opportunity to influence strategic activity as this will motivate them to become active, productive, innovative players in the strategy-making process. They are often capable of contributing creative new ideas because of their diverse experiences, which are closer to the heart of operations in the organization or to the customers served by it. As a result, both the effectiveness of new strategies and the likelihood of their successful implementation increase. Managers who are excluded (or who are included but are not allowed to influence strategic conversations) are, on the other hand, likely to be disaffected and alienated. At best, they are unable to contribute new ideas; at worst, they may hinder strategic initiatives.

Extrapolating these findings to the university setting, we can see that deans (and other members of the university community) can be a useful asset if they are included in strategy-making. Deans and department heads can promote central initiatives and help to secure broader support or, alternatively, to scuttle proposals through their influence on the university community. Deans gain power through their access to information and their impact on the university's senate. Since individual professors often identify with a faculty rather than with an institution, deans are important opinion leaders who can foster either institutional collegiality or parochial interests among faculty members. They can be a disruptive influence if they use their power to further individual goals, and institutional initiative will rely on their goodwill. Meaningful strategic planning can only be carried out if deans and other members of the university community relate to institutional needs rather than to vested interests, particularly in the context of funding cuts, which tend to provoke territorial conflicts.

Accordingly, when we talk of leadership in universities, we can rarely confine our attention to the president or even to central administrators, since these individuals seldom have the power to impose strategy on an institution and are forced to depend on the cooperation of other members of the university community (Sibley 1993). Even factors such as a crisis or a recent appointment rarely translate into absolute power. A crisis may legitimate a certain amount of central intervention but, overstep the mark and the university community may quickly resist. The honeymoon period of a new president may be limited in both time and scope if he or she is forced to make too many unpopular decisions early on, or if failure at an early stage damages credibility for further change. Leaders who circumvent procedures and work behind the scenes to implement change risk a backlash from faculty and administrators who feel frozen out of the process. Even charismatic leaders can leave succession and transition problems – if they leave or retire, or the institution grows, or the crisis for which they were hired is satisfactorily solved.

Highly centralized leadership is rare in university settings and may even be counterproductive. In addition, the specialization-and-diversity approach means that administrators may benefit from a more inclusive form of leadership, whereby individuals throughout the organization are involved in collective strategy-making processes. Central administrators sometimes balk at the idea of extensive decentralization. Much like business managers, they are concerned that an increase in participation could lead to a loss of control (see Westley 1990). Clearly, then, the broader involvement of organizational members in strategy-making

– or in any other form of "empowerment," for that matter – has political implications, and senior administrators are unlikely to surrender any more power than they have to.

Collective strategy-making does not, however, involve giving up power – it involves the replacement of the overt use of instrumental power with the more subtle use of symbolic power. There is no *surrender* of power, merely a *substitution* of different forms of power. This substitution of power techniques requires a very different approach to management – one on which the traditional literature is unable to shed much light because of its narrow conceptualization of power. It involves relatively sophisticated processes to manage meaning, as illustrated in the following example.

Roberts (1991) has described a situation in a divisionalized company – in some ways, not unlike a university and its faculties (Savenije 1992) – where plant managers were brought into the strategy-making process. To ensure they did not fall prey to parochial interests, a complex process was devised around an annual conference in which these managers were obliged to make a group presentation on the following year's strategic plan to subordinates across the company. The conference lasted two days and was preceded by a three-day rehearsal and other meetings. It accomplished a number of things. First, the conference and the meetings provided managers with opportunities to inform and be informed about what was happening in the company as a whole; partial insights could be integrated into a coherent picture of the whole, in which individuals could locate the significance of their actions. Thus the conference created a shared definition of reality. Second, it led to set of commitments that countered the potentially centrifugal forces of decentralization: when meetings raised conflicts, they were addressed by public agreements or "deals" between managers in different functions and factories, which facilitated continued cooperation following the conference. Third, the conference forced managers to clarify their thinking and reduced the likelihood of "bad" decisions since they had to submit their thinking and actions to the scrutiny of their subordinates. Thus the conference built shared understandings and knowledge, as well as a complex system of reciprocal rights and obligations.

In this way, a shared conception of strategic reality was constructed through a complex process of managing meaning, which was both a calculated technique and a social process into which the "controllers" were drawn. It constructed a credible picture of a shared reality, introduced new and diverse ways of dealing with that reality, and generated strong mutual commitment to strategic change. It was this collective view rather than the will and formal authority of the CEO that dictated subsequent actions. While it is often possible to resist the will of a single individual, it is difficult to resist a more pervasive, collective reality. Thus the need for senior managers to use instrumental power to bring people into line was reduced. If dissidents did continue to resist, there was widespread legitimacy and support for a tougher use of power. But most of the time, it was the use of power to manage meaning that defined reality, created legitimacy, and exercised control.

Elements of collective strategy-making were seen at Carleton University, where the deans were incorporated into a policy-making executive. They took part in regular discussions with central administrators through two committees that met regularly, and informal meetings were also held every week. The aim of these meetings was to increase communication and provide a forum for both a high degree of consultation and the opportunity for deans to influence decisions.

> The deans are consulted quite adequately. In my view there's almost too much consultation. I would sometimes have preferred a *fait accompli* for approval. The deans are involved at an early stage. It's a bit inefficient because it takes lots of time, but there has to be an excess of it some of the time in order for it to be adequate overall. (Dean)

This degree of openness in the administration prevented complaints and criticism from festering. Differences of opinion were aired and discussed.

> We never have the opportunity to build up any grievances: they are always resolved. (Dean)

The fact that the deans got on well together and understood each other's problems through communication made consensus relatively easy to achieve.

> There's a collective decision-making process. It's usually easy to arrive at consensus because it's a close working relationship. We operate on a solidarity basis. (Dean)

This process had a number of important components. First, the careful *selection* of new deans helped to form a cohesive group with which the central administration could work effectively. Second, deans were *socialized* into an institutional perspective through extensive interaction with the central administration. Third, deans were *included* in university decision-making. Fourth, deans were *given* more power to take decisions in their own faculties. So, as formal, instrumental controls were relaxed, informal, unobtrusive controls were substituted, which helped to create a collective vision of the university's problems and the best way of solving them.

CONCLUSIONS

Power can be used to influence outcomes by overcoming opposition through the use of instrumental power, or by trying to prevent opposition and conflict from occurring altogether through the use of symbolic power. This chapter has examined examples of the latter and shown how it can help to foster collegiality. This form of power influences attitudes by legitimating decisions and, in turn, reducing the likelihood of conflict and opposition. It focuses on influencing behaviour by changing attitudes rather than targeting behaviour directly. That is not to say that instrumental power is never used in universities – of course it is. The aim here is to draw attention to a different kind of power, which is featured less often in the literature but is nonetheless an important component in creating collegiality.

The sources of symbolic power are varied and embedded in a particular institutional context. The effectiveness of symbolic power rests on a detailed knowledge of that context and on the use of *appropriate* symbolic action. Thus the institutional context, which exerts some influence over the outcomes of retrenchment and other strategies, can be harnessed by organizational actors to direct that influence in a more deliberate fashion. We can see how context, strategy, and power are linked through political action (Figure 13.2). As shown in chapter twelve, the nature of the institutional context has some bearing on the way in which retrenchment (and other) strategies are realized. Organizational actors can intervene in that relationship by engaging in political action and drawing on power lodged in the context to influence strategic outcomes. These relationships are not simply one-way. One would imagine that specific strategic changes would have an effect on context and subsequent political actions. Moreover, as shown in the case studies, political actions can be used to change or modify the institutional context.

The use of symbolic power lends itself to collective strategy-making that is consistent with the bottom-up approach advocated in universities (e.g., Hardy et al. 1983; Shirley 1988; Swain 1988; Savenije 1989). It also shows how university actors can shape retrenchment by managing meaning (Chaffee 1984). By linking power to this process, it becomes possible to offer university actors with a means of influencing strategic outcomes. This has practical advantages over the existing models, which present strategy-making as either a bottom-up,

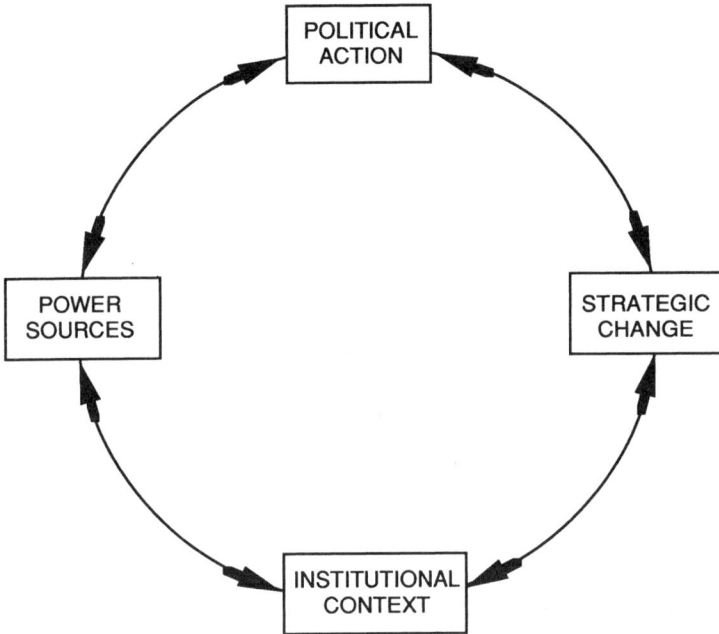

Figure 13.2
Linkages Between Political Action, Institutional Context, Strategic Change, and Power

emergent, but largely uncontrollable, process, or as a top-down, deliberate activity, which can be planned but rarely implemented.

While there are limits to leadership, formal leaders can clearly contribute to change through political action. Simon Fraser University and Carleton University had new presidents overseeing retrenchment. In neither case did they impose cutbacks but, by employing various forms of symbolic power, they were able to influence both retrenchment strategy and institutional context. New leaders arrived at the University of Montreal and the University of British Columbia after the cutbacks. The former indicated that he intended to work within the existing technocratic context and to harness it more effectively in order to make change. The latter used new procedures, processes, and positions to modify the institutional context. Context does, however, constrain leaders: the president of the University of Toronto voiced his frustration at being unable to transplant planning procedures that had been effective at his previous institution. Thus the effect of political action by leaders (at faculty, departmental, as well as central levels) on organizational change is not a simple, unidirectional matter, but the result of a complex interplay between context and power.

CHAPTER FOURTEEN

Conclusions

This final chapter summarizes some of the main issues raised by the present study. In general, it questions the move towards managerialism that has become so popular in the sphere of higher education. While it does not dispute that some university procedures can be made more efficient, nor that a more insightful understanding and analysis of the environment could produce more creative and innovative strategies, it does question the rational-analytic focus that underlies the managerialist ideology. Managerialism fails to take account of the political realities of university life and ignores the role of power in both confronting and preventing resistance. This study is an attempt to redress the balance by providing a more explicit understanding of power. It shows how power can be used to develop and implement strategies that nurture institutional loyalty (O'Briant 1991; Stetar and Jemmott 1991), and how institutional loyalty can help in developing and implementing strategies, for retrenchment in particular and for change in general.

The study illustrates the link between power, context, and collegiality. Institutional context, which encapsulates the distribution and use of power by various organizational actors, influences the way in which actions and decisions (in this case, those relating to retrenchment) are played out. By understanding context, organizational actors can intervene in this relationship by mobilizing the sources of power embedded within it to influence events. This use of power need not revolve around its more visible, coercive aspects. Actors can also use symbolic power to create legitimacy and support for their actions, thereby avoiding opposition and conflict. In this way, power can be used to create and sustain collegiality, which is not an inevitable, or even normal, state of affairs. Allegiances to particular disciplines tend to produce departmental subcultures rather than institutional identification. Consequently, institutional collegiality must be created by individuals capable of using power to substitute a common vision for parochial interests. Thus collegiality is part of a political process whereby power is mobilized to prevent conflict.

In this situation, collegiality becomes a strategic weapon. When moved by collegiality, individuals are willing to sacrifice personal or group interests in favour of an overarching identification to the institution. This loyalty makes interest groups willing to accept decisions that do not necessarily have any individual benefit but do have some institutional payoff. It also makes groups more understanding and receptive to the different circumstances experienced by other groups; avoids time-consuming conflict; and builds institutional loyalty, which helps to retain productive individuals who may have lucrative prospects elsewhere in the institution. It has been found, for example, that recovery from decline is mainly the result of agreement around the institutional mission rather than of specific turnaround strategies (Parker 1987).

The critique of managerialism is not meant to be an argument against change, whether as a result of funding restrictions or other factors. There is undoubtedly a "new reality" facing universities that must be addressed (Sibley 1993). Continued preoccupations with funding restrictions have now been supplemented with concerns stemming from an increasing interest in accountability. In 1993, six provincial governments were conducting in-depth studies of their university sectors (*University Affairs* May 1993: 16–17). Ontario had issued a report advising universities to strengthen their accountability and proposing the creation of an external monitoring agency (Ontario Task Force on Accountability 1993; also see ISGUG 1993), while the Quebec government recently announced the publication of comparative indicators concerning its universities. As other countries have become more directive by targeting their funding, determining student enrolments, and developing performance indicators, observers of the Canadian scene are arguing that universities must become more accountable if they want to preserve their autonomy (*University Affairs* March 1991: 3).

> In comparison with the experience in the u.k., Australia, and the u.s., Canadian universities have taken a bit of a beating on funding levels, but have emerged almost unscathed in terms of financial control (earmarking of funds, contracting of services) or accountability requirements (detailed reporting, external "value for money" audit). For universities, a window of opportunity appears to be open to shape the agenda and, perhaps, to disarm the funding weapon while meeting legitimate public concerns for greater candor and accountability. (Cutt and Dobell 1992: 29)

Since governments, business, and the public are becoming increasingly concerned with the quality of education and the way in which universities spend tax dollars, the university community has become increasingly dependent on these stakeholders (Watts 1992) and will have to respond to demands for change.[4]

If universities refuse to change, government frustration and business disillusionment are likely to cost them dearly in the form of increased controls and reduced corporate sponsorship. Thus Canadian universities must seriously consider new initiatives in the light of their changing environment. As the business world struggles with globalization, deregulation, recession, and new technology, so, too, must the university sector. University members in both the administration and professoriate must examine mechanisms for initiating responsive, innovative, and creative new developments. So far, the only mechanism to receive widespread attention has been the move towards managerialism, discussed at the beginning of this book. It is argued here that planning alone will have little success in meeting the objectives of either government or university because it is not possible to police our universities through the current financial constraints, let alone towards the responsive, innovative institutions that some people have in mind. Whether instigated by university administrators or imposed by government officials, the changes associated with managerialism are likely to have adverse effects on universities.

> Bureaucratic intrusion and overregulation interfere with basic university functions, lead to feelings of helplessness or, conversely, prompt a subversive "beat the system" approach. (Boone et al. 1991)

What is needed is a better understanding of alternative ways of bringing about strategic change (Figure 14.1). So, while managerialism focuses on deliberate strategies and blueprints for change, this book seeks to show how action-oriented approaches can be developed to address the emergent strategy-making processes characteristic of universities. In this way, the focus on formulating strategic intentions is supplemented with an understanding of how strategies can be realized, helping university members to develop the *additional* skills they need to bring about change.

ORGANIZATIONS FOR LEARNING AS LEARNING ORGANIZATIONS

The ability to secure and maintain excellence is unlikely to result from planned strategy alone. The move to adopt strategic planning in the

BLUEPRINT

INTENTION

MANAGERIALIST
LITERATURE

EMERGENT

DELIBERATE

THIS
STUDY

REALIZATION

ACTION PLAN

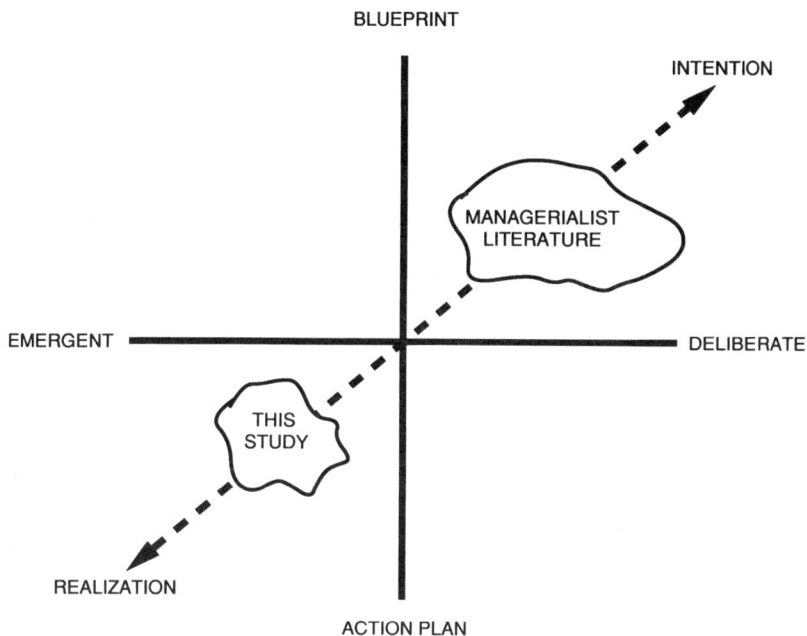

Figure 14.1
Alternative Models for Effecting Strategic Change

Adapted from Savenije 1989:8

university context stems from the idea that planned change is more likely to improve performance than unplanned change. But formal planning can have major drawbacks, especially in university settings (Hardy 1987a), and it has been argued that many of the supposed strategic turnarounds associated with u.s. liberal-arts colleges were, in reality, creative marketing techniques (Dill 1990). Part of the problem lies in the fascination with planning techniques rather than with the processes of implementing and realizing change.[5]

The planning approach to strategy tends to ignore the fact that institutional excellence and innovation require the ability to attract and hold on to *people* who are excellent and innovative. Planning may even jeopardize this: it produces homogenized procedures that often alienate productive professors by curtailing their autonomy, while unproductive faculty will always find a way around them. The centralized control that planning requires is often at odds with the autonomy and freedom needed to stimulate research.

There are, however, alternatives to the planning model, as an example from the business world will illustrate. Honda's highly successful bid to capture the u.s. motorcycle market in the 1960s was unplanned as the company adapted to a series of events and accidentally uncovered an untapped niche in the small (50 c.c.) motorcycle market, where it was able to compete successfully with established u.s. and European manufacturers (Pascale 1988). What made Honda successful was not the ability to plan but the ability to *learn*. The company was able to respond to events by recognizing them, assessing their potential, and adapting strategy to accommodate them. In fact, had the company stuck to its original plan to compete in the large motorcycle market, powerful rivals would have developed counter-strategies. As it was, Honda inadvertently located a new niche that all the planning in the world would not have located.

Proponents of the "learning school" (e.g., Mintzberg 1989) argue that the complex and dynamic nature of the environment precludes accurate forecasting and deliberate control. They argue that effective strategies can occur only with collective strategy-making, where a wide number of informed individuals, located throughout the organization, are involved. As a result, the key to success lies not so much in the ability of formal leaders to plan but in the ability of the organization as a collectivity to learn. In this situation, informed individuals throughout the organization contribute to strategic action, and learning proceeds in an emergent fashion as initiatives spring up from various locations and are either nurtured or left to founder. The role of leaders is not to preconceive deliberate strategies but to encourage the process of strategic learning and crafting strategy (Mintzberg 1987) by ensuring that the appropriate initiatives are encouraged.

If actors are to be successful in championing change in this fashion, they must pay particular attention to the nature of the institutional context in which they work. What is considered legitimate in one university may be perceived as counter-cultural in another. In other words, actors must locate the "on" switches in their particular institution. Understanding context is related to understanding the particular interest groups that exist in an institution, as well as the distribution of power among them and their use of it. If an accurate assessment can be made of the institutional context, actors are in a far better position to identify the levers they can use to realize strategies and bring about change. In this way, context represents a surrogate for culture: it can be ascertained more quickly than the underlying culture (and subcultures). Obviously, the more an actor understands about the organization's culture, the more successful, one would expect, would be the use of symbolic power. In the absence of such a detailed knowledge, however, an understanding of the institutional context appears to be a useful alternative.

The recognition that universities represent arenas of potentially conflicting groups will help external stakeholders to comprehend the difficulties involved in orchestrating change in this sector. Any inclination to increase the power of the central administration at the expense of other groups must be countered with the realization that many universities are successful *because* power is relatively decentralized. Moreover, any attempt by government to impose standardized systems across the higher-education sector is likely to weaken effective cultures and dispel institutional missions (Clark 1970). It would seem counter-productive to homogenize and dilute diverse institutional contexts in the light of findings in the business world which indicate that a strong culture can foster excellence (e.g., Peters and Waterman 1982).

University autonomy may frustrate policy-makers because of the abuses that are assumed to be taking place, but bureaucracy is not the solution because loopholes will always be found. Neither administrators nor policy-makers can afford to hide behind the security of standardized planning mechanisms. Universities require politically astute individuals who can manage conflict and create consensus; who know how to reward as well as how to control; who can tap the advantages of a strong culture or change an ineffectual one. They need discriminating management, not standardized management that ignores the complexity and diversity of university life.

A FINAL WORD

We must recognize that the conflicts experienced in the arena of higher education are not the result of miscommunication or misunderstanding, nor are they caused by aberrant individuals. They are the inevitable result of the presence of different groups which, while working under the same broad paradigm, often have incompatible goals. It is perhaps not a very attractive framework: we are often reluctant to acknowledge such inherent tensions within our society. Once we do recognize them, however, we are in a position to manage the differences and create some degree of consensus around the functioning of higher education. It is only by recognizing division that we can create unity. More to the point, attempts to introduce administrative and public policy based on the faulty assumptions associated with the unitary approach simply do not work (e.g., Hardy 1986).

It is an understanding of power and politics that is most helpful in this regard. Not only does it acknowledge the possibility of conflict resulting from the presence disparate interest groups, but it provides an analysis of why and how that possibility arises by reference to the political context of a particular situation, institution, or issue. It also indicates how power can be used to build consensus. It thus provides an indication of how competing interests, inside and outside the institution, can be managed.

The unitary perspective neither accurately describes the situation nor offers useful advice on how to deal with it. Ironically, the conditions associated with the unitary model – the existence of common goals – can be achieved, but often only *through the active deployment of power*. In other words, power is used to create consensus around common goals. This politicization of the unitary model is important, not only because it provides university actors with a mechanism for bringing about change, but also because it reminds us that power is at work, even when there is apparent cooperation. It unmasks the rhetoric that surrounds collegiality and shows it for what it is – a particular use of power that avoids conflict. This form of power, as with any other, can be both used and abused. By exposing the power behind collegiality, we are, at the very least, in a better position to ensure it is used wisely.

Methodology

This appendix describes the methodology used in the present study and assesses its implications. The research question concerned the nature of, and reasons behind, the retrenchment strategies adopted by six Canadian universities. The study was based on the use of comparative case studies, in which interviews were carried out with key actors and representatives of the various interest groups. Other forms of both university and third-party documentation were also collected and analysed.

All too often, qualitative case-study research is dismissed by social scientists who criticize its apparent lack of rigour and precision. One reason for this reaction is that case-study research has none of the technical complexity that seems to render statistical research more objective in the eyes of many academics (Yin 1984). As a result, this methodology has often been relegated to the status of an "exploratory" method – the first step to uncovering ideas that will be subsequently tested with the aid of more rigorous methodologies, or even rejected out of hand.

Despite these criticisms, this research strategy continues to be widely used in areas as diverse as political science, public administration, sociology, and urban planning, in addition to organization studies. It is particularly effective in situations characterized by an inability to control events and a high degree of complexity – when a "'how' or 'why' question is being asked about a contemporary set of events, over which the investigator has little or no control" (Yin 1984: 20). This description clearly fits the present study, in which the aim was to find out *how* different institutions responded to financial restraint and *why* they adopted certain strategies.

The case study is an empirical inquiry that investigates a contemporary phenomenon within its real life context, when the boundaries between phenomenon and context are not clearly evident (Yin 1984: 23). The examination of context was crucial to this study since the aim was to link the nature of the retrenchment strategies to the internal university context. The complexity of the phenomena under investigation was amenable neither to the control necessary for an experiment nor to the condensation required for a survey. Qualitative work is essential in this type of situation, where the investigator has to delve more deeply to be able to examine and understand the intangible aspects of process (Loffland 1971; Mintzberg 1979b; Pettigrew 1979; Van Maanen 1979).

Critics who argue that case studies are not "representative" are barking up the wrong tree since they confuse statistical and theoretical generalization (Yin 1984). Their sampling logic assumes that the respondents in a study represent a larger pool of respondents and that as a consequence, sample data can, subject to the appropriate statistical procedures, be considered as data from the whole pool. But since case-study research covers both phenomena and context, it inevitably has too many variables to allow statistical consideration. Cases are not meant to be representative – any more that social scientists design representative experiments – because they are not used to assess the incidence of a phenomenon. Their objective is the generalization of theory (analytic generalization), not the enumeration of frequencies (statistical generalization). In other words, the investigator is attempting to generalize findings to a theory in the same way that a scientist generalizes experimental results to a theory.

Case studies can be selected in one of two ways. The first makes the selection on the basis of the expectation of securing similar results (literal replication). The second chooses cases on the expectation of contrary results that can be explained with reference to the theory (theoretical replication). Eisenhardt (1989) points out that such use of "extreme" cases can help to render theoretical implications more transparent (also see Dutton and Dukerich 1991). In this way, the strength of a multiple case study design is clear – to build and expand theory.

This study uses a multiple-case design (six case studies) for a single unit of analysis (the university). Theoretical replication was used to select cases on the grounds that different university contexts would throw some light on different retrenchment responses. The relationship between the data from the case studies and the theory was an iterative one (see Sutton and Elsbach 1992). It was based on the generation of grounded theory (Glaser and Strauss 1967) and involved three main stages. First, an understanding of existing theories of university decision-making and governance was used to inform the data analysis, and the results of the latter were used to refine these theories. In this way, the university contexts, which represent a refinement of existing theories, were identified. Second, the retrenchment strategies were compared and related back to the context in a chain of causal links. At this points, gaps in the chain prompted additional data collection, in the form of verification through interviews, the collection of statistics, written documentation, and third-party reports. Third, the understanding of the role of power in creating collegiality evolved later, as the manuscript was in the latter stages of preparation, and was an indirect consequence of another research project on power as a factor in strategic change. A fresh look at the data, with a different set of theoretical issues in mind, led to a deeper understanding of how power can be mobilized to create collegiality.

THE CASE STUDIES

The study focused on six Canadian institutions – McGill University, the University of Montreal, the University of British Columbia (UBC), Simon Fraser University (SFU), the University of Toronto, and Carleton University. Data collection at McGill University and the University of Montreal began in 1984–85. These two institutions were chosen on the grounds that they would reflect two quite different contexts. While both are large, traditional research institutions with comparable formal structures, it was envisaged that they would operate quite differently because of their different linguistic and cultural traditions, and that these differences would be manifested in different power distributions and political arrangements. This "pilot" study also found differences in their responses to the budget cutbacks imposed by the Quebec government. Thus the comparison of the two universities indicated that the institutional contexts varied and that these variations appeared to have some bearing on the nature of the retrenchment strategy. As a result, the study was extended.

The objective in including the four remaining universities was twofold. One goal was to see whether the theoretical framework could be generalized to newer, smaller institutions (such as Carleton University and Simon Fraser University). The second objective was to assess whether larger and older institutions in provinces where fiscal restraint had taken a different form could be explained by the theory. The University of Toronto and the University of British Columbia were included for this reason. As explained earlier, the aim was not to produce a representative sample in the statistical sense but to provide a sufficient diversity of cases to extend the theory. The study is not intended to produce an inclusive typology to categorize all institutions

Table A.1
Number of Interviews Conducted in Each University

	McGill University	University of Montreal	University of British Columbia	Simon Fraser University	University of Toronto	Carleton University
Central administrators	11	8	9	8	10	6
Deans	12	11	10	7	12	5
Professors	6	5	4	4	8	7
Senators[1]	4	3	4	4	5	3
Board members	3	2	3	2	3	
Faculty association	2	2	2	3	2	2
Support staff	4	4	2	3	6	4
Total	42	35	34	31	43	30

1 The figure for the University of Toronto refers to representatives of the Governing Council.

Table A.2
Number of Interviews Conducted Outside the University, by Province

	Quebec	British Columbia	Ontario
Ministry officials	3	3	2
Intermediate-body representatives	2	3	2
University presidents[1]	4	2	5
CREPUQ/COU	2	–	3
Total	11	8	12

1 Figures include former presidents of the institutions covered in the study and presidents of other institutions.
– Not applicable.

– other university contexts may exist in Canada and have certainly been found elsewhere (Hardy 1990c) – but to demonstrate that the analysis of interest groups and the distribution of power in an institution provides an understanding of the nature of its specific context, and that, in turn, helps to explain the choice of retrenchment strategy.

Interviews were carried out with key organizational actors[6] (Tables A.1 and A.2). The initial contact usually involved the president, vice-presidents, or deans, because these individuals were easy to identify and could be expected to have been involved in resource allocations decisions. Other interviewees were identified as the interviews progressed, especially those on key committees and/or who played an important role in resource allocation. Representatives of the main interest groups (senate, board, faculty, and staff association) were also interviewed. In addition, individuals in the external community were interviewed, including representatives of the government, intermediary bodies, university associations, and other universities.

A database of quotations was prepared from the transcribed interviews. These quotations were grouped according to particular issues so as to ensure that they were illustrative of other interviewees' thoughts and attitudes rather than the idiosyncratic views of one individual. Thus the quotations presented in the case-study chapters do not simply represent the view of the particular individual but have been chosen specifically to reflect a broader base of opinion.

The interview data were supplemented with documentation, such as memoranda and reports from the various institutions, as well as a variety of archival records, including institutional records; statistical information from government, intermediary bodies, and university associations; media reports; and other third-party studies. A significant portion of the data also provided unobtrusive measures of the phenomena that helped to triangulate the data (Webb et al. 1966; Webb and Weick 1979) and confirm statements made by interviewees.

Formal permission for conducting interviews was not requested from the university president, in order to keep the study as independent as possible and to avoid any pressure being put on individual interviewees. Apart from a few cases, all the individuals who were approached consented to being interviewed. The only exceptions were one vice-president at the University of Toronto and two deans at the University of British Columbia. Some other individuals were unable to participate because of scheduling problems, but their number was small. The interviewing was conducted in three phases. The first took place in 1984–85 at McGill University and the University of Montreal. The second took place in 1986 at the remaining four universities. A final phase was carried out in 1991 to explore further certain issues that had arisen during the latter stages of data analysis.

The interviews were all taped (apart from one) and transcribed. They were semi-structured and lasted between one and three hours. A series of key questions concerning the various organizational actors, interest groups, and retrenchment strategies formed the nucleus of the interview, but considerable digression was used to allow interviewees to identify the issues that concerned them, present their thoughts in their own terms, and allow new information to emerge. Individuals participated on the basis of an agreement that they would not be identified. The central administrators of the six universities did not seek any power of veto over the study or the data and, in fact, were most helpful in providing documentation, statistics, and so on. In all cases, they were shown the final case-study report. In some cases, matters of "fact" were disputed, leading to further verification by the author, and changes were made where appropriate.

LIMITATIONS

While the case-study design was particularly well suited to the phenomena under study, there are nevertheless limitations to this methodology.

One important limitation is the cross-sectional nature of the data. Since there was only one major phase of interviewing in each institution, the data show a picture of each university at one point in time. It is unlikely that the contexts identified here are ephemeral and transitory phenomena, since aspects of them will certainly endure. For example, the fact that documentation written before and after the interviews support the interview data suggests that university contexts may last for a number of years. At the same time, chapter thirteen indicates that aspects of the institutional context can be changed. Beyond this, the study cannot say how individual institutions have or have not changed since the 1980s because it did not track them over time.

A second limitation concerns the single unit of analysis. The emphasis is on the university and how it reacts to its environment. It is assumed that environmental changes in the form of funding restrictions provoked some sort of reaction from university administrators. The study does not critically examine this relationship between the organization and its environment. It does not, for example, try to determine at what point administrators perceive funding to be constrained. Nor does it look at attempts by the university community to shape the external context. In other words, the environment is seen in a relatively simplistic sense as impinging on university decision-making, and the study does not analyse how universities enact, manage, or change their environments.

Third, there are potential limitations inherent in any project involving interviewing – namely, respondent bias and retroactive bias. Both were addressed by the use of multiple sources of evidence that enabled the investigator to check out discrepancies. Neither bias was found to be a particular problem here, since data from different sources matched up.

Notes

CHAPTER TWO

1 The 1987 *Commonwealth Universities Yearbook* lists fifty-six institutions, a number that does not include any affiliated or specialized institutions. The *Yearbook* notes that the Association of Universities and Colleges of Canada has over eighty members and that the Canadian higher-education system also includes nearly 200 colleges as well as other technical and vocational institutions. The subject of the present study is, however, the university sector; while it is recognized that "postsecondary" and "higher education" refer to more than just universities, the use of these terms here indicates a focus on universities.

2 The expressions "operating fund" and "grant" refer to the money provided by government to cover an institution's operating expenses. It typically covers the majority, but not all, of those expenses. Funding usually goes into base budgets on a continual basis, although funds may be tied to a specific, short-term program, in which case they are often called "soft" funds.

3 The ministry responsible for higher education went through a number of changes during the 1980s but was usually separate from the rest of the provincial education system (Cameron 1991).

CHAPTER FOURTEEN

4 On university-government relations, see Mullins 1990; Tavenas 1990 on university-government relations; and Tatel and Guthrie 1983. On the relationship between universities and business, see *Financial Post* 1983; Maxwell and Currie 1984; Smith 1984; Ashworth 1985; Williams 1986; Nelkin and Nelson 1987; Cerych 1989; Dinsmore 1990; and Fairweather 1990.

5 This fascination is not confined to higher education and is also to be found in business. According to a cd-rom search of ABI-Inform abstracts between

January 1989 and May 1993, over 27,000 articles on strategy have been written, but only 110 on strategic *change*.

APPENDIX

6 Interviews with department heads at McGill University and the University of Montreal were also carried out. An analysis of this data indicated that the understanding of *institutional* resource allocation decisions was not sufficiently enhanced to justify the additional time, effort, and money involved in these additional interviews. So, it was decided not to repeat these interviews at the remaining four institutions and they are not included in these tables.

Bibliography

Allison, G.T. 1971. *Essence of Decision: Explaining the Cuban Missile Crisis.* Boston: Little and Brown.

Allison, L. 1974. "On the Nature of the Concept of Power." *European Journal of Political Science* 2: 131–41.

Alvesson, M. 1984. "Questioning Rationality and Ideology: On Critical Organization Theory." *International Studies of Management and Organizations* 14 (1): 61–79.

Armour, J., and E. DesRosiers. 1974. *The Recent Evolution of Financial Planning and Management at McGill University.* Paper presented at the Annual Conference of the Canadian Association of University Business Officers, Halifax, June.

Arnold, L. 1981. *How Do We Cut the Cake.* Ottawa: Canadian Association of University Business Officers.

Ashworth, J.M. 1985. "What Price an Ivory Tower? University–Industry Relationships." *Higher Education Review* 17 (2): 31–43.

Astley, W.G. 1985. "Administrative Science As Socially Constructed Truth." *Administrative Science Quarterly* 30: 497–513.

Axelrod, P. 1982. *Scholars and Dollars.* Toronto: University of Toronto Press.

Bachrach, P., and M.S. Baratz. 1962. "The Two Faces of Power." *American Political Science Review* 56: 947–52.

Bachrach, S., and E. Lawler. 1980. *Power and Politics in Organizations.* London: Jossey Bass.

Baldridge, J.V. 1971. *Power and Conflict in the University.* London: Wiley.

Baldridge et al. 1978: see *Policy Making and Effective Leadership.*

Becher, T. 1981. "Towards a Definition of Disciplinary Cultures." *Studies in Higher Education* 6: 109–22.

Bélanger, C., and L. Tremblay. 1982. "A Methodological Approach to Selective Cutbacks." *Canadian Journal of Higher Education* 12 (3): 25–36.

Bélanger, C., and R. Lacroix. 1986. "Measuring the Effectiveness of Research Grant Getting." *Canadian Journal of Higher Education* 16 (1): 25–40.

Bess, J.L. 1988. *Collegiality and Bureaucracy in the Modern University: The Influence of Information and Power on Decision-making Structures*. New York: Teachers College Press.

Beyer, J.M. 1982. "Power Dependencies and the Distribution of Influence in Universities." *Research in the Sociology of Organizations* 1: 167–208.

Beyer, J.M., and T.M. Lodahl. 1976. "A Comparative Study of Patterns of Influence in United States and English Universities." *Administrative Science Quarterly* 21: 104–29.

Birnbaum, R. 1988. *How Colleges Work*. San Francisco: Jossey Bass.

Blau, P.M. 1973. *The Organization of Academic Work*. New York: Wiley-Interscience.

Blauner, R. 1964. *Alienation and Freedom*. Chicago: University of Chicago Press.

Boone, J.N., S. Peterson, D.J. Poje, and M. Scarlett. 1991. "University Autonomy: Perceived and Preferred Location of Authority." *The Review of Higher Education* 14 (2): 135–53.

Bowen, H.R. 1977. *Investment in Learning*. San Francisco: Jossey Bass.

Bresser, R.K. 1984. "Structural Dimensions of University Departments and Their Context: The Case of West Germany." *Organization Studies* 5 (2): 119–146.

Bruzzese, A. 1991. "What Business Schools Aren't Teaching." *Incentive* (March): 19–21.

Bryman, A. 1984. "Organization Studies and the Concept of Rationality." *Journal of Management Studies* 21 (4): 391–408.

Burns, T. 1961. "Micro-politics: Mechanisms of Institutional Change." *Administrative Science Quarterly* 6: 257–81.

Burrell, G., and G. Morgan. 1979. *Sociological Paradigms and Organizational Analysis*. London: Heinemann.

Business Week. 1984. "The New Breed of Strategic Planner." *Business Week* (17 September): 62–8.

Cameron, D. 1991. *More than an Academic Problem*. Halifax, N.S.: Institute for Research on Public Policy.

Cameron, K.S. 1985. "Institutional Effectiveness in Higher Education." *Review of Higher Education* 9 (1): 1–5.

– 1986. "Effectiveness as Paradox: Consensus and Conflict in Conceptions of Organizational Effectiveness." *Management Science* 32 (5): 539–53.

Campell, D.D. 1978. "Western Canada." In *Systems of Higher Education in Canada*.

Cerych, L. 1989. "University–Industry Collaboration: A Research Agenda and Some General Impacts on the Development of Higher Education." *European Journal of Education* 24 (3): 309–13.

Chaffee, E.E. 1983a. *Rational Decision Making in Higher Education*. Boulder, Colo.: National Centre for Higher Education Management Systems.

– 1983b. "The Role of Rationality in University Budgeting." *Research in Higher Education* 19 (4): 387–406.

– 1984. "Successful Strategic Management in Small Private Colleges." *Journal of Higher Education* 55 (2): 213–41.

– 1985. "Three Models of Strategy." *Academy of Management Review* 10 (1): 89–98.

Chaffee, E.E., and W.G. Tierney. 1988. *Collegiate Culture and Leadership Strategies*. New York: MacMillan.

Childers, M.E. 1981. "What is Political About Bureaucratic–Collegial Decision Making." *Review of Higher Education* 5: 25–45.

Clark, B.R. 1970. *The Distinctive College: Antioch, Reed and Swarthmore*. Chicago: Aldine.

– 1971. "Belief and Loyalty in College Organization." *Journal of Higher Education* 42: 499–520.

– 1972. "The Organizational Saga in Higher Education." *Administrative Science Quarterly* 17: 178–84.

– 1983. "Governing the Higher Education System." In *The Structure and Governance of Higher Education*, edited by M. Shattock. Guildford, U.K.: Society for Research into Higher Education, 19–45.

Clegg, S. 1975. *Power, Rule and Domination*. London: Routledge and Kegan Paul.

– 1989. *Frameworks of Power*. London: Sage.

Cohen, M.D., and J.G. March. 1974. *Leadership and Ambiguity*. New York: McGraw-Hill.

Committee of Vice-Chancellors and Principals. 1985. *Report of the Steering Committee for Efficiency Studies in Universities* (Jarratt Report). United Kingdom.

Corson, J.J. 1960. *Governance of Colleges and Universities*. New York: McGraw Hill.

Crozier, M. 1964. *The Bureaucratic Phenomenon*. Chicago: University of Chicago.

Cutt, J., and R. Dobell. 1992. *Universities and Government: A Framework for Accountability*. Halifax, N.S.: Institute for Research on Public Policy.

Cyert, R.M., and J.G. March. 1963. *A Behavioral Theory of the Firm*. Englewood Cliffs, N.J.: Prentice-Hall.

Dahl, R. 1961. *Who Governs: Democracy and Power in an American City*. New Haven: Yale University Press.

Darkenwald, G.G. 1971. "Organizational Conflict in Colleges and Universities." *Administrative Science Quarterly* 16: 407–12.

Davies, J.L., and A.W. Morgan. 1982. "The Politics of Institutional Change." In *Agenda for Institutional Change in Higher Education*, edited by L.

Wagner. Guildford, U.K.: Society for Research into Higher Education, 153–88.

Deal, T., and A.E. Kennedy. 1982. *Corporate Cultures*. Reading, Mass.: Addison-Wesley.

Deetz, S. 1992. *Democracy in an Age of Corporate Colonization: Developments in Communication and the Politics of Everyday Life*. Albany: State University of New York.

Dennison, J.D. 1987. "Universities Under Financial Crisis: The Case of British Columbia." *Higher Education* 16: 135–43.

Dill, D.D. 1982. "The Management of Academic Culture: Notes on the Management of Meaning and Social Integration." *Higher Education* 11: 303–20.

– 1990. *The Context and Process of Planning in American Academic Institutions*. Paper presented at the Workshop on Leadership and Strategy in the Collegial Institution, Montreal, February.

Dill, D.D., and K.P. Helm. 1990. "Faculty Participation in Strategic Policy Making." In *Higher Education: Handbook of Theory and Research*, edited by J. Smart. New York: Agathon Press, 4: 319–55.

Dinsmore, J. 1990. *University–Industry Links*. Paper presented at the Workshop on "Canadian Universities: Problems and Opportunities in the 1990s," Ottawa, November.

Dube, C.S., and A.W. Brown. 1983. "Strategic Assessment: A Rational Response to University Cutbacks." *Long Range Planning* 16: 105–13.

Dutton, J.E., and J.M. Dukerich. 1991. "Keeping an Eye on the Mirror: Image and Identity in Organizational Adaptation." *Academy of Management Journal* 34: 517–54.

Eastman, J.A. 1986. "Programme Structure and Academic Freedom: An Analysis of the 'New Programme' in Architecture at the University of Toronto, 1968–1983." *The Canadian Journal of Higher Education* 3: 13–29.

Eisenhardt, K.M. 1989. "Building Theories from Case Study Research." *Academy of Management Review* 14: 532–50.

Ellstrom, D. 1983. "Four Faces of Educational Organizations." *Higher Education* 12: 231–41.

Elsbach, K.D., and R.I. Sutton. 1992. "Acquiring Orgnaizational Legitimacy through Illegitiate Actions: A Marriage of Institutional and Impression Management Theories." *Academy of Management Journal* 35 (4): 699–738.

Etzioni, A. 1964. *Modern Organizations*. Englewood Cliffs, N.J.: Prentice Hall.

Fairweather, J.S., and D.F. Brown. 1991. "Dimensions of Academic Program Quality." *The Review of Higher Education* 14 (2): 155–76.

Financial Post. 1983. "Conference Report." *Financial Post* (14 May): C1–8.

Foggin, J.H. 1992. "Meeting Customer Needs." *Survey of Business* (Summer): 6–9.

Foucault, M. 1979. *Discipline and Punish: The Birth of the Prison*. New York: Vintage Books.

- 1980. *Power/Knowledge: Selected Interviews and Other Writings 1972–1977*, edited by C. Gordon. Brighton, U.K.: Harvester Press.

- 1982. "The Subject and Power." In *Michel Foucault: Beyond Structuralism and Hermeneutics*, edited by H.L. Dreyfus and P. Rabinow. Brighton, U.K.: Harvester, 208–26.

- 1984. *The History of Sexuality: An Introduction*. Harmondsworth: Penguin.

Fox, A. 1973. "Industrial Relations: A Social Critique of Pluralist Ideology." In *Man and Organization*, edited by J. Child. London: Allen and Unwin, 185–233.

French, J.R.P., and B. Raven. 1968. "The Bases of Social Power." In *Group Dynamics*, edited by D. Cartwright and A. Zander. New York: Harper and Row.

Friedberg, E., and C. Musselin. 1989a. *En quête d'universités. Étude comparée des universités en France et en RFA*. Paris: l'Harmattan.

- 1989b. "L'Université des professeurs." *Sociologie du travail* 31 (4): 455–76.

Frost, P.J., and C.P. Egri. 1991. "The Political Process of Innovation." *Research in Organizational Behaviour* 13: 229–95.

Frost, S.B. 1984. *McGill University for the Advancement of Learning: Volume 2*. Montreal: McGill-Queen's University Press.

Gaff, J.G., and R.C. Wilson. 1971. "Faculty Cultures and Interdisciplinary and Studies." *Journal of Higher Education* 42: 186–201.

Gaventa, J. 1980. *Power and Powerlessness: Quiescence and Rebellion in an Appalachian Valley*. Oxford: Clarendon Press.

Gerth, H., and C. Wright Mills. 1946. *From Max Weber*. Oxford: Oxford University Press.

Giddens, A. 1984. *The Constitution of Society: Outline of a Theory of Structuration*. Berkeley: University of California Press.

Goodman, P. 1962. *The Community of Scholars*. New York: Random House.

Government Strategies and Innovation in Higher Education, edited by F.A. Van Vucht. London: Jessica Kingsley, 1989.

Gumport, P.J. 1988. "Curricula as Signposts of Cultural Change." *The Review of Higher Education* 12 (1): 49–61.

Hardy, C. 1984. "The Management of University Cutbacks: Politics, Planning and Participation." *Canadian Journal of Higher Education* 14 (1): 79–89.

- 1985a. "The Nature of Unobtrusive Power." *Journal of Management Studies* 22 (4): 384–99.

- 1985b. *Managing Organizational Closure*. Aldershot, U.K.: Gower Press.

- 1986. "Management in the National Health Service: Using Politics Effectively." *Public Policy and Administration* 1 (1): 1–17.

- 1987a. "Strategic Planning?" In *Education Canada?*, edited by G. Paquet and M. Von Zur-Muehlen. Ottawa: Canadian Higher Education Network.
- 1987b. "Using Content, Context and Process to Manage University Cutbacks." *Canadian Journal of Higher Education* 17 (1): 65–82.
- 1988. "The Rational Approach to Budget Cuts: One University's Experience." *Higher Education* 17: 151–73.
- 1990a. "'Hard' Decisions and 'Tough' Choices: the Business Approach to University Decline." *Higher Education* 20 (3): 1–21.
- 1990b. *Strategies for Retrenchment and Turnaround: The Politics of Survival.* Berlin: De Gruyter.
- 1990c. *Managing Strategy in Academic Institutions: Learning from Brazil.* Berlin: De Gruyter.
- 1990d. "Leadership and Strategy Making for Institution Building: the Case of a Brazilian University." In *Management in Developing Countries*, edited by A. Jaeger and R. Kanungo. London: Routledge, 83–100.
- 1990e. "Putting Power into University Governance." *Handbook of Higher Education* 6: 393–425.
- 1990f. "Strategy and Context: Retrenchment in Canadian Universities." *Organization Studies* 11 (2): 207–37.
- 1991a."Pluralism, Power and Collegiality in Universities." *Financial and Accountability Management* 7 (3): 127–42.
- 1991b. "Configuration and Strategy Making in Universities: Broadening the Scope." *Journal of Higher Education* 62 (4): 363–93.
- 1992. "Retrenchment Strategies in Two Canadian Universities: A Political Analysis." *Canadian Journal of Administrative Sciences* 9 (3): 180–91.
- 1994. *Managing Strategic Action: Mobilizing Change.* London: Sage.
- [forthcoming]. "Managing Strategic Change: Power, Paralysis and Perspective." *Advances in Strategic Management.*

Hardy, C., A. Langley, H. Mintzberg, and J. Rose. 1993. "Strategy Formation in the University Setting." *Review of Higher Education* 6 (4): 407–33.

Hardy, C., and A.M. Pettigrew. 1985. "The Use of Power in Managerial Strategies for Change." In *Research on Technological Innovation, Management and Policy*, edited by R.S. Rosenbloom. Greenwich, Conn.: JAI Press, 2: 11–45.

Hass, M.E., and J.H. Philbrick. 1988. "The New Management: Is it Legal?" *Academy of Mangement Executive* 2 (4): 325–9.

Helsabeck, R.E. 1973. *The Compound System.* Berkeley: University of California, Center for Research and Development in Higher Education.

Hendrickson, R.M., and J.P. Bartkovich. 1986. "Organizational Systematics: Toward a Classification Scheme for Postsecondary Institutions." *Review of Higher Education* 9 (3): 303–24.

Heydinger, R.B. 1982. *Using Program Priorities to Make Retrenchment Decisions: The Case of the University of Minnesota.* Minnesota: Southern Regional Education Board.

Hickson, D.J., C.R. Hinings, C.A. Lee, R.E. Schneck, and J.M. Pennings. 1971. "A Strategic Contingencies Theory of Intraorganizational Power." *Administrative Science Quarterly* 16 (2): 216–29.

Hickson, D.J., R.J. Butler, D. Cray, G.R. Mallory, and D.C. Wilson. 1986. *Top Decisions: Strategic Decision-making in Organizations.* San Francisco: Jossey-Bass.

Hill, W.W., and W.L. French. 1967. "Perceptions of the Power of Department Chairmen by Professors." *Administrative Science Quarterly* 11: 548–74.

Holdaway, E.A., J.F. Newberry, D.J. Hickson, and R.P. Heron. 1975. "Dimensions of Organizations in Complex Societies: The Educational Sector." *Administrative Science Quarterly* 20: 37–58.

Holmes, J. 1978. "The Atlantic Provinces." In *Systems of Higher Education In Canada.*

ISGUG. 1983. *Governance and Accountability.* Report of the Independent Study Group on University Governance. Ottawa: Canadian Association of University Teachers.

Jones, C. 1986. "Universities, on Becoming What They Are Not." *Financial Accountability and Management* 2 (2): 107–19.

Kerr, C. 1964. *The Uses of the University.* Cambridge: Harvard University Press.

Kiechel, W. 1982. "Corporate Strategies." *Fortune* 106: 34–39.

Knights, D., and H. Willmott. 1985. "Power and Identity in Theory and Practice." *Sociological Review* 33 (1): 22–46.

Knights, D., and G. Morgan. 1991. "Strategic Discourse and Subjectivity: Towards a Critical Analysis of Corporate Strategy in Organisations." *Organization Studies* 12: 251–73.

Kort-Krieger, U., and P. Schmidt. 1982. "Participation and Legitimacy Conflict at West German Universities." *Organization Studies* 3 (4): 297–319.

Kymlicka, B.B. 1978. "Ontario." In *Systems of Higher Education in Canada.*

Langlois, H.O. 1980. "Shrinking School Systems: Some Fiscal Considerations." *Education Canada* 20 (2): 11–15.

Lawler E.E., and A. Mohrman. 1987. "Unions and the New Management." *Academy of Management Executive* 1 (3): 293–300.

Lee, R.A., and J.A. Piper. 1988. "Organizational Control, Differing Perspectives: The Management of Universities." *Financial Accountability and Management* 4 (2): 113–28.

Leiba, C, and C. Hardy. 1994. "Employee Empowerment: A Seductive Misnomer." In *Managing Strategic Action: Mobilizing Change,* edited by C. Hardy. London: Sage, 256–271.

Leslie, L.L. 1980. "The Financial Prospects for Higher Education in the 1980s." *Journal of Higher Education* 51: 1–17.

Lindblom, C.E. 1959. "The Science of 'Muddling Through'." *Public Administration Review* 19: 79–88.

Linder, J.C., and H.J. Smith. 1992. "The Complex Case of Management Education." *Harvard Business Review* 70 (5): 16–33.

Lodahl, J.B., and G. Gordon. 1972. "The Structure of Scientific Fields and the Functioning of University Graduate Departments." *American Sociological Review* 37: 57–62.

– 1973. "Funding Sciences in University Departments." *Educational Record* 54: 74–82.

Loffland, J. 1971. *Analysing Social Settings*. Belmont. Cal.: Wadsworth.

Lukes, S. 1974. *Power: A Radical View*. London: Macmillan.

Lutz, F.W. 1982. "Tightening Up Loose Coupling in Organizations of Higher Education." *Administrative Science Quarterly* 27: 653–69.

March, J.G., and J.P. Olsen. 1976. *Ambiguity and Choice in Organizations*. Bergen, Norway: Universitetsfolaget.

Masland, A.T. 1985. "Organizational Culture in the Study of Higher Education." *Review of Higher Education* 8 (2): 157–68.

Maxwell, J., and S. Currie. 1984. *Partnership for Growth: Corporate–University Cooperation in Canada*. Montreal, Corporate–Higher Education Forum.

Mayhew, L.B. 1979. *Surviving the Eighties*. San Francisco: Jossey-Bass.

Millett, J.D. 1962. *The Academic Community*. New York: McGraw Hill.

Mingle, J.R. 1981. *Challenges of Retrenchment*. San Francisco: Jossey-Bass.

Mintzberg, H. 1979a. *The Structuring of Organizations*. Englewood Cliffs, N.J.: Prentice Hall.

– 1979b. "An Emerging Strategy of Direct Research." *Administrative Science Quarterly* 24 (4): 582–589.

– 1987. "Crafting Strategy." *Harvard Business Review* 65 (4): 66–75.

– 1988. "The Professional Bureaucracy." In *The Strategy Process*, edited by H. Mintzberg, J.B. Quinn, and R.M. James. Englewood Cliffs, N.J.: Prentice-Hall, 638–648.

– 1989. *Mintzberg on Management*. New York: Free Press.

Mouzelis, N.P. 1967. *Organisation and Bureaucracy*. Chicago: Aldine.

Mullins, G. 1990. "*The University/Government Interface: A Deputy Minister's Perspective*. Paper presented at the Annual Conference of the Canadian Society for the Study of Higher Education, Victoria, June.

Musselin, C. 1987. "Système de gouvernement ou cohésion universitaire. Les capacités d'action collective de deux universités allemandes et de deux universités françaises." Ph.D. thesis, Institut d'Études politiques de Paris.

Nelkin, D., and R. Nelson. 1987. "Commentary: University–Industry Alliances." *Science, Technology and Human Values* 12 (1): 65–74.

O'Briant, W.H. 1991. "Professional Loyalty and the Scholarly Community: Reflections toward a Philosophy for Fostering Faculty." *The Review of Higher Education* 14 (2): 251–62.

Ontario Task Force on University Accountability, 1993. *Task Force on University Accountability: Progress Reports and Issues Papers.* Toronto, June.

Ouchi, W.G. 1981. *Theory Z.* New York: Avon Books.

Padgett, J.F. 1980. "Managing Garbage Can Hierarchies." *Administrative Science Quarterly* 25: 583–604.

Parker, B. 1987. *Discriminants for Recovery from Decline.* Paper presented at the Annual Meeting of the Association for the Study of Higher Education, San Diego.

Parsons, T. 1967. *Sociological Theory and Modern Society.* London: Collier-MacMillan.

Pascale, R.T. 1988. "The Honda Effect." In *The Strategy Process,* edited by J.B. Quinn, H. Mintzberg, and R.M. James. Englewood Cliffs, N.J.: Prentice Hall, 104–113.

– 1990. "The Renewal Factor: Constructive Contention." *The Planning Forum* 17 (6).

Pearce, J., E.B. Freeman, and R.B. Robinson. 1987. "The Tenuous Link Between Formal Strategic Planning and Financial Performance." *Academy of Management Review* 12 (4): 658–75.

Pedersen, K.G., and T. Fleming. 1984. "Education under Siege: Academic Freedom and the Cult of Efficiency." *Journal of Business Administration* 14: 13–40.

Peters, T.J., and R.H. Waterman. 1982. *In Search of Excellence.* New York: Harper and Row.

Pettigrew, A.M. 1973. *The Politics of Organizational Decision Making.* London: Tavistock.

– 1977. "Strategy Formulation as a Political Process." *International Studies of Management and Organizations* 7 (2): 78–87.

– 1979. "On Studying Organizational Cultures." *Administrative Science Quarterly* 24: 570–81.

– 1985a. *The Awakening Giant: Continuity and Change in Imperial Chemical Industries.* Oxford: Basil Blackwell.

– 1985b. "Contextualist Research and the Study of Organizational Change Processes." In *Research Methods in Information Systems,* edited by E. Mumford. Amsterdam: Elsevier, 53–77.

Pfeffer, J. 1981a. *Power in Organizations.* Marshfield, Mass.: Pitman.

– 1981b. "Management as Symbolic Action." In *Research in Organizational Behavior,* edited by L.L. Cummings and B.M. Staw. Greenwich, Conn.: JAI Press, 3: 1–52.

Pfeffer, J., and W.L. Moore. 1980. "Average Tenure of Academic Department Heads: The Effects of Paradigm, Size, and Departmental Demography." *Administrative Science Quarterly* 25: 387–406.

Pfeffer, J., and G.R. Salancik. 1974. "Organizational Decision Making as a Political Process." *Administrative Science Quarterly* 19: 135–51.

Pfeffer, J., G.R. Salancik, and H. Leblebici. 1976. "The Effect of Uncertainty on the Use of Social Influence in Organizational Decision Making." *Administrative Science Quarterly* 21: 227–45.

Platt, G.M., and T. Parsons. 1968. "Decision-making in the Academic System: Influence and Power Exchange." In *The State of the University*, edited by C.E. Kruytbosch and S.L. Messinger. Beverly Hills, Cal.: Sage, 133–80.

Policy Making and Effective Leadership, edited by J.V. Baldridge, D.V. Curtis, G.P. Ecker, and G.L. Riley. San Francisco: Jossey-Bass, 1978.

Ranson, S., R. Hinings, and R. Greenwood. 1980. "The Structuring of Organizational Structure." *Administrative Science Quarterly* 25 (1): 1–14.

Roberts, J. 1990. "Strategy and Accounting in a U.K. Conglomerate." *Accounting Organization And Society* 15: 107–26.

Sabatier, P. 1978. "The Acquisition and Utilization of Technical Information by Administrative Agencies." *Administrative Science Quarterly* 23: 396–447.

Salancik, G., and J. Pfeffer. 1974. "The Bases and Use of Power in Organizational Decision Making." *Administrative Science Quarterly* 19: 453–73.

Satow, R.L. 1975. "Value-Rational Authority and Professional Organizations: Weber's Missing Type." *Administrative Science Quarterly* 20: 526–31.

Savenije, B. 1989. *University Strategy: Creation and Implementation*. Paper presented at the European Association for Institutional Research, Trier, August.

– 1992. *The University as a Divisionalized Structure: the Role of the Centre*. Paper presented at the European Association for Institutional Research, Brussels, September.

Schein, E.H. 1968. "Organizational Socialization." *Industrial Management Review* 9: 1–15.

– 1985. *Organizational Culture and Leadership*. San Francisco: Jossey Bass.

Sheffield, E. 1978: see *Systems of Higher Education in Canada*.

Shirley, R.C. 1988. "Strategic Planning: an Overview." In *Successful Strategic Planning: Case Studies*, edited by D.W. Steeples. New Directions for Higher Education 64. San Francisco: Jossey-Bass.

Shirley, R.C., and J.F. Volkwein. 1978. "Establishing Academic Program Priorities." *Journal of Higher Education* 49 (5): 972–88.

Sibley, W.M. 1982. *The Role of Intermediary Bodies in Postsecondary Education*. Address to Council of Ministers of Education, Canada Conference on Postsecondary Education Issues in Canada for the 1980s, Toronto, October.

– 1993. "The University in the 1990s: Crisis or Predicament?" *Canadian Journal of Higher Education* 23 (1): 114–32.

Simon, H.A. 1955. "A Behavioral Model of Rational Choice." *Quarterly Journal of Economics* 69 (1): 99–118.

Sizer, J. 1987. *Institutional Responses to Financial Reductions in the University Sector: Final Report*. Loughborough, U.K.: Department of Education and Science.

– 1988a. "British Universities' Responses to Events Leading to Grant Reductions Announced in July 1981." *Financial Accountability and Management* 4 (2): 79–98.

– 1988b. "The Management of Institutional Adaptation and Change under Conditions of Financial Stringency." In *Restructuring Higher Education: Proceedings of the Annual Conference 1987*, edited by H. Eggins. Milton Keynes, U.K.: Society for Research into Higher Education and Open University, 80–92.

Skolnik, M.L. 1986. "If the Cut is So Deep, Where Is the Blood? Problems in Research on the Effects of Financial Restraint." *The Review of Higher Education* 9 (4): 435–55.

Skolnik, M.L., and N.S. Rowen. 1984. *Please Sir, I Want Some More: Canadian Universities and Financial Restraint.* Toronto: Ontario Institute for Studies in Education.

Skousen, M. 1991. "Roaches Outlive Elephants: An Interview with Peter F. Drucker." *Forbes* (19 August): 72–4.

Smith, K.A. 1984. "Industry–University Research Programs." *Physics Today* 37 (2): 24–9.

Southern, L. 1987. "Politics and Its Limits on Government, Intermediaries and Universities." In *Governments and Higher Education: The Legitimacy of Intervention.* Toronto: The Ontario Institute for Studies in Education, Higher Education Group.

Southern, L., and J.D. Dennison. 1985. "Government–University Relations: IMB or No IMB? A Comparative View of Alberta and British Columbia." *The Canadian Journal of Higher Education* 2: 75–89.

Statistics Canada. 1978. *From the Sixties to the Eighties: A Statistical Portrait of Canadian Higher Education.* Ottawa: Statistics Canada.

Stetar, J.M., and J.N. Dorset. 1991. "Fostering Faculty: Institutional Loyalty and Professional Rewards." *The Review of Higher Education* 14 (2): 263–72.

Stroup, H.M. 1966. *Bureaucracy in Higher Education.* New York: Free Press.

Swain, D.C. 1988. "The University of Louisville." In *Successful Strategic Planning: Case Studies*, edited by D.W. Steeples. New Directions for Higher Education 64, San Francisco: Jossey Bass.

Systems of Higher Education in Canada, edited by E. Sheffield. International Council for Educational Development, 1978.

Tatel, D.S., and R.C. Guthrie. 1984. "The Legal Ins and Outs of University–Industry Collaboration." *Educational Record* 64 (2): 19–25.

Tavenas, F. 1990. *Managing the Political Environment.* Paper presented at the Workshop on Leadership and Strategy in the Collegial Institution, Montreal, February.

Taylor, W.H. 1983. "The Nature of Policy-making in Universities." *Canadian Journal of Higher Education* 13 (1): 17–31.

Thompson, D.C. 1977. "The State of Planning at McGill." *McGill Journal of Education* 12 (1): 42–56.

Tierney, W.G. 1987. "Facts and Constructs: Defining Reality in Higher Education Organization." *Review of Higher Education* 11 (1): 61–73.

– 1988. "Organizational Culture in Higher Education." *Journal of Higher Education* 59 (1): 1–21.

– 1989. "Symbolism and Presidential Perceptions of Leadership." *Review of Higher Education* 12 (2): 153–66.

Van Maanen, J. 1979. "Reclaiming Qualitative Methods for Organisational Research: a Preface." *Administrative Science Quarterly* 24 (4): 520–26.

– 1983. "Golden Passports: Managerial Socialization and Graduate Education." *Review of Higher Education* 6 (4): 435–55.

Van Maanen, J., and E.H. Schein. 1979. "Toward a Theory of Organizational Socialization." In *Research in Organizational Behavior*, edited by B. Staw and L.L. Cummings . Greenwich, Conn.: JAI Press.

Van Vught, F.A. 1989: see *Government Strategies and Innovation in Higher Education*.

Walsh, K., R.C. Hinings, R. Greenwood, and S. Ranson. 1981. "Power and Advantage in Organizations." *Organization Studies* 2 (2): 131–52.

Watson, T.J. 1982. "Group Ideologies and Organizational Change." *Journal of Management Studies* 19 (3): 259–75.

Watts, R. 1992. "Universities and Public Policy." In *Universities and Government: A Framework for Accountability*, edited by J. Cutt and R. Dobell. Halifax, N.S.: Institute for Research on Public Policy.

Webb, E.J., D.T. Campbell, R.D. Schwartz, and L. Sechrest. 1966. *Unobtrusive Measures: Non-reactive Research in the Social Sciences*. Chicago: Rand McNally.

Webb, E.J., and K.E. Weick. 1979. "Unobtrusive Measures in Organizational Theory: A Remainder." *Administrative Science Quarterly* 24 (4): 650–59.

Webster, J.L., W.E. Reif, and J.S. Bracker. 1989. "The Manager's Guide to Strategic Planning Tools and Techniques." *Planning Review* 17 (6): 4–13.

Weick, K.E. 1976. "Educational Organizations as Loosely Coupled Systems." *Administrative Science Quarterly* 21: 1–19.

Weiss, R.M. 1983. "Weber on Bureaucracy: Management Consultant or Political Theorist?" *Academy of Management Review* 8 (2): 242–48.

Westley, F.R. 1990. "Middle Managers and Strategy: Microdynamics of Inclusion." *Strategic Management Journal* 11: 337–51.

Williams, J.C. 1986. "Industry–University Interactions: Finding the Balance." *Engineering Education* 76 (6): 320–25.

Yin, R. 1984. *Case Study Research: Design and Methods*. Newbury Park, Cal.: Sage.

Index

Page references to tables or figures are in italic type.

academic statistics, 14
accountability, 3, 199
administrative skills, 5–6, 8, 10
Alberta, 18, 19
Association of Universities and Colleges of Canada (AUCC), 20, 211n.1
attrition: Carleton University, 157, 176; McGill University, 40, 74; Simon Fraser University, 114; University of British Columbia, 91; University of Montreal, 61–2, 74; University of Toronto, 132
AUCC (Association of Universities and Colleges of Canada), 20, 211n.1
Australia, 3, 199

Bishop's University, 16
Board of Governors: Carleton University, 33, 147, 155–6, 176; McGill University, 33, 35, 175; Simon Fraser University, 33, 110–11, 117, 177; University of British Columbia, 33, 81, 118, 180–1; University of Montreal, 33; University of Toronto, 33
Bovey Commission (1983), Ontario, 26
Brandon University, 18
British Columbia: government view of universities, 92, 103–4, 116; restraint legislation, 79–81, 101, 120, 180; university system history, 18, 19, 29–31, 211n.3
British North America Act, 16
Brock University, 18
bureaucratic institution model. *See* professional-bureaucracy institutional model
business world: collegiality, 191–2; fascination with strategic planning, 211–12n.5; managerialism, 4; relations with universities, 200, 211n.4

Canadian Association of University Teachers (CAUT), 20
Carleton University: as centralized collegium, 176, 177; case study, 11, 207–9; collegiality, 150–3, 176; compared with McGill University, 177; compared with Simon Fraser University, 177; created, 18, 147; deans, 33, 149–53, 158, 176, 195–6; faculty, 33, 150, 155, 156–7; financial problems, 147–49; governance structure, 147, 148, 153–6, 176, 177, 192, 197; institutional context, 34, 149–53, 176; planning, 151–2, 158–9, 161; presidents, 147–8, 149, 150–1, 153–5; resource allocation, 157–8, 161, 176; retrenchment outcomes, 161–2; retrenchment strategy, 34, 156–9, 161, 176, 195; Senate, 33, 147–8, 154, 156, 176; statistics (1984–86), 33, 34, 147; vice-presidents, 33, 151–2, 153–5, 176
case study methodology, 205–10